Earnings Inequality, Unemployment, and Poverty in the Middle East and North Africa

Earnings Inequality, Unemployment, and Poverty in the Middle East and North Africa

Edited by WASSIM SHAHIN
and GHASSAN DIBEH

Contributions in Economics and Economic History,
Number 215

GREENWOOD PRESS
Westport, Connecticut • London

Library of Congress Cataloging-in-Publication Data

Earnings inequality, unemployment, and poverty in the Middle East and North Africa /
edited by Wassim Shahin and Ghassan Dibeh.
    p. cm.—(Contributions in economics and economic history, ISSN 0084–9235 ; no. 215)
    Papers presented at the Conference on Earnings Inequality, Unemployment, and
Poverty in the Middle-East and North Africa (MENA), 1998 in Byblos, Lebanon.
    Includes bibliographical references and index.
    ISBN 0–313–30977–9 (alk. paper)
    1. Poverty—Arab countries—Congresses. 2. Wages—Arab countries—Congresses.
3. Income distribution—Arab countries—Congresses. 4. Unemployment—Arab
countries—Congresses. I. Shahin, Wassim N., 1957– II. Dibeh, Ghassan, 1963–
III. Conference on Earnings Inequality, Unemployment, and Poverty in the Middle-East
and North Africa (1998 : Jubayl, Lebanon) IV. Series.
HC498.9.P6 E18 2000
330.917'49270828—dc21   99–046153

British Library Cataloguing in Publication Data is available.

Library of Congress Catalog Card Number: 99–046153
ISBN: 0–313–30977–9
ISSN: 0084–9235

First published in 2000

Greenwood Press, 88 Post Road West, Westport, CT 06881
An imprint of Greenwood Publishing Group, Inc.
www.greenwood.com

Printed in the United States of America

The paper used in this book complies with the
Permanent Paper Standard issued by the National
Information Standards Organization (Z39.48–1984).

10 9 8 7 6 5 4 3 2 1

Contents

List of Figures and Tables

Preface

The idea for this book germinated in the School of Business, Byblos at the Lebanese American University, Lebanon and flourished in the conference on Earnings Inequality, Unemployment, and Poverty in the Middle East and North Africa (MENA), held on November 5–7, 1998 in Byblos, Lebanon. Numerous papers were presented by international scholars and experts and a few were selected through a thorough refereeing process to appear in this book.

The aim of this book is to shed additional light on poverty, unemployment, and income inequality in selected MENA countries by presenting the magnitude of these problems and recommending policies to alleviate and reduce them.

The importance of addressing the issues researched and studied in this book manifests itself in the following 1996 data and figures from the United Nations. The number of people below the absolute poverty line constitutes 49 percent of the population in sub-Saharan Africa, 41 percent in South and Southeast Asia, 36 percent in Latin America, and 32 percent in the MENA region. The average for the developing world is 30 percent and the number of poor is 1,438 million persons. The degree of income inequality is reflected in the following figures on the share of global income. In 1960, the share of global income of the poorest 20 percent was 2.3 and the share of the richest 20 percent was 70.2. In 1990, the figure worsened. The share of the poorest 20 percent was 1.4 and the share of the richest 20 percent was 82.7. According to these numbers, the ratio of income of rich to poor moved from 30 to 1 in 1960 to 59 to 1 in 1990.

The reality of these statistics extends beyond the economic loss to threaten political stability and social cohesion. The causes of these problems are still researched, discussed, studied, and debated. The studies in the book aim at enhancing our understanding of the issues for policy recommendations. The topics addressed have gained international recognition as reflected in the October 1998 selection of Amartya Sen by the Royal Swedish Academy of Sciences for the Nobel Prize. Sen achieved major research in welfare economics addressing the issue of poverty and recommending major structural solutions for this problem.

The book is organized into 10 major studies by international scholars and an introductory chapter highlighting some remarks and observations on poverty and earnings inequality in the Arab world by Elias Tuma, of the University of California, Davis. Dr. Tuma comes up with a set of logical conclusions and resolutions to combat poverty and inequality based on the salient features of the Arab social, political, and economic structure and environment.

The second chapter, by Sourushe Zandvakili, of the University of Cincinnati, surveys various measures of inequality by stressing that the views regarding the framework necessary to investigate economic inequality are not unanimous. The author discusses the relevant factors in inequality measurement, presents welfare considerations and the selection criteria of inequality measures, introduces specific inequality measures, and discusses the effect of accounting interval upon the measured inequality, long-run inequality, and mobility and the statistical inference for measures of inequality.

The third chapter, by Ayman Kandeel and Jeffrey Nugent, of the University of Southern California, deals with the unraveling of the paradox in Egypt's trends in income inequality and poverty. The authors separately explain the changes in both the Gini coefficients and Kuznets ratios as indexes of inequality and the indexes of poverty and then compare the two sets of results.

The fourth chapter, by Hans Lofgren, of the International Food Policy Research Institute, deals with trade reform and the poor in Morocco in a rural-urban general equilibrium analysis. The author explores, quantitatively, the short-run impact of agricultural deprotection on the Moroccan economy in general and on disaggregated household welfare and the rural economy in particular. The analysis also addresses the use of complementary policies aimed at protecting the incomes of vulnerable parts of the rural population. The contribution of this study stems from its focus on the impact of trade and complementary policies on the rural world using a model that captures salient characteristics of Morocco's rural-urban divide including large skill and wage gaps, labor market segmentation, and difference in sectoral structure.

The fifth chapter, by E. Mine Cinar, of Loyola University of Chicago, addresses earning profiles of women workers and education in the Middle East. The author examines life-cycle labor force participation of unskilled women in formal labor markets by discussing the earnings stream of women over time and analyzing human capital development and related proxy indexes. The results show that the Middle East still lags behind the rest of the world in terms of gender development and gender disparity. The lack of developed human capital, especially when it comes to women, in many countries in the region has to be overcome before gender disparities can get smaller.

The sixth chapter, by Muhammad Islam, of St. Louis University, deals with fiscal policy and social welfare in selected MENA countries. The author describes the various fiscal instruments in use in these countries. Then, he looks at the structure of government expenditure to examine how certain forms of spending can be successfully used to promote distributional equity and to ameliorate poverty. The results reached suggest that governments ought to prioritize expenditures so that the benefit to the poor is the greatest, especially in Bahrain, Kuwait, Tunisia, and Egypt.

The seventh chapter, by Karen Pfeifer, of Smith College, investigates the relationship between structural adjustment and unemployment by comparing four International Monetary Fund programs in Egypt, Jordan, Morocco, and Tunisia. The results reached suggest that structural adjustment programs at best returned these economies to their precrisis levels of investment, economic growth, debt, and debt-service burdens. The major change occurring in these countries as a result of structural adjustment is in the shift from public to private centrality in investment decisions and the shift from the inward orientation to outward orientation characterized by a disproportionate growth in financial and trade activity relative to real production.

The eighth chapter, by Salim Chishti and Badria Khalaf, of the Kuwait Institute for Scientific Research, deals with the relationship between earnings, education, experience, and gender in Kuwait. The focus of the study is on the human capital earnings profile of Kuwaiti labor. The authors perform separate analysis for men and women to capture the gender differentials towards the earnings profiles. The results show that the returns to education are higher for female employees whereas the returns to experience are lower for women.

The ninth chapter, by Zafiris Tzannatos, of the World Bank, addresses the reasons behind earnings inequality in Jordan and the way in which labor policies can help reduce poverty. In this respect, the study estimates the effects of a wage increase upon poverty as well as of introducing old age assistance or increasing existing pensions. The main conclusion reached is that policies that operate more or less directly through the labor market have severe fiscal implications and reduce poverty by a small amount. The chapter also examines whether earnings inequality arises from the demographic composition of workers, the return to education, public and private sector differences, or gender.

The tenth chapter, by Berch Berberoglu, of the University of Nevada, Reno, examines the relationship between unemployment, low wages, income inequality, and poverty in selected MENA countries. The author, using a socioeconomic analysis and a comparative historical perspective, argues that rapid urbanization accompanied by economic stagnation and a decline in the standard of living have led to an increase in poverty among the local population of the suburbs and the cities. The chapter provides an analysis of the major sources of poverty and attempts to explain its depth and extent.

The eleventh chapter, by Fatemeh Moghadem, of Hofstra University, deals with ideology, economic restructuring, and women's work in Iran focusing on the postrevolutionary period. The author argues that the structural changes in the economy resulting from growth, migration, urbanization, and education have impacted women's participation. State policy and ideology have also impacted labor force participation and occupational segregation. The study concludes that the structural adjustment policies, together with the specific institutional, demographic, and ideological characteristics of the Iranian economy in the 1990s, have not allowed for a significant impact stemming from privatization and liberalization policies.

In addition to the deficits we have been running with the Lebanese American University for funding the conference and providing administrative and moral support, we incurred numerous debts in organizing the conference on Earnings Inequality, Unemployment, and Poverty in the MENA region and in putting together this book. We owe a great deal of gratitude to all the international scholars and experts who flew to Lebanon from the rest of the world to present papers and participate in discussions. We would also like to thank our graduate students in the M.B.A. program in the School of Business, Byblos, namely Dina Assaf Bou Saba, Eliane Bacha, and Rania Tohme, for their help in the conference, and Sylvie Mitri, Dalina Slaiby, and Hisham Haddad, for editorial assistance.

We feel lucky to have Roula Hawwa Ghosn, the secretary in the School of Business, as a dedicated associate. Her tolerance for hard work and multiple demands and her penchant for sophistication were instrumental in improving the quality of the presentation of the manuscript.

Finally, we address the policy recommendations of the conference to policymakers, academicians, and students of economics. However, we dedicate this work to the greatest source of concern: the poor and unemployed of the world.

Wassim Shahin and Ghassan Dibeh
Byblos, Lebanon

1

Some Introductory Observations on Poverty and Earnings Inequality in the Arab World

Elias H. Tuma

INTRODUCTION

Poverty and inequality are functions of the economic system and the ideals and policies that drive the economy and society. They are relative conditions of well-being, depending on the standards by which they are measured, such as national plans and expectations, international standards, or certain absolute values of what counts as poverty or inequality. In this context, poverty may be computed relative to international standards. One such measure is the percentage of people in a country who live on $1 (ppp) or less a day (ppp= purchasing power parity of the currency in constant dollars).[1] Another measure is the percentage of people who enjoy less than a specified minimum of longevity, knowledge, and "decent" living.[2] Inequality of earnings may be interpreted in three ways, namely: it may be perceived as differential earnings because of different qualifications, jobs, or performance; it may be perceived as the result of discrimination because of differences in race, ethnic origin, or gender; it could also be due to market forces that favor certain income earners over others. I shall be concerned with the societal framework of all three forms of inequality.[3]

Poverty and inequality in the Arab world do not seem to be high on the list of concerns as suggested by the small number of Arab countries that survey and publish data on these conditions; less than half publish any data at all in the international sources.[4] However, poverty and inequality in the Arab countries are less extreme than in many other regions with a high degree of variation across Arab nations. Inequality in Egypt, for example, is lower than in many European countries and compares favorably with the distribution in the Netherlands. Arab countries may consider poverty and inequality as a normal social condition driven by forces discussed later in this chapter.

The chapter is organized as follows. The next section presents a conceptual framework for the analysis. In the following section I shall explain poverty and inequality in the Arab countries within that framework. The last section explores ways to reduce poverty and inequality to a feasible minimum.

BEHAVIORAL STRUCTURE: A CONCEPTUAL FRAMEWORK

According to philosopher A. C. Grayling, "Humanity lives by ideas, and many if not indeed most of the conflicts, turmoils, revolutions and resurgences that mark history are driven by philosophies—often half-baked, usually less than half-understood, dreadfully oversimplified when turned into slogans for mass consumption and invariably destined to harden into stone if adopted by ruling establishments, so that to disagree with them is to risk punishment, including death."[5] However, while change is driven by philosophies and ideas, society as a system is also held together by philosophies and ideas that spell out the ideals and expectations of the given society—or country. These ideals may be represented by religious beliefs, economic and political principles, moral and ethical standards, or a combination of these. Major institutions are then established to reflect, promote, and sustain those ideals. These institutions include the national constitution, if there is a written one, criminal and civil laws, religious rules and regulations, the educational system and curriculum, and unwritten accepted rules of behavior. An administrative machinery, including government, school authorities, religious hierarchies, business organizations, and the family, serves and protects the institutions. The administrative machinery sees to it that the laws and rules of behavior are interpreted and enforced through an army of field workers, such as the postman, the policeman, the teacher, and so forth. For a policy to be fully implemented, it has to be consistent with the philosophy of society and its institutions, and it has to be acceptable to the administrative machinery and field workers. The philosophy, institutions, administrative machinery, and field workers together, set in descending order of significance, form what I call *behavioral structure*.[6] Conflict between the policy and any component of the behavioral structure could spell doom for that policy, unless change in the behavioral structure is enforced to bring it into harmony with the proposed policy.

The problem becomes more complicated if the policy is consistent with one component of the behavioral structure but not with others. The most difficult situation is when policy is in conflict with the philosophy, followed by conflict with institutions, and then with the administrative machinery. The reason is that changing the philosophy is most difficult compared with other components of the behavioral structure. Similarly, changing institutions is more difficult than reforming the administrative machinery. However, conflict with any of the components of the behavioral structure is bound to reduce the probability of successful implementation of the policy.

To summarize, as long as the behavioral structure and peoples' expectations are consistent with the existing conditions, there is little chance for those conditions to change. Similarly, any conflict between a policy to change conditions and any component of the behavioral structure will reduce the probability of implementing that policy, more so if the conflict involves the philosophy of society regarding the contents of that policy.

POVERTY AND INEQUALITY IN THE ARAB WORLD

The existence of poverty and inequality in the Arab world is not in doubt. Poverty exists both as a percentage of the people living on $1 (ppp) a day or less in all the countries reporting. Poverty also exists as a percentage of people who do not enjoy the minimum standard of longevity, knowledge, and decent living. Though most Arab countries do not report such data, the existence of poverty and inequality is not contested. Furthermore, all evident efforts against these conditions try to reduce poverty rather than eliminate it. However, few efforts fight inequality seriously enough to make a difference, lip service and public proclamations to the contrary notwithstanding.[7] Hence both poverty and inequality persist also because they are consistent with the behavioral structure and few people expect them to go away.

The philosophy or social doctrine in Arab society honors the wealthy and in many ways tolerates the poor only on the assumption that it must be God's will if some are wealthy and some are poor. Another common belief is that if you try hard, God will help you, thus suggesting that poverty is the result of failure on the part of the poor and it is God's will. These beliefs are reflected in literature, poetry, historical anecdotes, and everyday communications. The fact that some people may not have had the opportunity or that they are not qualified because of circumstances beyond their control does not seem to make a difference. Policymakers and experts explain poverty as the result of market conditions, low marginal productivity of the worker, and competition, on the assumption that the market is fair and neutral. However, the market is blind to the differences in opportunities available to people and to the initial starting point long before these people enter the market. Therefore, the fabric of society is woven into economic classes, with visible differentiation between them, and the "poor" as an integral permanent part of society.

Given that the ideals of Arab society do not preclude poverty and people's expectations are consistent with the existence of the poor, institutions of Arab society are equally in harmony with poverty. Civil and religious laws as well as the standards of ethics and morality do not exclude the existence of poverty and the poor. Arab people, in principle, care about the poor as reflected in the calls for charity to the poor and needy. Charity is considered a good deed and a religious act in all religions of the Arab countries. Welfare programs by government and charitable organizations also reflect concern for the poor, but not for poverty. Even when a minimum wage is legislated, it is usually below the income required to climb above the poverty level. Hence, poverty continues in spite of these programs and because it is consistent with the behavioral structure of society.[8]

Poverty is sustained also by economic forces in the Arab world. On one hand, market forces, regardless of how imperfect the market is, tend to aggravate relative poverty inasmuch as the market favors those who enter it well equipped with physical and human resources and the promise of relatively high productivity. On the other hand, most Arab countries have low average productivity and income, making the lower-income groups relatively poor. This dilemma is exacerbated by the high rate of population growth in Arab society, especially among the less equipped and less skilled workers who are responsible for the livelihood of large families with many dependents.[9]

The persistence of poverty is reinforced by the existence of unemployment, in its various forms. Unemployment in the non-oil-rich countries sometimes affects a quarter of the labor force, in which case relative poverty is almost unavoidable.

Both low productivity and high unemployment are sustained in part by the existing behavioral structure, which fails to guarantee a reasonable minimum income and full employment.

The problem of inequality of earnings is more complex than that of poverty but the two are closely related. Inequality usually results from a combination of social, economic, and political factors. On the economic side, inequality may be explained by inequality of individual merits and qualifications, and inequality in the ability to accumulate capital and generate earnings independently of merit and qualifications from inheritance and private ownership. Capital earnings influence inequality in at least two ways: they augment earnings directly, and they redistribute opportunities for acquiring skills and qualifications before entering the market. These economic dynamics are fully consistent with the existing behavioral structure and therefore economic inequality is expected to exist.[10]

On the social level, inequality is inherent in racial, ethnic, and gender discrimination in the marketplace, in the family, and in the behavioral structure. Discrimination against racial and ethnic minorities (minorities in power terms) is common throughout the Arab world. Discrimination against females, from the day they are born, is a fact of life in most Arab countries, even though people try to rationalize that behavior in the name of religion, social relations, or tribal traditions. As a result, inequalities of merit, qualifications, and productivity are predetermined long before members of minorities and females enter the market.

Inequality is also predictable as a result of inequality in the distribution of political power. In most of the Arab world, political power is prescribed, either by tradition or by the new regimes of government that have come to power in the post–World War II period. These regimes have virtually institutionalized the distribution of power in favor of certain groups: the military, the technocrats, and, since the *Infitah* (opening of the market), the wealthy. These regimes pay lip service to democracy and welfare of the workers and peasants, but do little to equalize opportunities or incomes. Therefore, those who are in the less favored situations continue to form a class of poor and unequal. Of course, certain individuals do manage to climb out of that predicament, but a class of poor and underprivileged continues to exist.

As already noted, these conditions are predictable by the behavioral structural model. The philosophy and expectations of Arab society tend to promote inequality. These expectations are inherited through history, which describes people as not equal, and are contained in the teachings of religion, which assign equality to people only on the basis of faith and the other world or before God. But such equality does not extend to economic or earning equality in this world.

Given the discriminatory philosophy of Arab society, it is to be expected that the institutions that reflect that philosophy and the administrative machinery provide little to remove discrimination and equalize opportunities and earnings even in the once-called Islamic or Arab Socialist countries. To illustrate, laws of inheritance and private property tend to protect and augment the status quo, which is discriminatory. The military, which usually is the most equalizing institution, excludes women from service, except in rare situations. Free compulsory education is another equalizing institution. However, in most Arab countries, the quality and availability of public education are less than adequate, as shown by the high illiteracy rates and lack of skills that still prevail. The same inequalities apply to health services and nutrition in the early stage of life of large numbers of people so that underprivileged children grow up as underqualified workers and thus less than equal income earners. The failure to guarantee a decent minimum of basic needs to all children is at the root of both poverty and inequality, especially inequality of opportunities.

Still another institution that tends to perpetuate inequality is the system of taxation. Some Arab countries levy no income tax and thus they do not even pretend to deal with inequality through progressive taxation. Other countries have fairly progressive tax systems but the tax laws have many loopholes and enforcement is so lax that the equalization impact of these laws has been quite limited. In other words, not only do the philosophy and institutions of Arab society tend to sustain inequality, but the administrative machinery also tends to augment these tendencies by failing to implement even the modest equalization measures that are in existence.

IS THERE A WAY OUT?

The most logical conclusion of this analysis is that a change in the behavioral structure is necessary before poverty and inequality can be arrested and contained. The ideal change would instill a behavioral structure that dictates equality of earnings according to an approved definition, and the absence of poverty. Yet, though such a change is logical and theoretically valid, it would be naïve to expect it to happen in the present state of the world in general and the Arab world in particular. Leaders and policymakers have shown little indication that they would support or consider such a change. Whenever issues of poverty and inequality are on the table, the focus is on how to help the poor and how to rationalize inequality. Therefore, a more practical resolution that is not in conflict with the behavioral structure may have a better chance of consideration and support. Such a resolution should have positive effects in the short run as well as an impact on expectations in the long run, as follows:[11]

1. Probably the first step should be to increase awareness of the existence of both poverty and inequality, and their negative effects not only on their victims, but also on society and the economy as a whole. It can and should be shown clearly that inequality and poverty reduce incentives and capacities to produce by the large segment of the labor force suffering from them.

2. The concepts of poverty and inequality seem somewhat vague when measurement and policymaking are considered. Therefore, it is necessary for each country or society to formulate its own conceptions of the minimum level of earning that is acceptable and the minimum level of inequality that will be tolerated. In the process of formulating these concepts, the level of awareness will also be increased and policymaking and implementation become more feasible.

3. An attack on unemployment in its various forms may be the most important immediate step to take as both poverty and inequality may be easier to tackle in a full-employment economy than in one that suffers from unemployment. Increasing productive investment is the most direct way to deal with unemployment; if the private sector is unable to perform that function, then the public sector should be ready to do so.

4. In order to increase labor productivity and total output, there should be emphasis on improving technology and training workers in new skills in advanced technology. These two processes would render the workers

and the economy in general more productive and more competitive in the global market.

5. To combat the bias tradition, unfair competition, and the market, steps are necessary to guarantee minimum incomes and basic needs to all people. These steps will aid the poor, raise their morale, increase their level of energy and incentives, and thus increase total output.

6. Dealing with inequality may take two different forms, in the short and the long run. In the short run, instruments of fiscal policy may be the most effective, including progressive taxation and targeted public expenditure. While progressive taxation will help to reduce the gap between rich and poor, targeted public expenditure will promote equality of opportunity through retraining workers and increasing employment.

7. All these measures depend on the will of the political leaders and policymakers, and awareness of the people. Therefore, in the long run, modification of the behavioral structure is essential. The philosophy and institutions of the Arab countries may be modified through formal and informal education so that poverty and inequality become unacceptable in principle and in practice. It should be made clear that a guarantee of equal opportunity for all children even before they are born is the best guarantee for reducing poverty and inequality to the unavoidable minimum. Such a measure would be most effective in reducing bias while relating earnings to merit and qualifications, regardless of race, ethnic origin, or gender.

8. Finally, to be effective, measures to combat poverty and inequality, whether in the short or the long run, ought to be made public, and data on actions and results should be collected and published. Only then can we assess the intensity of these problems and the effectiveness of measures to reduce them.

NOTES

This is a revised version of a paper presented at the Conference on Earnings Inequality, Unemployment, and Poverty in the Middle East and North Africa at the School of Business, Lebanese American University, Byblos, Lebanon, November 5–7, 1998.

1. *World Development Report*, 1997.
2. *Human Development Report*, 1997.
3. See Tuma 1995.
4. See Tuma 1980, Amin 1974, and El-Ghonemy 1998.
5. *New York Times* "Review of Books," 1998.
6. For more details see Tuma 1987.
7. El-Ghonemy 1998.
8. See Chaudhry 1997 on the importance of institutions.
9. See Wilson 1995.
10. For details, see Tuma 1995, chapter 7.
11. For a different set of recommendations, see El-Ghonemy 1998.

8   Earnings Inequality, Unemployment, and Poverty

REFERENCES

Amin, Galal (1974). *The Modernization of Poverty*. Leiden: E. J. Brill.
Chaudhry, Kiren Aziz (1997). *The Price of Wealth, Economies, and Institutions in the Middle-East*. Ithaca: Cornell University Press.
El-Ghonemy, Riad (1998). *Affluence and Poverty in the Middle-East*. London and New York: Routledge Press.
Human Development Report (1997). United Nations.
New York Times. "Review of Books" (1998), Sept. 27, p. 20.
Tuma, Elias (1987). *Economic and Political Change in the Middle-East*. Palo Alto, CA: Pacific Books.
————(1995). *The Persistence of Economic Discrimination*. Palo Alto, CA: Pacific Books.
————(1980). "The Rich and Poor in the Middle-East," *Middle-East Journal* 34 (Autumn): 413–437.
Wilson, Rodney (1995). *Economic Development in the Middle-East*. London and New York: Routledge Press.
World Development Report (1997). World Bank.

2

Measurement of Inequality: Motivation and Survey

Sourushe Zandvakili

INTRODUCTION

Economic inequality has been one of the most important social issues for most, if not all, societies. For centuries philosophers have debated the co-existence of great wealth and poverty. More recently, social scientists have been preoccupied with the connection between political influence and economic affluence with one aspect being the current debate on the control over economic resources within and across economic boundaries. Although economists have continually identified efficiency and equity as the most important factors guiding economic policy designed to enhance economic well-being, there is lack of awareness as to the connection between them and economic inequality.

Economic inequality can be analyzed in the context of public policy decisions and their consequences. Some policy decisions are made as a result of economic conditions and some are the result of social and political pressures. Opinions regarding the efficacy or desirability of government policy are not unanimous. However, there is agreement that public policy can influence economic inequality and mobility.

In most countries it is generally accepted that all individuals should be able to maintain some minimum standard of living. However, there is disagreement on how to establish the minimum, and various income maintenance programs have been introduced by governments in response to the desire to establish this minimum. The objectives of these programs are to protect the total income of families from declining due to factors beyond their control. Policies such as social security for retirement, aid to families with dependent children, and unemployment compensation are alternative ways of addressing the problem of economic inequality. Some countries have introduced benefits in the form of cash and goods and services such as medical benefits, public housing, child care, and so forth. These policies are basically a form of social insurance, which allow families to maintain their existing economic status. A more serious approach in addressing income inequality requires a proper taxation mechanism to alter the distribution of income and wealth.

The objective of public policy, generally, has been to increase the economic means of those in the lower end of distribution. Consequently issues such as discrimination have been of great concern recently. Furthermore, skill, a factor that is closely tied to the issue of efficiency and in turn to economic standing, has received a great deal of attention. This is because some policymakers and economists believe economic growth is the fundamental solution to the whole problem of inequality. Subsequently substantial emphasis was placed on accumulation of human capital (training programs and education) to overcome the problem of economic inequality. However, the benefits of educational programs take time to accrue, and a shift in policy will tend to have effects upon the "size distribution" of income over time.

Macroeconomic policies also influence the general condition of the economy and the size distribution of income (inequality). The effect of public policy for the purpose of recovery from such conditions is an empirical question. More recently, globalization of markets and trade has issued another challenge for public policy makers and analysts alike. The welfare and distributional implications of trade within and across countries are not yet fully understood.

Regardless of the motivation for the investigation of economic inequality, one has to understand the proper approach in the measurement of inequality. There are a number of measurement issues that need to be addressed. It is the objective of this survey to present measurement of inequality within the context of short-run inequality, long-run inequality, and income stability (mobility), e.g., changes in "size distribution of income over time." This approach allows consideration of characteristics of the household such as age, education, ethnicity, race, sex, and income level.

Views regarding the framework necessary to investigate economic inequality are not unanimous. A brief discussion regarding relevant factors in inequality measurement is presented. Welfare considerations and the selection criteria of inequality measures are presented next, and specific inequality measures are introduced and discussed. The impact of accounting interval on measured inequality is presented, followed by measurement of long-run inequality and mobility. A brief discussion regarding statistical inference for measures of inequality is presented. Concluding remarks follow.

FACTORS OF INTEREST

Measurement of inequality requires special attention to factors such as income source, income unit, equivalence scale, the time duration, and weights. Each of these factors alters our view of the observed inequality, and influences how we evaluate economic well-being. Although the focus of this survey is measurement of inequality, a note regarding these factors is very useful.

A quick review of inequality literature reveals that the most commonly used variable in the analysis of inequality is income. However, there are different variations of income that can be used for measurement purposes such as both pre-and posttax and transfer income. We can also measure inequality based on earnings, expenditures, and wealth. The choice of income source needs to be justified on the basis of the general objective of the research question.

The proper choice of an income unit is very critical in the measurement of inequality. The choice of individuals is a poor choice of an income unit. Generally, households and families are better choices for measurement purposes. Although nonworking spouse and children do not have their own income, they are direct beneficiaries of the household income. Thus, measurement of inequality at the individual level provides a misleading picture. At the same time, a measure based on per capita household or family income is not proper as within households, not all individuals enjoy the same economic well-being. This requires addressing the problem through an equivalence scale.

The use of an equivalence scale requires deflating household or family incomes for each extra member in the economic unit. Equivalent income for a family or a household is equal to the observed income divided by the equivalence scale value for households or families of similar type. The derivation of such scales is a problem. The choice is normative and needs to be justified based on some consensus regarding the minimum level of consumption for households or families of similar type.

The time horizon for measurement of inequality is another complicating factor, and is of paramount importance. This issue has not received much attention in the literature. However, an analyst has to decide the nature of the problem. If permanent and chronic inequality is an issue, then one has to adopt a long-run time horizon. This requires the use of aggregation techniques for the purpose of measurement. However, the current literature is dominated by short-run annual measures of inequality. These measures contain transitory components and need to be used with caution. I will provide a solution to this problem.

The emergence of micro data at the unit level has generated another variable that requires some attention. It is important to use the proper weighting scheme to assure that the observed data are representative of the population under consideration in particular when long-run measures of income are considered. The use of panel data to generate long-run measures of income is problematic, as attrition and changes in demographic composition of the population affect most panels.

WELFARE CONSIDERATIONS

The approach to the theoretical framework of the concept and measurement of inequality (inequality of attributes in general, and income inequality in particular) is the starting point for this survey. The type of inequality measure used will reflect upon the measured short-run inequality, long-run inequality, and income mobility. Choice of such measures embodies normative judgment about inequality in welfare, and positive gesture concerning efficiency.

Some economists have centered their discussions on the marginal productivity theory. They have been concerned with variables influencing income-generating factors. This approach assumes that these variables depend upon "ability," which defines and guides an overall distribution. Moreover, this approach has been extended by assuming that ability is a function of investment in human capital. Thus ability is an asset for which there is a market. The problem inherent in this approach is the measurement of a unit of human capital.

Others have been preoccupied with the notion of efficiency with some reference to equity. They have separated the two ideas, indicating that a move from a non-Pareto optimal position to a Pareto optimal one will make the society as a whole better off. Thus they imply that more efficiency is always desirable. Public policy that benefits those with higher income and has no impact upon the poor will fall into this category. I am sure that many economists do not subscribe to the above notion. Some have moved on to look at the distribution along the Pareto curve, which is not only efficient, but also maximizes social welfare.

What one says about different social states implies some form of value judgment. One also has to define equity, and the type of social welfare function. The objective is to overcome the problem of ranking income distributions based on using a social welfare function. Shorrocks (1980) investigated this problem. His approach was to impose restrictions on the social welfare function that are weak enough to command a wide degree of support and yet are strong enough to produce some conclusive ranking. He indicated that the assumption that social welfare function is equality preferring (in the sense of being Schur-concave) and using a nondecreasing function of incomes for the purpose of efficiency will achieve such an objective. His choice of the welfare is, however, one among many with different valuations of equality and efficiency.

SELECTION CRITERIA FOR MEASUREMENT

The choice of inequality measure represents an important aspect in computing short-run inequality, long-run inequality, and stability profile. The characteristics of inequality measures are such that each varies in its degree of sensitivity to different parts of the distribution. This feature alters the weights attached to the income fluctuations of individuals in computations of inequality. There is no unique rule for the selection of an appropriate inequality measure. The ranking of inequality measures is not feasible, although the selection process is of interest to us, because each of these inequality measures satisfies some desirable properties. The axiomatic approach to inequality measurement proposed by Shorrocks (1980), Cowell and Kuga (1981a,b), and Maasoumi (1986) is a step in this direction. It is desirable for inequality measures to be a real valued function for a population, and to satisfy a set of the following properties.

Mean Independence (Income Homogeneity)

The inequality measure will be sensitive to proportional changes in all incomes. The inequality measure $I(S,n)$ should be a real valued function, which may depend on the population size n, defined on the space of income shares:

$$S \varepsilon S^n = [S(S_1, \ldots, S_n) \geqslant 0], \sum_i S_i = 1 \tag{1}$$

where inequality is independent of the unit of measurement of income.[1]

Anonymity (Symmetry)

This condition requires the inequality index to be independent of labels, which are assigned to income shares of the population:

$$I(S,n) = I(PS,n), S \varepsilon S^n \tag{2}$$

where P is an arbitrary permutation matrix of size $n \times n$. Thus inequality does not change as shares are permuted.

Pigou-Dalton Principle of Transfer

This property requires that a transfer from a rich person to a poor person should reduce inequality, provided the transfer is not so large as to reverse their positions.[2] The reverse also holds true. Vector Y is obtained from vector S by a regressive transfer on individuals i and j, if (1) $S_i \leqslant S_j$, (2) $Y_j - S_j = S_i - Y_i > 0$, (3) $Y_h = S_h$ for all $h \neq i$ and j. So S and Y

are identical except for a positive transfer of income from "poor person i" to the "richer person j"; then $I(Y) > I(S)$.

Principle of Population

This condition ensures that the inequality measures depend on relative densities rather than the absolute density. If a replication of Y is given by S then $I(Y) = I(S)$. Thus, a distribution and its replications have the same level of inequality. Furthermore, "given that the proportion of the population receiving each income level is fixed, changing (e.g., doubling) the population size has no effect on the measured level of inequality."

Decomposability

For any subdivision of a population such that $n>3$ and $n>2$, we may find transformations of inequality measures $I(S_1,n_1)$ and $I(S_2,n_2)$ as functions G and H, possibly depending on n_1,n_2; such that:

$$I(S,n) = F[G(S_1,n_1),H(S_2,n_2); n_1,n_2,\sigma_1,\sigma_2] \tag{3}$$

A decomposable measure is defined as one in which the total inequality in the distribution of income of a population can be broken down into a weighted average of the inequality existing within subgroups of the population and the inequality between the groups. The functions G and H may be transformations of $I(S_1,n_1)$ and $I(S_2,n_2)$, the measures of inequality defined on the appropriate spaces for the groups N_1 and N_2. The group shares in total income are given by σ_1 and σ_2. The intergroup inequality is incorporated in the explicit dependence of F upon these group shares. The decomposable measures differ only by the weights given to the inequality within the subgroups of the population. Decomposability is a useful property, but not all decomposable measures are good measures of inequality. Those inequality measures that satisfy decomposability as well as the set of desirable properties discussed above are of special interest while some inequality measures that violate any one of these requirements could be used in special cases (Gini coefficient, which is not additively decomposable). The weights given to the inequalities within the various subgroups distinguish the additively decomposable measures. Population and income shares are usually used for the weights. Following is an evaluation of some of the measures of inequality with regard to these desirable properties.

EVALUATION OF INEQUALITY MEASURES

A number of measures have been proposed in the literature. These measures fall into two categories as indicated before. There are conventional measures with no explicit reference to the concept of social welfare, and measures that are based on some formulation of the social welfare function. I will define and evaluate some of these measures with specific reference to the desirable properties indicated. The conventional measures most commonly used in research include the following:[3]

The Variance

$$V = \left(\frac{1}{n}\right)\sum_i (y_i - \mu)^2 \tag{4}$$

where μ is the mean income and y is the income of individual i, $i = 1, \ldots n$.

The Coefficient of Variation

$$C = \frac{\sqrt{V}}{\mu} \tag{5}$$

or its square:

$$C^2 = \frac{V}{\mu^2} \tag{6}$$

Unlike the variance, C is independent of the mean income level. Analogous measures, using log of income, can be based on the formula:

$$H = \left(\frac{1}{n}\right)\sum_i [\log(y_i) - \log(\delta)]^2 \tag{7}$$

when $\delta = \mu$, H equals logarithmic variance. If $\delta \neq \mu$, and $\delta = \theta$, where θ is the geometric mean, then H equals the variance of the logs.

The Gini Coefficient

$$G = \left[\frac{1}{[2n^2\,\mu]}\right]\sum_i\sum_j \left| y_i - y_j \right| \tag{8}$$

In reference to "income homogeneity," the above measures are unaffected by equal proportional changes in all incomes with the exception of the variance. Variance is not defined relative to the mean; thus it violates the mean independence property. A utility function is assumed to be quadratic (equivalent to) if the distributions are ranked according to the mean and variance. This implies increasing relative and absolute inequality aversion. According to Atkinson (1983a), this means equal absolute increases in all incomes give rise to the equally distributed equivalent income by less than the same amount. The coefficient of variation and the Gini coefficient are sensitive with regard to the Pigou-Dalton condition of transfer; i.e., a transfer from a richer person to a poorer person always reduces their value. The standard deviation of logarithm violates the principle of transfer occasionally. This can happen when there is a transfer from a rich individual to a poor individual at very high levels of income. In reference to the relative sensitivity, the coefficient of variation is equally sensitive at all levels of income. The Standard Deviation of Logarithms is more sensitive for transfers in the lower income brackets and rather insensitive to transfers among the rich. In the case of the Gini coefficient, a higher weight is attached to the transfers in the center of the distribution than at the two tails. Also with reference to the decomposition property, the Gini coefficient is not additively decomposable.

It has been shown that the conventional summary measures violate some of the desirable properties indicated in the previous section. It would be a better approach to examine social welfare functions that we would like to employ directly, rather than through implicit value judgments with each of these statistical summary measures.

The inequality measures, which are homogeneous, symmetric, decomposable, and satisfy the Pigou-Dalton condition of transfer, are the class of Generalized Entropy measures. They are defined as:

$$I(S,n) = f[\mu_\gamma (S)] \tag{9}$$

where γ is defined as the inequality aversion parameter. For $\gamma \neq 0$ and -1 the Generalized Entropy measures are ordinally equivalent to Atkinson indices of inequality (Atkinson 1970). I_0 and I_1, are Theil's two information measures.

Type of welfare function is defined by choosing γ, which is a measure of the degree of inequality aversion and relative sensitivity to transfers at different income levels. As γ falls, we attach more weight to transfers at the lower end of the distribution and less weight to transfers at the top.

MEASURED INEQUALITY AND THE ROLE OF ACCOUNTING INTERVAL

The extension of the duration of accounting for our purpose has added a new dimension to the measured inequality. It is important to be aware of the implications of this new dimension, i.e., time. Following is a brief insight into the extension of time and its effect upon inequality.

Let $Y = \left(Y_1/Y*, \ldots, Y_n/Y*\right)$ and $Y* = \sum_i Y_i$, where $Y_i = \sum_t Y_{it}$. Let $I(\bullet) = g(\bullet)$ denote a measure of relative income inequality where $g(\bullet)$ is convex and homogeneous. It may be verified that:

$$I(Y) \leqslant \sum_t \alpha_t I(Y^t) \tag{10}$$

where $Y^t = (y_{1t}, \ldots, y_{nt})$ and $y_{it} = Y_{it}/\sum_i Y_{it}$. Also $I(Y^t)$ denotes inequality at time t, and $\alpha_t = \mu_t/\mu$ represents the proportion of the aggregate T-period income in period t, where $\sum_t \alpha_t = 1$. The above notion indicates that the T-period inequality can never exceed the weighted sum of single-period inequality values. This indicates that for most of the common inequality measures, the inequality values fall as the length of the accounting interval is extended. This result finds support in the work of, for example, Shorrocks (1978), who has shown that inequality is reduced to some extent as the period of accounting is extended beyond one period. The exception is the result based on the Gini coefficient that suggests income inequality can actually increase with longer measurement intervals. However, this arises because the Gini coefficient is a nonconvex function of relative incomes.

To overcome this kind of problem, Shorrocks (1978) indicates that an appropriate comparison be made between long-run inequality and a weighted average of the annual inequalities. A more detailed statement is useful here.

Consider the time interval (t_1, t_T), which is divided into T subperiods. Also total income to individual i over the interval (t_{t-1}, t_t) is given by $Y_i(t_{t-1}, t_t)$. The appropriate mean over the subperiod is $\mu(t_{t-1}, t_t)$, and $I[Y(t_{t-1}, t_t)]$ is the associated inequality measure. For the whole time period we can define total (aggregate) income such that:

$$Y(t_1, t_T) = \sum_t Y(t_{t-1}, t_t) \tag{11}$$

and

$$\mu(t_t, t_T) = \sum_t \mu(t_{t-1}, t_t) \tag{12}$$

Thus, comparison of aggregate inequality index $I[Y(t_t, t_T)]$ with the index value $I[Y(t_{t-1}, t_t)]$ for the T subperiods is possible. From the above we have:

$$I[Y(t_1, t_T)] = g\left(Y/\mu\right) \tag{13}$$

$$= g\left(\left.\frac{\sum_t Y(t_{t-1},t_t)}{}\middle/\mu(t_1,t_T)\right.\right) \tag{14}$$

$$= g\left(\sum_t \alpha_t \left.\frac{Y(t_{t-1},t_t)}{}\middle/\mu(t_{t-1},t_t)\right.\right) \tag{15}$$

$$\leqslant \sum \alpha_t g\left(\left.\frac{Y(t_{t-1},t_t)}{}\middle/\mu(t_{t-1},t_t)\right.\right) \text{ by convexity of } g(\bullet) \tag{16}$$

where $\alpha_t = \left.\frac{\mu(t_{t-1},t_t)}{}\middle/\mu(t_1,t_T)\right.$ is the proportion of aggregate income received in subperiod t and it is normalized. This demonstrates that the T-period inequality does not exceed a weighted sum of the single-period inequality values. Equality holds above if and only if $\left.\frac{Y(t_{t-1},t_t)}{}\middle/\mu(t_{t-1},t_t)\right.$ is independent of the accounting period. However, it is evident that this method of aggregating income over time reduces income inequality since some income fluctuations (mobility) are smoothed out in this process of aggregation. The problem that we wish to address is whether the same phenomenon holds under different aggregation rules, i.e., with different $Y(t_1,t_T)$ and different α_t.

MEASUREMENT OF LONG-RUN INEQUALITY

Household income is a measure of economic well-being. It is usually given for a specific point in time, but this is only a snapshot of an attribute, which is hard to define, and which changes over time. Such a static view of economic well-being contains positive information, although it should be analyzed with some caution. One's view of these short-run pictures can be misleading. Recognition of this is particularly important since individuals move up and down the scale of income distribution over their life cycles, i.e., in the long run. Analysis of the "snapshots" for the purpose of public policy has created some concern on our part since most public policy decisions should consider the long-run implications as to the economic well-being of each individual.

Several factors are involved in measurement of long-run earnings inequality. First, the appropriate method of aggregating earnings needs to be selected. There are several approaches. A number of aggregation methods must be used to gauge the sensitivity of the long-run inequality to the method of aggregation in order to minimize the influence of normative preferences. Second, an appropriate index of inequality that possesses a set of desirable properties designed to minimize the normative judgments involved in selection must be selected.

Consider a population of N households ($i = 1, \ldots, N$) with earnings received for T consecutive accounting intervals, ($t = 1, \ldots, T$). The earning of individual i at time t is Y_{it}, and $Y_i = \sum_t Y_{it}$ is total earnings for individual i over the entire accounting period. Maasoumi (1986) developed a class of aggregator functions that place distinct weights on different attributes. If earnings at different points in time are viewed as distinct, different weights need to be used at different moments over the accounting interval. The aggregator functions should have distributions approximating T earnings distributions over the accounting interval. Theil (1967) and Maasoumi (1986) have formalized this notion of "*closeness*" in information theory. Consider:

$$S_i(Y_{i1}, \ldots, Y_{it}) = \left[\sum_t \eta_t Y_{it}^{-\beta} \right]^{-1/\beta} \qquad \beta \neq 0, -1 \tag{17}$$

$$= \Pi_t Y_{it}^{\eta_t} \qquad \beta = 0 \tag{18}$$

$$= \sum_t \eta_t Y_{it} \qquad \beta = -1 \tag{19}$$

where S_i is the aggregate composite measure of earnings over the accounting interval. η_t are the weights given to earnings in each period and $\sum_t \eta_t = 1$. As the period of accounting is extended, a new aggregate share measure for the ith individual is calculated. Note that $S^* = (S^*_1, \ldots, S^*_N)$, where ($S^*_i = S_i/\sum_j S_j$ is the ith share of aggregate earnings. β is related to the elasticity of substitution σ, and by the following relation $-\beta = 1 - 1/\sigma$. S^* can be regarded as a measure of intertemporal utility or an evaluation of households' economic well-being given β and η. The relative inequality in S^* is computed by the Generalized Entropy family of measures as:

$$I_\gamma(S) = \sum_i \left[(NS^*_i)^{1+\gamma} - 1 \right] \Big/ N\gamma(1 + \gamma) \qquad \gamma \neq 0, -1 \tag{20}$$

$$= \sum_i S^*_i \log(NS^*_i) \qquad \gamma = 0 \tag{21}$$

$$= \sum_i N^{-1} \log(1/NS^*_i) \qquad \gamma = -1 \tag{22}$$

where $\gamma = -(1 + \beta)$, and its choice determines the sensitivity to the two tails of income distribution. I_0 and I_{-1} are Theil's first and second measures of inequality, respectively. Theil's measures are special cases for linear and Cobb-Douglas-type aggregation. This family includes the monotonic transformation of the family of measures introduced by Atkinson (1970).

The decomposition of $I_\gamma(S)$ to "between-group" and a weighted average of "within-group" inequality for any partitioning of the population is desirable as well. The usefulness of the additive decomposition property of Generalized Entropy measures in this context is discussed in Maasoumi and Zandvakili (1990). For example, Theil's second measure of inequality can be decomposed to:

$$I_{-1} = I_{-1}(S) + \sum_r P_r I_{-1}(S^r) \tag{23}$$

where P_r is the population share of the rth group, $r = (1, \ldots, G)$. Note that S^r is the rth group's share vector and S is the vector of group means. The first term on the right-hand side is the "between-group" component of the measured inequality. The second term is a weighted average of "within-group" inequalities.

To measure stability over a subset of the accounting period M, $M \leq T$ period, the corresponding long-run inequality $I_\gamma(S)$, and a weighted average of short-run inequalities in each period, $\sum_t \mu_t I_\gamma(Y_t)$, is calculated. A measure of stability over the M periods is derived from the following relationship:

$$R_M = I_\gamma(S)/\sum_t \mu_t I_\gamma(Y_t) \tag{24}$$

where μ_t is the weight given to earnings at different time periods. If $\sum_t \mu_t = 1$, then μ_t can be replaced by η_t. As M approaches T, the profile generated by R_M reflects changes in the distribution of earnings (stability). The choice of $I_\gamma(S)$ affects the computation of R_M because inequality measures vary in their sensitivity to transfers in the distribution of earnings. Therefore, several inequality measures and aggregation methods were used. For some S_i, the restriction $0 \leq R_M \leq 1$ holds for all convex measures if $\sum_t \mu_t = 1$, where $\eta_t = \mu_t/\sum_t \mu_t$. This restriction holds for other functions following the propositions 1 and 2 in Maasoumi (1986) such that $-\gamma = (1 + \beta)$. Accordingly, R_M decomposes into the "between-group" and average "within-group" component such that:

$$R_B = \left. I_\gamma(S) \middle/ \sum_t \mu_t I_\gamma(Y_t) \right. \tag{25}$$

and

$$R_w = \left. \sum_t P_r^{-\gamma} S_r^{1+\gamma} I_\gamma(S^r) \middle/ \sum_t \mu_{tr} I_\gamma(Y_t^w) \right. \tag{26}$$

where $R_M = R_B + R_W$. Group-specific stability profiles are derived from the following expression:

$$R^w = \left. I_\gamma(S^w) \middle/ \sum_t \mu_{tr} I_\gamma(Y_t^w) \right. \tag{27}$$

where the earnings share of the ith household in the rth group at time t is Y_{tri} with the relative weights given as μ_{tr}. The value of R^W ranges between 0 and 1.

The "earnings-share matrix" y has a typical element $y_{it} = Y_{it}/\sum_j Y_{jt}$. The composite measure of earnings S^* based on Maasoumi (1986) is "closest" to the $y_t = (y_{1t}, \ldots, y_{nt})$ when:

$$D_\beta (S^*, y;\mu) = \sum_t \mu_t \sum_i S_i^* \left[(S_i^* / y_{it})^{-\beta} - 1 \right] \Big/ \beta(\beta + 1) \tag{28}$$

It can be demonstrated that $0 \leq R_M \leq 1$ for all S_i when $-\gamma = (1 + \beta)$. For example:

$$I_0 (S) = \sum_t \mu_t I_0(Y_t) - D_{-1}(S^*, y;\mu) \leq \sum_t \mu_t I_0(Y_t) \tag{29}$$

The second term in (29) is positive by definition. Long-run inequality, therefore, is less than a weighted average of short-run inequalities, and the measure of stability is between the bounds established for linear-type aggregation functions. In the same fashion, it can be shown that:

$$I_{-1} (S) = \sum_t \mu_t I_{-1}(Y_t) - D_0 (S^*,y;\mu) \leq \sum_t \mu_t I_{-1} (Y_t) \tag{30}$$

holds for Cobb-Douglas-type aggregation functions. Equation (29) and (30) establish that R_M must be between the bounds established as benchmarks for our measure of stability. This enables the analyst to detect the changes in the size distribution of earnings over time. This is particularly important in understanding the nature of the observed movements (permanent or transitory).

STATISTICAL INFERENCE FOR MEASURES OF INEQUALITY

The measures cited above are most frequently used for dynamic comparisons of inequality such as comparing inequality measures across time, and policy analysis comparing the redistributive effects of tax policy. A major shortcoming to this literature is the lack of statistical inference; in most studies, no attempt is made to determine the statistical significance of observed differences in the computed values of a particular measure, despite the availability of asymptotic methods.[4]

The problem with conducting statistical inference for any of the measures of inequality used in the literature is that they are all nonlinear functions of a random variable (usually income). As a result, the interval estimates available from asymptotic theory may not be accurate and the small sample properties of these intervals are not known. Further, all the decomposable inequality measures used in the literature are bounded (e.g., the Gini coefficient lies in the [0, 1] interval), so application of standard asymptotic results may lead to estimated intervals that extend beyond the theoretical bounds of a particular measure (e.g., a negative lower bound for Gini).

An alternative method for computing probability intervals is to bootstrap. The bootstrap provides interval estimates drawn from the small sample distribution. These intervals have been shown to be superior to asymptotic intervals both theoretically and in a variety of applications; see, e.g. Burr (1994), Freedman and Peters (1984), and Hall (1992). Bootstrap intervals are computationally inexpensive and easy to calculate. The same method applies to all the inequality measures used in the literature, and the bootstrap method automatically takes into account any bounds that apply to a particular measure. Furthermore, bootstrap intervals computed using the percentile method provide a straightforward solution to the Behrens-Fisher problem of comparing means from two distributions. Given the potential advantages of bootstrapping, it appears worthwhile to consider its use as a tool for statistical inference for inequality measures.

The bootstrap is a method for recovering the distribution of a statistic by employing simulation methods to approximate the small sample distribution.[5] The bootstrap provides a numerical approximation to the distribution of interest, F, that is similar to a high-order Edgeworth expansion. Edgeworth expansions can represent considerable improvements over Normal approximations, and the bootstrap is often superior to a practically calculable Edgeworth expansion.[6]

Tail probability values for hypothesis tests can be calculated directly from the bootstrap distribution in the same manner as probability intervals. Often, however, we are more interested in comparing different values of an inequality measure, such as for different points in time. The following test for this case, analogous to the comparison of two means from two different samples can be used. Consider the statistic $D = H_1 - H_2$, where H_1 and H_2 are the two values of the inequality measure we wish to compare. The distribution of D can be bootstrapped in the same manner used to obtain distributions for H_1 and H_2. Tail probability values for hypothesis regarding D can be calculated directly from the bootstrap distribution F(D). A confidence interval can thus be constructed using the values of D associated with appropriate tail probabilities. Exploiting the relationship between confidence intervals and hypothesis tests then allows us to conduct an hypothesis test for $D = 0$.[7]

Note that the hypothesis test using the statistic D involves the comparison of means of two distributions, which has become known as the Behrens-Fisher problem. The problem is a very difficult one within the classical hypothesis-testing framework and consequently there is no generally accepted classical procedure for this problem. By contrast, the Bayesian procedure is straightforward. The bootstrap method is a simple implementation of this Bayesian procedure.[8] The bootstrap performs well in this situation, and represents an important advantage of bootstrap methods over the use of asymptotic interval estimates as shown in Mills and Zandvakili (1997).

CONCLUDING REMARKS

This survey was set forth with two broad objectives and their interaction in mind. The first dimension involves measurement of inequality and mobility. The second objective refers to how the choice of inequality measures influences the degree of inequality. In the process, I addressed some questions with regard to the measurement of inequality. They involved (1) the importance of factors such as income source, income unit, equivalence scale, weighting, and so forth; (2) the choice of the degree of inequality aversion and its effect upon the measured short-run inequality, long-run inequality, and income stability; (3) the choice of the "weights" used for the calculation of weighted average of short-run inequality, long-run inequality, and measured stability; (4) the effect of accounting interval upon the measured inequality; and (5) the measured value for the stability profile and its interpretations, and the role of statistical inference in measurement of inequality. I hope that this survey can contribute to more important endeavors for the analysis of inequality and related policy questions.

NOTES

This is a revised version of a paper presented at the Conference on Earnings Inequality, Unemployment, and Poverty in the Middle East and North Africa at the School of Business, Lebanese American University, Byblos, Lebanon, November 5–7, 1998.

1. See Cowell and Kuga (1981a, and b) and Bourguignon (1979).

2. See Dalton (1920) and Cowell and Kuga (1981).

3. See Sen (1973a) and Atkinson (1970).

4. Some notable exceptions are Bishop et al. (1988, 1989), Cowell (1989a), Gastwirth et al. (1986, 1989), and related work. See Maasoumi (1997) for a more complete list of references.

5. See Efron (1979, 1982), Efron and Tibshirani (1993), Hall (1988, 1992), and Freedman and Peters (1984) for detailed expositions of the bootstrap.

6. Bhattacharya and Qumsiyeh (1989) show that the bootstrap estimate of F outperforms the short Edgeworth approximation in and L^p metric.

7. See Efron and Tibshirani (1993) for a clear exposition of this approach.

8. The bootstrap distribution is a close approximation to the posterior density from Bayesian inference with a Dirichlet process prior. See Efron (1982) and Rubin (1981).

REFERENCES

Atkinson, A. B. (1970). "On the Measurement of Inequality," *Journal of Economic Theory* 2: 244–263.

————(1983a). *The Economics of Inequality*. New York: Oxford University Press.

————(1983b). *Social Justice and Public Policy*. Cambridge: MIT Press.

Atkinson, A. B. and F. Bourguignon (1982). "The Comparison of Multi-dimensioned Distributions of Economic Status," *Review of Economic Studies* 49: 183–201.

Bhattacharya, R. N. and M. Qumsiyeh (1989). "Second Order L^p-Comparisons Between the Bootstrap and Empirical Edgeworth Expansion Methodologies," *Annals of Statistics* 17: 160–169.

Bishop, J. A., S. Chakraborti, and P. D. Thistle (1989). "Relative Inequality, Absolute Inequality, and Welfare: Some Statistical Tests," *Economic Letters* 26: 291–294.

Bishop, J. A., J. P. Formby, and P. D. Thistle (1989). "Statistical Inference, Income Distributions, and Social Welfare," *Research on Economic Inequality* 1: 49–82.

Blackorby, C. and D. Donaldson (1978). "Measures of Relative Equality and Their Meaning in Terms of Social Welfare," *Journal of Economic Theory* 18: 58–90.

————(1984). "Ethical Social Index Numbers and the Measurement of Effective Tax/benefit Progressivity," *Canadian Journal of Economics* 17: 683–694.

Bourguignon, F. (1979). "Decomposable Income Inequality Measures," *Econometrica* 47: 901–920.

Burr, D. (1994). "A Comparison of Certain Bootstrap Confidence Intervals in the Cox Model," *Journal of the American Statistical Association* 89: 1290–1302.

Chakravarty, S. R. (1988). "Extended Gini Indices of Inequality," *International Economic Review* 29: 147–156.

Chakravarty, S. R. and B. Dutta (1987). "A Note on Measures of Distance between Income Distributions," *Journal of Economic Theory* 41: 185–188.

Cowell, F. A. (1977). *Measuring Inequality*. Oxford: Philip Allan.

————(1980). "On the Structure of Additive Inequality Measures," *Review of Economic Studies* 47: 521–531.

————(1985). "Measurement of Distributional Change: An Axiomatic Approach," *Review of Economic Studies* 52: 135–151.

————(1989a). "Sampling Variance and Decomposable Inequality Measures," *Journal of Econometrics* 41: 27–41.

————(1989b). "Analysis of Income Distribution Using Microcomputer Technology," *Research on Economic Inequality* 1: 249–267.

Cowell, F. A. and K. Kuga (1981a). "Additivity and the Entropy Concept: An Axiomatic Approach to Inequality Measurement," *Journal of Economic Theory* 25: 131–143.

————(1981b). "Inequality Measurement: an Axiomatic Approach," *European Economic Review* 15: 287–305.

Cowell, F. A. and F. Mehta (1984). "The Estimation and Interpolation of Inequality Measures," *Review of Economic Studies* 43: 273–290.

Creedy, J. (1977). "The distribution of lifetime earnings," *Oxford Economic Papers* 29: 412–429.

————(1985). *The Dynamics of Income Distribution*. Oxford: Blackwell.

Dalton, H. (1920). *The Inequality of Incomes*. London: Routledge.

Dasgupta, P., A. Sen, and D. Starrett (1973). "Notes on the Measurement of Inequality," *Journal of Economic Theory* 6: 180–187.

DeGroot, M. H. (1986). *Probability and Statistics*, 2nd edition. Reading, MA: Addison-Wesley.

Donaldson, D. and J. A. Weymark (1983). "Ethically Flexible Indices for Income Distributions in the Continuum," *Journal of Economic Theory* 29: 353–358.

Ebert, U. (1984). "Measures of Distance between Income Distributions," *Journal of Economic Theory* 32: 266–274.

———(1987). "Size and Distribution of Incomes as Determinants of Social Welfare," *Journal of Economic Theory* 41: 23–33.

Efron, B. (1979). "Bootstrap Methods: Another Look at the Jackknife," *Annals of Statistics* 7: 1–26.

———(1982). *The Jackknife, the Bootstrap and Other Resampling Plans*. Philadelphia: SIAM.

Efron, B. and R. J. Tibshirani (1993). *An Introduction to the Bootstrap*. New York: Chapman & Hall.

Fisher, F. M. (1987). "Household Equivalence Scales and Interpersonal Comparisons," *Review of Economic Studies* 54: 519–524.

Foster, J. E. (1985). "Inequality Measurement," in H. P. Young, ed. "Fair Allocation," *Proceedings of Symposia in Applied Mathematics*, volume 33, American Mathematical Society.

Foster, J. E. and Shorrocks, A. F. (1988). "Poverty Orderings," *Econometrica* 56: 173–177.

Freedman, D. A. and S. C. Peters (1984). "Bootstrapping an Econometric Model: Some Empirical Results," *Journal of Business and Economic Statistics* 2: 150–158.

Gastwirth, J. L. (1972). "The Estimation of the Lorenz Curve and Gini Index," *Review of Economics and Statistics* 54:306–316.

Gastwirth, J. L., T. K. Nayak, and A. N. Krieger (1986). "Large Sample Theory for the Bounds on the Gini and Related Indices from Grouped Data," *Journal of Business and Economic Statistics* 4:269–273.

Gastwirth, J. L. and J. L. Wang (1989). "Statistical Properties of Measures of Between-Group Income Differentials," *Journal of Econometrics* 42:5–19.

Hall, P. (1988). "Theoretical Comparison of Bootstrap Confidence Intervals" (with discussion), *Annals of Statistics* 16:927–985.

———(1992). *The Bootstrap and Edgeworth Expansion*. New York: Springer-Verlag.

Jaynes, E. T. (1976). "Confidence Intervals vs. Bayesian Intervals," in W. L. Haper and C. A. Hooker, eds. *Foundations of Probability Theory, Statistical Inference, and Statistical Theories of Science*. Dordrecht: D. Reidel Publishing Co.

Jorgenson, D. W. and D. T. Slesnick (1984). "Inequality in the Distribution of Individual Welfare," *Advances in Econometrics* 3:67–130.

Kakwani, N. C. (1977a). "Applications of Lorenz Curves in Economic Analysis," *Econometrica* 45:719–727.

———(1977b). "Measurement of Tax Progressivity: An International Comparison," *Economic Journal* 87:71–80.

Khetan, C. P. and S. N. Podder (1976). "Measurement of Income Tax Progressivity in a Growing Economy: The Canadian Experience," *Canadian Journal of Economics* 4:613–629.

Kiefer, D. W. (1985). "Distributional Tax Progressivity Measurement," *National Tax Journal* 37: 497–513.

Lambert, P. J. (1989). *The Distribution and Redistribution of Income: A Mathematical Analysis.* Oxford: Basil Blackwell.

Lillard, L. A. and R. Willis (1978). "Dynamic Aspects of Earnings Mobility," *Econometrica* 46:985–1012.

Maasoumi, E. (1986). "The Measurement and Decomposition of Multi-Dimensional Inequality," *Econometrica* 54:991–997.

———(1997). "Empirical Analysis of Inequality and Welfare," in P. Schmidt and H. Persaran, eds. *Handbook of Applied Microeconomics.* Oxford: Basil Blackwell.

Maasoumi, E. and S. Zandvakili (1986). "A Class of Generalized Measures of Mobility with Applications," *Economics Letters* 22:97–102.

———(1989). "Mobility Profiles and Time Aggregates of Individual Incomes," *Research on Economic Inequality* 1:195–218.

———(1990). "Generalized Entropy Measures of Mobility for Different Sexes and Income Levels," *Journal of Econometrics* 43:121–133.

Maasoumi, E., S. Zandvakili, and J. Mills (1998). "Consensus Ranking of US Income Distribution: A Bootstrap Application of Test for Stochastic Dominance," working paper.

Mills, J. and S. Zandvakili (1997). "Statistical Inference via Bootstrapping for Measures of Economic Inequality," *Journal of Applied Econometrics* 12:1–18.

Moyes, P. (1989). "Some Classes of Functions that Preserve the Inequality and Welfare Orderings of Income Distributions," *Journal of Economic Theory* 49:347–359.

Pechman, J. A. (1987). "Tax Reform: Theory and Practice," *Journal of Economic Perspectives* 1:11–28.

Rubin, D. B. (1981). "The Bayesian Bootstrap," *Annals of Statistics* 9:130–134.

Sen, A. (1970a). *Collective Choice and Social Welfare.* San Francisco: Holden-Day.

———(1970b). "Interpersonal Aggregation and Partial Comparability," *Econometrica* 40:393–409.

———(1973a). *On Economic Inequality.* Oxford: Clarendon Press.

———(1973b). "On Ignorance and Equal Distribution," *American Economic Review* 63:1022–1024.

———(1974). "Informational Bases of Alternative Welfare Approaches," *Journal of Public Economics* 3:387–403.

———(1976). "Poverty: An Ordinal Approach to Measurement," *Econometrica* 44:219–231.

———(1977). "On Weights and Measures: Informational Constraints in Social Welfare Analysis," *Econometrica* 45:1539–1572.

Shorrocks, A. F. (1978). "Income Inequality and Income Mobility," *Journal of Economic Theory* 19:376–393.

———(1980). "The Class of Additively Decomposable Income Inequality Measures," *Econometrica* 48:613–625.

————(1982a). "Inequality Decomposition by Factor Components," *Econometrica* 50:193–211.

————(1982b). "On the Distance between Income Distributions," *Econometrica* 50: 1337–1339.

————(1982c). "Inequality Decomposition by Factor Components," *Econometrica* 50:193–211.

————(1983a). "Ranking Income Distributions," *Economica* 50:3–17.

————(1983b). "The Impact of Income Components on the Distribution of Family Incomes," *Quarterly Journal of Economics* 98:311–326.

————(1984). "Inequality Decomposition by Population Subgroups," *Econometrica* 52:1369–1386.

Shorrocks, A. F. and J. Foster (1987). "Transfer Sensitive Inequality Measures," *Review of Economic Studies* 54:485–497.

Silber, J. (1989). "Factor Components, Population Subgroups and the Computation of the Gini Index of Inequality," *Review of Economics and Statistics* 71: 107–115.

Slottje, D. J., ed. (1989). *Research on Economic Inequality, 1*. Greenwich, CT: JAI Press.

Theil, H. (1967). *Economics and Information Theory*. Amsterdam: North-Holland.

Yitzhaki, S. (1979). "Relative Deprivation and the Gini Coefficient," *Quarterly Journal of Economics* 93:321–324.

————(1983). "On an Expression of the Gini Index," *International Economic Review* 24:617–628.

Zandvakili, S. (1995). "Decomposable Measures of Income Tax Progressivity," *Applied Economics* 27:657–660.

————, "Inequality and Taxation," Guest editor (1997). *Research on Economic Inequality, 7*. Greenwich, CT: JAI Press.

Zandvakili, S. and J. Mills (1998). "Statistical Inference via Bootstrapping: An Application to the Distributional Implications of Taxes and Transfer Programs in US," *Proceedings of the American Statistical Association*: Section on Social Statistics, 101–106.

3

Unraveling the Paradox in Egypt's Trends in Income Inequality and Poverty

Ayman Kandeel and Jeffrey B. Nugent

INTRODUCTION

Income inequality and poverty have recently risen as both policy and re-search priorities in the economics of development for several reasons. First, development has frequently been associated with increasing inequality. Second, poverty has been reduced by growth but increased by income inequality, implying that poverty can be assuredly reduced only if a country is able to achieve growth without raising income inequality. Third, in contrast to dominant development thinking of the 1950s and 1960s in which inequality was believed to be favorable to growth and development,[1] the new thinking views inequality as hurting development,[2] implying that it is important to reduce inequality in order to raise the chances for growth and development.

As shown in column (4) of Table 3.1, as measured by the Gini coefficient, income inequality in Egypt has fallen rather steadily between 1959 and 1991 and then again between 1990/91 and 1995/96. While the Gini coefficient puts more weight on the middle range of the distribution than do other measures of inequality, at least between the latter two years, the same downward trend in inequality can also be observed in the Kuznets ratio,[3] a measure that relates only the extremes of the distribution as shown in column (5) of the same table. This is a significant finding for three reasons. First, it is based on data of relatively high quality and comparability so as to be included in the Deininger and Squire (1997) data set, the best compilation of inequality indexes yet assembled. Second, the fact that the trend

Table 3.1
Growth Rates of Income and Population, Gini Coefficients, and Poverty Indexes 1959–1996

Year	Rate of Real Income Growth	Rate of Population Growth	Gini Coefficient of Income Inequality	Kuznets Ratio	Head Count Ratio P_0	Poverty Gap P_1	Inequality-Weighted Poverty Gap P_2
1959			42.0				
1965	7.40	2.66	40.0				
1975	3.97	2.05	38.0				
1985	8.37	2.55					
	3.89	2.27					
1990/91	4.49	1.92	32.0/34.61	9.008	26.01	6.44	1.03
1995/96			/ 33.12	7.334	42.13	8.06	1.71

Source: For income and population growth rates: United Nations MEDS, World Bank, *World Development Indicators,* CD-ROM. Gini coefficients, P_0, P_1 and P_2 for all years prior to 1990/91 from Deininger and Squire (1997) and the second set of estimates for 1990/91 and 1995/96 computed from CAPMAS (1990/91 and 1995/96).

is continuous over this period of more than 35 years contrasts with the new stylized fact that instead of long-term trends or inverted-U patterns in income inequality indexes, most countries show fluctuations, or a series of different distributional "episodes." Indeed, the Gini coefficient, the most commonly used index of income inequality, has decreased by over 25 percent over the period. Third, at least for the most recent period, the decline in the Gini coefficient is accompanied by a decline in the Kuznets ratio.nd 1995/96, which is the subject of this chapter.

At the same time, as shown in column (2) of the table, growth rates in real income have fluctuated and while comparable poverty rate indexes are unavailable before 1990, as shown in columns (6), (7), and (8) of the table, all three different poverty rate indexes (P_0, P_1, and P_2)[4] have increased sharply between 1990/91 and 1995/96. The contrast between the trend in income inequality and poverty, the former falling and the latter rising, at least between 1990/91 and 1995/96, was identified in a recent paper by Cardiff (1997). Yet, he made no attempt to explain the paradox.

The purpose of this chapter, therefore, is to explain the paradox by separately explaining the changes in both the Gini coefficients and Kuznets ratios as indexes of inequality and indexes of poverty and then comparing the two sets of results. In each case, the overall changes are disaggregated into various components, such as age, education, public goods supply, region, and an unexplained residual.

The organization of the chapter is as follows. The next section describes the changes in the Egyptian economy, especially over the years 1990–1995/96, that could have affected either income distribution or poverty. The next section identifies the data used in the study and the measures of poverty and income inequality. The following section describes the methods used, presents descriptive statistics, and contains the results of the regression analysis for both income inequality and poverty. That analysis is based on a pooling of cross-section data for 40 regions (the urban and rural regions separately of each of Egypt's 26 governorates) for each of two periods: 1990/91 and 1995/96.[5] The regression coefficients are then combined with the changes in the explanatory variables to determine the extent to which each such variable "contributes to" the observed changes in income inequality and poverty. The final section contains our conclusions.

CHANGES IN THE EGYPTIAN ECONOMY AND POLICY OVER THE 1990–1995/96 PERIOD

From the mid-1970s to the mid-1980s Egypt enjoyed an acceleration in its growth rate, attributable to several favorable factors. Among these were (1) a gradual opening up of the economy, (2) the return of the Sinai and the reopening of the Suez Canal, (3) the indirect effects of the oil boom in the Gulf realized through exports of goods and services to the Gulf and the remittances from Egyptian workers in the Gulf, and (4) substantial flows of external assistance and credit, which alleviated the balance-of-payments constraints. Over the decade, however, the fiscal deficit mushroomed to some 20 percent of gross domestic product (GDP), the foreign debt virtually exploded, and inflation accelerated.

By the mid-1980s, Egypt's day of reckoning had come. Credit constraints again became binding, income growth rates fell to virtually zero, unemployment rates increased, some large nonbank financial institutions failed, and investment rates fell sharply. Inflation continued to accelerate until it hit a rate of 22.7 percent per annum in 1989. As shown in Table 3.1, even fertility rates and population growth rates were reduced substantially. With the need for debt rescheduling, under these pressures, Egypt agreed to undertake some reforms. Until 1991, however, by which time the country's international reserves had virtually disappeared, little was accomplished. After 1991, reforms began in earnest; government spending was trimmed, including various kinds of subsidies, some of which were focused on the poor. As a result, the public sector's share in GDP fell from 47 percent to 26.5 percent between 1991 and 1996 (Abol-Kheir, 1996). The gradual and partial removal of food subsidies had the effect of raising food prices and the reduction in public expenditures and modern sector employment had the effect of putting a squeeze on real income of relatively low-wage public sector jobs. All these effects could be expected to raise income inequality and poverty rates between 1991 and 1996.

Yet, one of the reforms implemented after 1991 was a tax reform (the Global Income Tax Law of 1993), which featured tax exemptions for the poor. Even more important, however, was a financial reform that raised interest rates on bank deposits in domestic currency and had the effect of reversing the dollarization trend that had taken place since the mid-1980s. The reduced inflation presumably helped the poor, who had less access to dollars and held more of their assets in the form of domestic currency. This also allowed the Central Bank to accumulate dollar reserves and since then to effectively stabilize the exchange rate.

With exchange rate stabilization has come increased foreign investment. While the reforms were expected to bring substantial pain for several years, in fact only 1990 and 1991 were really years of stagnation. Real income growth per annum accelerated from 1 percent in 1992 to 4.7 percent in 1996 and 4.9 percent in 1997. As a result, per-capita income is estimated to have increased from $610 in 1991 to about $765 in 1996 (World Development 1996), and to an estimated $1,090 in 1997. For the first time in modern history, Egypt has moved into the middle-income category (*Social Indicators* 1996). Egypt's modest recovery occurred sooner than many had expected, in part because of the surprisingly effective financial reform and, in part also, due to the debt reduction that followed Egypt's active participation in the Gulf War. A negative external shock, however, was the continuing decline in real oil prices, once oil had become so prominent in Egypt's exports. The oil price decline also had the indirect effect of reducing transfers from Egyptian workers in the Gulf.

Hence, the 1991–1996 period was clearly one of major changes in policy as well as external shocks that had differing effects on poverty and income distribution and resulted in the paradoxical findings reported in Table 3.1 of gradual recovery in growth, decreasing inequality but sharply increasing poverty.

DATA AND MEASURES USED

Before describing the Egyptian data, it should be recognized that certain rather demanding criteria have to be satisfied to assure that a given economic data set would be appropriate for measuring household characteristics in general and income distribution and poverty in particular (Kakwani 1990): First, the sample must be randomly selected so that each member of the population has an equal chance of being selected. Second, the sample has to be representative; i.e., its structure has to be an image of the true population. Third, the observations should be independent to ensure that there are no sample biases. Fourth, the data set must be "sufficiently" large to assure that slight changes in the selected sample would not substantially affect the results.

Usually, all these requirements cannot be satisfied in a household survey, and there are measurement errors in all surveys of this type due both to the fact that a sample can never completely represent a population and to human error/bias (Foster et al. 1985). The question of which variable to use—income or expenditure—as the basis for measures of poverty and income inequality has received much attention in the economics literature in general, and in development studies in particular. As a general rule, the decision on which to use depends on the objectives of the analysis (Atkinson 1970; Kakwani 1990).

By general agreement, however, data on incomes are most appropriate for determining income inequality whereas for measuring poverty over an extended period of time, it is common to use expenditure data as a measure of "living standards." The use of income data for poverty calculations is also rather common. In either case, however, to compare poverty over time or even at one point in time over space, the expenditures must be in real terms, thereby requiring an appropriate and reliable Consumer Price Index.

Given that they are based on a large and nationally representative national sample and that an appropriate consumer price index is available, the surveys used in this study are the Egyptian Household Income, Expenditure, and Consumption Surveys (HIECS) of 1990/91 and 1995/96. The HIECS data set is a household survey on expenditure, income, and consumption in Egypt. Sponsored by both USAID and Egypt's Central Agency for Public Mobilization and Statistics (CAPMAS), these two surveys are to be followed by other similar ones every five years. Hence, the findings reported here based on these surveys should also be useful in future comparisons. The samples are "sufficiently" large for serious quantitative analysis, allowing an assumption of sample mean convergence.

Some shortcomings in the surveys and their comparability, however, are evident. For example, according to the CAPMAS description of the survey, one area, namely the area inhabited almost exclusively by Bedouin nomads, has been omitted because of time and transportation constraints. Even at most, however, the Bedouin population could not account for as much as 2 percent of the entire population of Egypt.

Another potential problem can arise if there are differences in the way different surveys are carried out, e.g., in the time of year, the phrasing of questions, definitions, and so forth. While in the Egyptian case under study, considerable care was taken to avoid such barriers to comparability, even so, there was one change that makes the results somewhat less than perfectly comparable. In particular, to increase the response rate, the survey was streamlined somewhat in 1995/96 relative to 1990/91. As pointed out by Cardiff (1997), the result was apparently an increase in the response rate among the rural poor. This latter difference would seem to have increased the number of poor and hence increased poverty rates. It might also have affected income inequality in one direction or another. Hence, despite the care that was taken to make the two studies as comparable as possible, they are still neither perfectly comparable nor fully representative. Yet, the magnitude of any such bias would appear to be very small, and swamped by the effect of rural-urban migration during the period.

The part of the survey that was most streamlined was that dealing with details on expenditures, generally aggregating more items into an "other" category. For this reason, the expenditures data between the two surveys could be less comparable than the income data. Therefore, despite the more common use of expenditures data in constructing poverty indexes, to maximize comparability in this study we focus on income data even in the poverty index calculations.

In any case, the income data for the two surveys are certainly very close to being both fully comparable and representative and are clearly the best available for assessing changes in poverty and income inequality over this important period of reform. For the 1990/1991 HIECS, annual income and expenditure data are available for a sample of 5,880 households in urban areas and 8,352 in rural areas. In the 1995/1996 HIECS sample there were 6,622 urban households and 8,183 rural ones, the difference between the two surveys reflecting the continuing rural-urban migration. The 1995/1996 HIECS represents a total of about 73,939 individuals, 24,944 of whom earned income during or before the period of the survey. Sources of income are classified in various categories and included transfers from both relatives and government. All categories are comparable over both surveys. In both surveys, the head of the household was asked to record all sources of income and items of expenditure by him- or herself and by all other family members. Wherever possible, the other family members earning income were questioned separately. The primary objective of the survey was to obtain a precise account of itemized income and expenditures by type of expenditure, of each household, and each income-earning individual within the household. The 1995/1996 HIECS gives expenditure budget shares to over 600 items. Among the other information obtained for household heads are their gender, education, occupation, home ownership or rental arrangement, location by rural and urban as well as governorate, and access to infrastructure such as electricity or sewerage.

The indexes of poverty and income inequality used in this analysis are as follows:

Poverty

Two common measures of poverty are used: the head-count ratio (P_0) and the depth-of-poverty measure (P_1). These are sometimes referred to as measures of absolute and relative poverty, respectively. The method for calculating them is that of Foster-Greer-Thorbecke (FGT) (1985) used also for Egypt by Cardiff (1997) and for other countries in many other studies. The P_0 measure describes the incidence of poverty, and is simply the proportion of the total count within a specific group having an expenditure level less than some defined poverty level. In other words, it simply measures the proportion of those below a certain poverty level. The other measure, P_1, is used to measure the "depth" of poverty or the poverty gap, specifically, how far below the poverty line the poor fall (on average). To visualize the difference, suppose that all other households have the same income in each of two periods but that one poor household becomes poorer in the second period than in the first period. If so, P_0 would remain unchanged because the number of households below the poverty line remains unchanged. Yet, P_1 would increase since the relative degree of poverty or the poverty gap would have increased. A related index is P_2, which integrates inequality among the poor with the poverty gap or relative poverty.[6] Although the change between 1990/91 and 1995/96 in this index is reported in Table 3.1 along with P_0 and P_1, since this index combines inequality (which we treat separately from poverty), we do not analyze it. Not surprisingly, as shown in Table 3.1, its change was between the doubling of the poverty rates and the slight decline in income inequality. In particular, it increased by a little less than 70 percent over the period 1991–1996.

To define the indexes P_0 and P_1, as well as to measure the degree of income inequality, it is necessary to order the incomes or expenditures

$y = (y_1, y_2, \ldots, y_n)$ from highest to lowest, and define a poverty line $L >$ 0, where n is the total number of households in the population. Note that more than one L could be defined over the range of n, if we had evidence of significant variation in the value of the poverty line across governorates. However, this complicates the analysis, so we will ignore this possibility. Let $q_i = L - y_i$ be the amount by which the ith household's income or expenditure falls below the poverty line. Note that now we will consider only the subset of the population that is poor, namely, those who fall below the poverty line. Consider the subset of households f where $f = f(y, L/q_1 > 0)$, i.e., households that fall below the poverty line. The form of the FGT poverty index is a weighted sum of incomes (or expenditures) below the poverty level:

$$P_\alpha = (1/n) \sum_{i=1}^{q} (q_i/L)^\alpha \tag{1}$$

where α denotes a "poverty aversion" parameter. Obviously, the value of the index would vary with the choice of alpha. Normally, alpha is chosen to be 0, 1, or 2.

If $\alpha = 0$,
$$P_0 = L/n \tag{2}$$

which measures the absolute level of poverty, or the head-count ratio, simply the proportion of the population having an expenditure or income level less than a previously defined poverty line.

If $\alpha = 1$,
$$P_1 = (1/n) \sum_{i=1}^{q} (q_i/L) \tag{3}$$

P_1 constitutes a relative poverty measure. As we can see, P_1 is generally preferred to P_0 as a measure of poverty because it is sensitive to the income or expenditure deficits of the poor. Unlike the P_0 measure, P_1 will change if one poor household gets poorer, other household income levels held constant.

If $\alpha = 2$,
$$P_2 = (1/n) \sum_{i=1}^{q} (q_i/L)^2 \tag{4}$$

This is the other measure of relative poverty. It takes into consideration differences in the extent to which different members of the poor fall below the poverty line. It gives a higher level of the poverty index, the larger is the degree of inequality of income among the poor.

The P_0 measure is distributed bivariate normal with zero mean and variance $P_0(1 - P_0)/n$. The other P_α measures have variances $P_{2\alpha} - P_\alpha^2$. Kakwani (1990) provides the methodology for testing the significance of the poverty index, P_α, by testing the significance of the difference between the indexes for two independently drawn samples.[7]

Income Distribution

Since there is no unique or always preferred method for reducing information on the entire distribution of income to a single number, several different indexes of income inequality are in common use. In some situations the rankings obtained by comparing two or more distributions are sensitive to the use of different indexes. Nevertheless, as noted above, this turned out not to be the case for the Egyptian HIECS of 1990/91 and 1995/96 employed in this study wherein the Gini coefficient and Kuznets ratio moved in the same direction. Nevertheless, because the determinants of these two different indexes of inequality could be quite different, both are employed in the subsequent analysis. It should be remembered that the Gini coefficient weighs more heavily incomes in the middle of the distribution whereas the Kuznets ratio (defined as the percent of income of the richest 25 percent of the population divided by that of the poorest 25 percent) weighs only the rich and the poor, i.e., the tails of the distribution of households by income. The Gini coefficient is also useful because of the ability to make comparisons with the Gini coefficients used for many other countries, regions, and time periods.[8] Its common use arises in part because of its close conceptual relation to the Lorenz curve, i.e., the curve showing the relationship between the cumulative share of income belonging to the accumulated share of the population starting from the poorest, and is also in part due to the fact that it is decomposable into income sources and so forth.[9]

As mentioned at the outset, the paradox to be investigated was revealed in Table 3.1. In particular, income inequality seems to have fallen slightly between 1990/91 and 1995/96 but the poverty measures (P_0, P_1, and P_2) have all increased substantially. As mentioned above, for both P_0 and P_1, the increase is 100 percent or more. The observed increase in the poverty indexes are clearly too large to be attributable to the aforementioned increase in the response rate among the rural poor in the 1995/96 survey relative to that of 1990/91.

METHODS USED, DESCRIPTIVE STATISTICS, AND REGRESSION RESULTS

A common procedure is to decompose the indexes of poverty and income distribution into their component parts, a procedure that can be accomplished only when one has access to the microlevel data set. Since such access is often not possible and was not in this case, the method used here is regression analysis based on a pooling of the 40 regions for each of the two periods surveyed, i.e., 1990/91 and 1995/96, forming a pseudo panel data set. The explanatory variables are dummy variables for urban location (URBAN), various characteristics of the household head, and the degree of access of the household to infrastructure. While access to various types of infrastructure was relevant, the one used is access to sewerage; specifically, the variable (NOSEWER) takes the value one if there is *no sewerage* connected to the housing unit. The variables describing the head of household's characteristics included in the analysis are those representing the age of the household head being over 65 years (HAGE1) or under 35 (HAGE2), the household head having no education (HEDUC0), having primary education only (HEDUC1), some secondary education (HEDUC4), or college and above education (HEDUC3). (HOCUP1) represents the percent of heads of households who are self-employed, while (HOCUP2) represents the percent of those who were unemployed at the time of the survey.

Table 3.2 presents the means of the variables used in this chapter. Note that the changes in the poverty and income distribution measures are slightly different from those indicated in Table 3.1 inasmuch as those in Table 3.2 are based on means of regional means rather than means of all households in the sample. Nevertheless, the means for the left-hand-side variables—P_0, P_1, Gini, and Kuznets—once again show significant changes from 1990 to 1995 in the same direction as those in Table 3.1. Both P_0 and P_1 increased fairly sharply while both Gini and Kuznets declined. Our estimates for the overall Gini coefficient show a decline from 34.61 in 1990 to about 33.12 in 1995, a result that is consistent with the Deininger and Squire estimates (Deininger and Squire 1996), although smaller than that indicated by Cardiff (1997).

Turning next to the means of the explanatory variables, note that HAGE1 and HAGE2 show the highest rate of change among all the right-hand-side variables. The first decreases by 6 percent, whereas the second increases by more than 6 percent, between 1990/91 and 1995/96. HAGE1, the percent of heads of households above 65 years of age, shows a decline from 28.1 percent in 1990 to 22.1 percent in 1995, while the mean for HAGE2, the percent of heads of households below 35 years of age, increased from 19.8 percent to 26 percent during the same period. Once more, the additional weight given to rural households in the 1995/1996 HEICS data set may be playing a role: one would expect a lower HAGE1/HAGE2 ratio in rural areas, and indeed a lower life expectancy, due to disadvantages in health care provision. The urbanization index (URBAN) is the percent of urban households in the survey. Although the educational characteristics suggest an improvement in the overall level of education, the change is relatively slow compared to the changes in all other variables. This is of course attributable to the fact that, over a period of only five

Table 3.2
Means for All Variables

Variable	1990	1995	Change 1995-1990
Gini	32.56	31.85	-0.71
Kuznets	9.01	7.33	-1.67
Po	0.26	0.42	0.1604
P1	0.06	0.08	0.0207
HAGE 1	0.281	0.221	0.06
HAGE 2	0.20	0.27	0.07
HEDUC0	0.44	0.41	-0.03
HEDUC1	0.31	0.32	0.01
HEDUC3	0.051	0.054	0.003
HEDUC4	0.20	0.21	0.02
NOSEWER	0.52	0.50	-0.02
HOCUP1	0.24	0.25	0.01
HOCUP2	0.05	0.06	0.01
URBAN	0.41	0.43	0.02

Source: HEICS 1990/1991 and 1995/1996.

years, the levels of education would be changing primarily only within the relatively young age group in the population. In particular, HEDUC0, representing the percent of illiterate heads of households, declined from 43.8 percent to about 41.1 percent. A closer look at the decomposition of these figures between rural and urban areas and across regions shows that these estimates rely heavily on the fact that illiteracy rates in rural upper Egypt remain above 80 percent. On the other hand, illiteracy seems to have been reduced to less than 10 percent in several urban areas. HEDUC1, the percent of heads of households with some or complete primary education, increased from 31.9 percent to about 32.6 percent while HEDUC3 increased from 5.1 percent to about 5.4 percent. The percentage of households without access to sewerage (NOSEWER) fell from 51.7 percent to 49.5 percent between 1990/91 and 1995/96. Finally, from the occupation of the household head variables, it can be seen that the percent self-employed fell by 0.3 percent while the percent of heads who were unemployed increased by 0.4 percent.

For simplicity, linear relationships are assumed, although given our focus on explaining changes over time, the effects of several of the explanatory variables (those with "D" in front of them, such as DEDUC0, DEDUC3, etc. in Table 3.3) are allowed to vary between periods. Also, in the case of the inequality measures, these measures were converted to logarithms because this improved the fits marginally. The estimating equations used are thus of the following general form:

$$
\begin{aligned}
Pj_{it} = {} & \beta_0 + D_1 + \beta_1 DEDUC0_{it} \\
& + \beta_2 DEDUC3_{it} + \beta_3 HEDUC1_{it} + \beta_4 HEDUC3_{it} + \beta_5 HAGE_{it} \\
& + \beta_6 HOCUP1_{it} + \beta_7 HOCUP2_{it} + \beta_8 NOSEWER_{it} + REGION_{it} + \varepsilon_{it} \\
& j = 0,1 \\
& i = 1,2,\ldots,40 \\
& t = 1,2
\end{aligned}
\tag{5}
$$

$j = 0$ denotes the poverty head-count ratio, P_0, $j = 1$ denotes the poverty gap, P_1. REGION is a dummy variable that takes a value one if the region is urban.

Because of the multiple use of the D_1 dummy variable including its interactions with the other explanatory variables, there is considerable collinearity among some of the right-hand-side variables. To mitigate such problems and to check the sensitivity of the results to changes in specification, several of the variables indicated have been omitted in the results reported below for the inequality indexes. Also, to explain income inequality, as opposed to poverty, the definitions of certain explanatory variables were changed as indicated below. The following represents the general specification used to estimate the model for income inequality. The inequality indexes to be explained are the logs of the Gini index and the Kuznets ratio.

$$
\begin{aligned}
INEQ_{it} = {} & \alpha_0 + D_1 + \alpha_1 DEDUC1_{it} + \alpha_2 DEDUC4_{it} + \alpha_3 HEDUC0_{it} \\
& \alpha_4 HEDUC3_{it} + \alpha_4 HEDUC4_{it} + \alpha_5 NOSWRVR_{it} + \alpha_6 URBAN_{it} + v_{it} \\
& i = 1,2,\ldots,20 \\
& t = 1,2
\end{aligned}
\tag{6}
$$

Table 3.3

Regression Results for the Head-Count Ratio, P_0, and for the Poverty Gap, P_1

Variable	P0 1	P0 2	P0 3	P1 1	P1 2	P1 3
Constant	0.3008	0.3183	0.3117	0.1197	0.1128	0.1180
	(0.0993)***	(0.1047)***	(0.1014)***	(0.0352)***	(0.0360)***	(0.0350)***
D1	0.0712	0.0269	0.0226	-0.0734	-0.0697	-0.0662
	-0.0895	(0.0901)	(0.0882)	(0.0316)**	(0.0310)**	(0.0304)**
DEDUC0	0.4431	0.5289	0.5406	0.2664	0.2612	0.2519
DEDUC3	-1.2813	-1.2079	-1.2144	0.1494	0.1343	0.1395
	(0.6872)*	(0.7066)*	(0.7017)*	(0.2429)	(0.2433)	(0.2422)
HEDUC1	-0.3387	-0.3435	-0.3208	-0.1780	-0.1626	-0.1807
	(0.1791)*	(0.2012)*	(0.1829)*	(0.0633)***	(0.0692)**	(0.0631)***
HEDUC3	-0.38349	-0.52458	-0.51857	-0.43074	-0.40584	-0.41063
	-0.5415	(0.5534)	(0.5494)	(0.1914)**	(0.1906)**	(0.1896)**
HAGE	-0.2560	-0.1452	-0.1375	0.0191	0.0075	0.0014
	(0.1492)*	(0.1441)	(0.1406)	(0.0527)	(0.0496)	(0.0485)
HOCUP1	0.2667			-0.0397		
	(0.1202)**			(0.0460)		
HOCUP2		0.1132			-0.0902	
		(0.4044)			(0.1393)	
SEWER	0.1874	0.2223	0.2262	0.0626	0.0599	0.0568
	(0.0594)***	(0.0596)***	(0.0576)***	(0.0210)***	(0.0205)***	(0.0199)***
REGION	-0.0493	-0.0323	-0.0297	-0.0213	-0.0222	-0.0242
	(0.0363)	(0.0372)	(0.0358)	(0.0128)	(0.0128)**	(0.0124)*
R-Sq (adj)	0.790	0.778	0.781	0.773	0.772	0.774
N	80	80	80	80	80	80

where NOSWRVR is the variance of NOSEWER around its mean. Table 3.3 presents some preferred regression results for both poverty indexes P_0 and P_1, respectively. Similarly, in Table 3.4 are some results obtained for the Gini coefficient (multiplied by 100 and converted to natural logs) and for the logs of the Kuznets ratios.

Let us turn first to the results for the head-count ratio P_0 given in the

Table 3.4
Regression Results for Gini Coefficients and Kuznets Ratios (in logs)

Variables	LOGGINI	LOGGINI	LOGKUZ	LOGKUZ
Constant	8.150	8.112	1.495	2.304
	(0.0635)***	(0.0609)***	(0.5003)***	(0.3545)***
D1	-0.0708	0.0155	-0.0359	0.0415
	(0.0646)	(0.0730)	(0.1587)	(0.1535)
DEDUC1		-0.1048		
		(0.2544)		
DEDUC4	0.2970			
	(0.3071)			
HEDUC0			0.7474	
			(0.8893)	
HEDUC1	-0.0915	-0.0477		-1.7225
	(0.1375)	(0.1730)		(0.8674)*
HEDUC3			0.9930	
HEDUC4	-0.0637	-0.4970		1.3241
	(0.2502)**	(0.2076)**		(1.2958)
SEWERVR		0.0700		
	(0.0295)**	(0.0298)**	(0.2164)	(0.1861)
URBAN	0.1886	0.1915	0.1406	-0.4198
	(0.0746)**	(0.0753)**	(0.4556)	(0.4699)
R-Sq (adj)	0.161	0.144	0.055	0.141
N	40	40	40	40

first three columns of Table 3.3. The difference between the different specifications is limited to the occupational variables (HOCUP1 and HOCUP2). The results in column (1) are obtained when HOCUP1 is used, those in (2) when HOCUP2 is employed, and those in (3) when neither is included. The numbers in parentheses represent standard errors of the coefficients immediately above them and the asterisks indicate levels of significance.[10]

One clear finding from all three columns is that once one accounts for education, age, access to sewerage, and urban residence, the occupation variables have no significant effect on P_0. Neither does the dummy variable for urban residence (REGION) even though the coefficient is consistently negative. Similarly, households headed by older heads (i.e., those over 60 years of age, HAGE2), who presumably have accumulated more nonhuman wealth than other households, have consistently (and sometimes marginally significantly) slightly lower poverty rates than other households. The higher is the percentage of households living in communities with no access to sewerage (NOSEWER), the larger is P_0. Other findings are that none of the coefficients of the time dummy variable for 1995/96 (D 1) have effects on P_0 that are statistically significant at the 5 percent level though in fact they are consistently positive. While HEDUC3 has a consistently negative but insignificant effect on P_0, the effects of the interaction term DEDUC3 are negative and significant. This indicates that the poverty-reducing effect of higher education increased over this five-year period. By the same token, the effect of the interaction term DEDUC0 on P_0 is consistently positive and highly significant, indicating that the penalty in the labor market for having no education was increasing over the period 1990/91–1995/96. Even regions with more heads with primary education (HEDUC1) have lower P_0 than those whose heads have no education. Notice also that in most cases, the aforementioned statistically significant coefficients, i.e., those for DEDUC0, DEDUC3, HEDUC1, HAGE2, and NOSEWER are robust to the different changes in specification. The direction of all the effects is as expected and the values of the adjusted R^2 are reasonably high.

Next we turn to the results for the poverty gap measure P_1 given in the last three columns of Table 3.3. The specifications of the estimating equations are identical to those in the first three columns of the table for P_0. Broadly speaking, and as might be expected given the similarity of the measures P_0 and P_1, the results are fairly similar to those for P_0. In particular, the effects of DEDUC0 and NOSEWER are both positive and again highly significant while those of HEDUC1 and HEDUC3 are negative and significant. The fact that the significance levels of both these variables increased but that DEDUC3 is no longer significant is also not too surprising given the difference between P_0 and P_1. For both measures it is clear that the various measures of education of the head and their interactions with the time dummy $D1$ are the major determinants. Lack of education, as measured by DEDUC0, has become an increasingly strong contributor to poverty. Higher education, as measured by HEDUC3, remains a strong, negative influence on both P_0 and P_1 and, in the case of P_0 at least, this influence strengthened between 1990/91 and 1995/96.

Table 3.4 presents the preferred results for both measures of income inequality, for the log of the Gini coefficient (LOGGINI) in the first two columns of the table and for the log of the Kuznets ratio (LOGKUZ) in the last two columns. Since the determinants of inequality are presumably somewhat different than those for poverty, there are some notable differences in specification from Table 3.3. In this case the specifications are somewhat different than those in Table 3.3. Slightly different education variables are used and the variable URBAN (as opposed to REGION) represents the percentage of households in the governorate that live in urban areas as opposed to a mere dummy variable for urban (as in the case of REGION). Likewise, SEWERVR is a variance measure (rather than a mean) representing the square of the difference between the region's percent of households lacking access to sewerage and the national mean relative to the national mean. Another significant difference in the results presented here, as noted in the row for number of observations (N), is that there are only 40 instead of 80 observations. This is because the observations are now limited to one for each governorate (20) and time period (2).

Once again, the head's occupational variables had no significant effects and are therefore omitted from the specifications. Neither did the time dummy variable ($D1$). Nor are the interaction terms DEDUC1 and DE-DUC4 statistically significant. Both SEWERVR and URBAN have significant positive influences on LOGGINI but in the case of LOGKUZ the effects of these same variables, while generally positive, are not statistically significant. The only education-related variables that are statistically significant are HEDUC4 in the case of LOGGINI and HEDUC3 in the case of LOGKUZ. The latter differences are altogether plausible considering that in LOGGINI the emphasis is more on the middle range of incomes whereas in the case of LOGKUZ attention is exclusively focused on the tails of the distribution. Thus, the finding that the effect of secondary education (HEDUC4), an intermediate level of education, has a negative effect on LOGGINI is not unexpected. Likewise, the positive effect of both extremes of the head's education HEDUC0 and HEDUC4 on LOGKUZ are as expected. In addition to the smaller number of observations available in this table, note that the values of R^2 are also much lower.

Next, turn to Table 3.5. The entries in the second and fifth columns of this table are the values of the regression coefficients taken from the regression results given in column (3) of Table 3.3 for P_0 and from those of column (1) for P_1. The changes in the relevant explanatory variables between 1990/91 and 1995/96 from the two surveys are given in column (3) and repeated in column (6) of Table 3.5. Each corresponding entry in the "Coefficient" column is then multiplied by its corresponding entry in the "Change" column. The results of this multiplication are given in the third column of each side of the table, i.e., columns (4) and (7), and represent the estimated "contributions" of the changes in the variables identified in column (1) to the change in the dependent variable. At the bottom of these "Contributions" columns are both the sum of these estimated contributions and the actual change in the poverty indexes.

The striking result is that in both cases the most important factor contributing to the observed increase in the poverty index between 1990/91 and 1995/96 is the increase in the income penalty associated with lack of any education. Indeed, this single factor explains more than 100 percent of the increase in poverty in each case. Virtually all the other factors, led by

Table 3.5
Accounting for the Change in the Head-Count Ratio and in the Poverty Gap

Variable		P0 Coefficient	P0 Change	P0 Contribution To Total Change		P1 Coefficient	P1 Change	P1 Contribution to Total Change
D1		0.0226	1.0000	0.0226		-0.0734	1.0000	-0.0734
DEDUC0		0.5406	0.4107	0.2220		0.2664	0.4107	0.1094
DEDUC3		-1.2144	0.0539	-0.0654		0.1494	0.0539	0.0080
HEDUC1		-0.3208	0.0104	-0.0033		-0.1780	0.0104	-0.0018
HEDUC3		-0.5186	0.0026	-0.0013		-0.4307	0.0026	-0.0011
HAGE		-0.1375	0.0672	-0.0092		0.0191	0.0672	0.0013
NOSEWER		0.2262	-0.0216	-0.0049		0.0626	-0.0216	-0.0014
REGION		-0.0297	1.0000	-0.0297		-0.0213	1.0000	-0.0213
HOCUP1						-0.0397	0.0072	-0.0003
Predicted Change				0.1307				0.0194
Actual Change				0.1604				0.0207

the increasing urbanization rate and the increase in the percentage of household heads with higher education, have had the effect of lowering poverty. After controlling for education, neither the change in the age structure of household heads nor their occupational status played much of a role.

Finally, in Table 3.6 we present the corresponding decomposition of the contributions of different factors to the observed declines in LOGGINI and LOGKUZ. In this case, the entries in the "Coefficient" columns are taken from the second specification of the equations for LOGGINI and LOG-KUZ, respectively. Once again, each corresponding entry in the "Coefficient" column is multiplied by the corresponding entry in the "Change" column to obtain the entry in the "Contribution" column. For the change in LOGGINI, the result is similar to that obtained for the poverty measures inasmuch as it is the change in the impact of a single household head education variable, i.e., DEDEUC1, that most strongly contributes to the decline in LOGGINI. Indeed, again this change contributes more than 100 percent of the total decline. This influence is supplemented by very small contributions to the reduction in LOGGINI by the changes in HEDUC1, HEDUC4, and NOSEWRVR. The increasing urbanization rate, by itself, has the effect of slightly increasing LOGGINI and the residual (represented by D1) has a stronger positive effect on LOGGINI.

Table 3.6
Accounting for the Change in the Gini Coefficient and in the Kuznets Ratio

Variable		LOGGINI Coefficient	LOGGINI Change	LOGGINI Contribution To Total Change		LOGKUZ Coefficient	LOGKUZ Change	LOGKUZ Contribution To Total Change
D1		0.015	1.00	0.015		0.041	1.00	0.041
DEDUC1		-0.105	0.303	-0.032				
HEDUC1		-0.048	0.083	-0.004		-1.723	0.082	-0.141
HEDUC4		-0.497	0.004	-0.002		1.324	0.004	0.005
NOSWRVR		0.070	-0.077	-0.005		0.217	-0.0765	-0.017
URBAN		0.191	0.023	0.004		-0.420	0.023	-0.010
Predicted Change				-0.023				-0.121
Actual Change								

In the case of LOGKUZ, however, the largest factor contributing to the reduction in the Kuznets ratio is the increasing relative importance of household heads with primary education. Note also that the contribution of the rising value of URBAN in this case is a small negative number.

CONCLUSIONS

The results go at least a substantial way toward explaining the paradoxical result wherein between 1990/91 and 1995/96 inequality continued its secular decline at the same time that poverty increased. In particular, the following variables had opposite influences: The increase in the income penalty of household heads with no education increased poverty very significantly but had no effect on either of the inequality measures. The decreasing income penalty of household heads with primary education contributed very strongly to the reduction in LOGGINI but not to poverty. The increasing percentage of household heads with higher education significantly lowered poverty but had no effect on the inequality measures. Increasing urbanization reduced both poverty measures but increased LOGGINI slightly.

Methodologically, this demonstrates a way in which regressions can be used to decompose poverty and inequality indexes when (as is often the case) detailed data on individual incomes are unavailable. Since the detailed data on individual incomes were not available for Egypt,[11] there is little alternative to such a method in the case of Egypt.

At the same time, the preliminary and illustrative character of these findings should be stressed. Among the several existing shortcomings are the sensitivity of the results to differences in specification and the inability to use a more dynamic specification in which the poverty or income inequality indexes in period t would depend in part on those in period t-1. Both of these shortcomings can only be overcome with additional data. The bad news is that no such data are at present available; the good news is that with the appearance of data from the next survey to be carried out in 2000 that extra data will soon be available. For one thing, because of the small number of observations and collinearity among the explanatory variables, the regression results were relatively sensitive to small changes in specification.

If, contrary to the rumor mentioned in note 11, the microlevel data on household income and other characteristics should be forthcoming, further testing of these important hypotheses with the full microlevel data set should be attempted. This would afford an opportunity to compare results obtained from the two different decomposition methods for Egypt as well as those obtained from microlevel decompositions in other countries.

Whether or not the microlevel data should become available, as time goes on and more comparable surveys become available for Egypt, it should be possible to add fixed effects and other control variables to the analysis. In this way one could better see whether the variables included in the analysis are picking up effects that should more properly be attributed to the effects of omitted variables.

NOTES

This is a revised version of a paper presented at the Conference on Earnings Inequality, Unemployment, and Poverty in the Middle East and North Africa at the School of Business, Lebanese American University, Byblos, Lebanon, November 5–7, 1998.

The authors express their appreciation to Salwa Soliman of Cairo University and Hafez Shaltout of USAID/Egypt for assistance in obtaining the data employed in the study. They also express their appreciation to Boris Arabadjiev, Caroline Betts, Sriped Motiram, and several participants at the conference for useful comments and suggestions.

  1. From Kuznets (1955) and Lewis (1954), it was believed that the major constraint on growth in LDCs was capital and that inequality would raise savings and investment rates and hence growth.

  2. The new thinking focuses on the detrimental effects of inequality on investment and human capital growth from political economy considerations (Alesina and Perotti 1994; Alesina and Rodrik 1994; Persson and Tabellini 1994) and buoyed by empirical support from cross-section growth regressions.

  3. The Kuznets ratio is here defined as the share of the top 25% of the population divided by that of the poorest 25%.

4. These indexes are defined and explained below.

5. The 40 regions are arrived at as follows: Five of the smallest governorates in terms of population (Matrouh, Red Sea, North Sinai, South Sinai, and Wady Al Jadeed) are combined into one because of small samples in each. This would make for 44 regions. Yet, 4 of the remaining 22 governorates (Suez, Port Said, Cairo, and Alexandria) have only urban areas, thereby reducing the total number of regions to 40.

6. Specifically, P_2 is constructed by squaring negative changes in expenditure values per observation. In this sense, P_2 weighs poor households with the largest shortfall in expenditure below the poverty line more heavily than others.

7. It is assumed in the present exercise that the results are significant. The scope of this chapter could be extended to include testing for significance of the derived indexes, using the methodology used by Kakwani.

8. Other measures of income inequality include the coefficient of variation, the relative mean deviation, and the standard deviation of logarithms of income.

9. In particular, the Gini coefficient measures the area between the 45-degree line and the Lorenz curve as a fraction of the total area under the 45-degree line.

10. One asterisk (*) indicates statistical significance at the 10% level, while ** and *** indicate significance at the 5% and 1% levels, respectively.

11. Even though (as noted above) Cardiff (1997) was able to make use of this microlevel data, to our knowledge no other individual (including the present authors) has been able to gain access to that data. It is rumored that the reason for this is that an important minister requested that such data be destroyed when it was found to show an increase in the poverty rate between 1990/91 and 1995/96.

REFERENCES

Abol-Kheir, H. (1996). "Towards Privatization of the Egyptian Economy." Cairo: Report to the Ministry of Finance.

Alesina, A. and R. Perotti (1994). "The Political Economy of Growth: A Critical Survey of the Recent Literature," *World Bank Economic Review* 8 (3): 351–371.

Alesina, A. and D. Rodrik (1994). "Distributive Politics and Economic Growth," *Quarterly Journal of Economics* 41: 19–43.

Atkinson, A. B. (1970). "On the Measurement of Income Inequality," *Journal of Economic Theory* 2 (September): 244–263.

———. (1991). "Comparing Poverty Rates Internationally: Lessons from Recent Studies in Developed Countries," *World Bank Economic Review* 5:3–22.

———. (1997). "Bringing Income Distribution in from the Cold," *Economic Journal* 107 (March): 297–321.

Cardiff, Patrick W. (1997). "Poverty and Inequality in Egypt," *Research in Middle East Economics* 2: 1–38.

Central Agency for Public Mobilization and Statistics (CAPMAS) (1997). *Statistical Yearbook*. Nasr City, Egypt: CAPMAS.

Champemowne, D. G. "A Comparison of Measures of Inequality of Income Distribution," *Economic Journal* 84: 787–816.

Deininger, Klaus and Lyn Squire (1997). "A New Data Set Measuring Income Inequality," *World Bank Economic Review* 10: 565–591.

Foster, J., J. Greer, and E. Thorbecke (1985). "A class of Decomposable Poverty Measures," *Review of Economics and Statistics* 67: 151–156.

Kakwani, N. C. (1990). *Income Inequality and Poverty: Methods of Estimation and Policy Analysis*. New York: Oxford University Press.

Kuznets, S. (1955). "Economic Growth and Inequality," *American Economic Review* 45 (March): 1–28.

Lewis, W. A. (1954). "Economic Development with Unlimited Supplies of Labour," *Manchester School of Economic and Social Studies* 22 (May): 139–191.

Persson, T. and G. Tabellini (1994). "Is Inequality Harmful for Growth?" *American Economic Review* 84 (3): 600–621.

World Development Indicators. Washington, DC: World Bank, 1996.

Social Indicators of Development. Washington, DC: World Bank, 1996.

4

Trade Reform and the Poor in Morocco: A Rural-Urban General Equilibrium Analysis of Reduced Protection

Hans Lofgren

INTRODUCTION

In this chapter, a Computable General Equilibrium (CGE) model is used to explore quantitatively the short-run impact of agricultural deprotection on the Moroccan economy in general and on disaggregated household welfare and the rural economy in particular. In addition to trade policies per se, the analysis also addresses the use of complementary policies aimed at protecting the incomes of vulnerable parts of the rural population.

The next section provides a brief background on the Moroccan economy and economic policy, with a focus on agriculture and rural areas. In the following section, the CGE model and its data base are presented. The next section is devoted to simulations, followed by a summary of the results and the policy implications. Appendices to the chapter, available upon request, include a mathematical model statement as well as additional background data and simulation results.

BACKGROUND

The focus of this chapter is justified by the fact that Morocco's pervasive and sharp rural-urban divide remains in place. According to data from the early 1990s, rural per-capita consumption is around half the urban level. While rural areas house less than 50 percent of the population, they account for 70 percent of the poor. Rural areas are also strongly disfavored according to other indicators such as access to electricity and safe water, literacy, and school enrollment, with the female population standing out as particularly disadvantaged. Low educational achievement is reflected in a labor force that for the most part is "unskilled" (in the sense that most jobs require no formal education). The skill gap is a major source of inequality between rural and urban areas; on average skilled workers earn six to seven times the wage of unskilled workers (Karshenas 1994). Relatively unfavorable rural conditions have led to rapid rural-urban migration, which provides an important outlet for the rural labor force (absorbing the bulk of its natural growth), but exacerbates urban unemployment and puts downward pressure on urban wages. The rural economy is dominated by agriculture, which represents close to 80 percent of total employment and may account for some 60 percent of total rural value-added. In terms of the economy as a whole, agriculture provides somewhat less than 20 percent of GDP but as much as 45 percent of total employment, attesting to its relatively high labor intensity. While agricultural GDP is highly variable, since the early 1980s, the sector has discontinued an earlier secular decline in its share of the economy. The agricultural sector is itself marked by considerable heterogeneity, perhaps most importantly between relatively prosperous irrigated zones (17 percent of the cultivated area in the early 1990s) and disfavored rain-fed zones that, inter alia, suffer from frequent but irregular droughts. Moreover, the rain-fed areas differ greatly in terms of average annual rainfall.

Morocco's agriculture plays an important role in the country's relatively diversified foreign trade. When processed agricultural products are included, it accounts for around 30 percent of exports and 20 percent of imports. The most important agricultural exports are fish, fruits, and vegetables. Wheat and sugar are the major agricultural imports (Royaume du Maroc 1997; EIU 1998, pp. 54–55).[1]

Since the early 1980s, Morocco has gradually reformed its economy in the direction of trade liberalization and increased reliance on market forces and the private sector. Morocco's macroeconomic management has since the mid-1980s been more successful than in most other countries in the Middle East and North Africa according to indicators such as rate and volatility of inflation, level of the budget deficit, and stability of the real exchange rate (Page and Underwood 1997, pp. 104–105). In the trade area, the level and dispersion of tariffs have been reduced while quantitative restrictions have been eliminated (Alonso-Gamo et al. 1997, p. 24; IMF 1997, p. 7). Compared to most structural adjustment-oriented countries, Morocco was successful in combining positive growth with rapid restoration of internal and external balance (Karshenas 1994, pp. 47–48). Nevertheless, compared to the 1970s, economic growth decelerated in the 1980s and even more so during the period 1990–96.

In spite of far-reaching trade reforms, Morocco still has significant trade barriers with a high degree of dispersion across sectoral protection rates.

The agricultural trade regime was, as of the mid-1990s, particularly distorted, especially for cereals and animal products.

In 1996, Morocco signed an Association Agreement with the European Union (EU), which is Morocco's predominant trading partner, representing 64 percent of exports and 57 percent of imports (Royaume du Maroc 1997, p. 572). In the agreement, Morocco committed itself to a gradual elimination of its barriers to industrial imports from Europe in exchange for aid, technical assistance, and a slight improvement in access to the EU market for its agricultural exports.[2] At this point, major items on the policy agenda include the design of policies that complement the EU agreement.

As Morocco reduces its tariffs on industrial imports from the EU, a major question is whether it will unilaterally pursue general agricultural and industrial import liberalization vis-à-vis the rest of the world. While such policies may have a positive impact on aggregate economic performance, they may also be accompanied by welfare losses for parts of the population. The policy dilemma may be severe given that agriculture is both the most heavily protected sector and the sector that provides the bulk of the income of many of the rural poor with limited economic mobility. Moroccan policymakers are well aware of the link between rural welfare and agricultural crop prices—in March 1998, in the very first decree he signed, Morocco's new prime minister, Youssoufi, imposed a sharp increase in tariff rates on imported wheat to counteract a recent drastic fall in world prices (EIU 1998, p. 20). In fact, it may be more appropriate to consider agricultural trade liberalization in the context of complementary policies. As an example of policies that can be pursued in the short run, Mexico introduced an income transfer program (PROCAMPO) where farmers were compensated for reduced protection of agricultural markets. By making payments proportional to assessments of past earnings in agriculture, the program aimed at being nondistorting in terms of current production decisions (World Bank 1997c, p. 40). Over a longer time horizon, options include support for an educational system that is attuned to labor market conditions and the development of an infrastructure that facilitates the development of rural nonagricultural activities.

In this chapter, we will use a rural-urban CGE model to explore some of these issues with special emphasis on the impact of trade reforms and complementary policies on the rural economy, the labor market, and the rural poor.

MODEL STRUCTURE AND DATA

The current model, which draws on existing economy-wide models of Morocco, is distinguished by an explicit separation of activities, factors, and households into rural and urban.[3] The disaggregation aims at identifying the rural poor, as well as the factors and activities from which they earn their incomes. Hence, the model has a detailed treatment of aspects that are most closely linked to the rural economy and the welfare of the rural poor, including agricultural and other rural activities, and rural factors of production. Although the treatment of the urban production is more aggregated, the model also permits an analysis of the impact on the urban poor of policies and exogenous shocks. Moreover, the resulting economy-wide perspective permits us to avoid the fallacy of viewing the rural economy as an isolated island. This is important since the rural and urban economies and the welfare of their households are interdependent with numerous linkages, inter alia in the markets for commodities and factors.

Model Disaggregation

Among the 41 activities in Morocco, 34 are rural and 7 urban. Most rural sectors are part of crop or livestock agriculture. The nonagricultural sectors of the economy (disaggregated into the major types of industrial and service sectors) are classified as rural or urban.

Rural activities use rural factors whereas urban activities use urban factors.[4] All activities use capital and labor. Agricultural activities demand additional factors: livestock makes use of pasture-fallow land; crop activities rely on rain-fed land; irrigated crop activities also use water. Outside agriculture, the labor force of each activity includes both skilled and unskilled labor whereas for all agricultural activities except fishing and forestry, the labor force is made up of a separate category of (unskilled) agricultural labor.

In crop and livestock agriculture, most activities produce multiple commodities and most commodities are produced by two activities, one in rain-fed and one in irrigated areas. Fodder by-products are produced by most crop activities. Livestock activities produce meat and milk (disaggregated by animal type) and, for the cow activities, manure. Multiple-output activities produce their commodities in fixed physical proportions.

Outside crop and livestock agriculture, each activity produces only one commodity. Given that service commodities tend to have location-specific characteristics, rural and urban service activities are viewed as producing distinct commodities. For industrial and agricultural commodities, markets are treated as integrated across regions (irrigated and rain-fed agricultural zones or rural and urban regions) and with international trade.

The model includes four household types, disaggregated by region (rural and urban) and income level (poor and nonpoor). The other institutions consist of the government and the rest of the world, divided into the European Union (EU) and non-EU in the area of goods trade. The rest of the world is thus disaggregated given that one purpose of the analysis is to

Figure 4.1
Technology for Production Activities

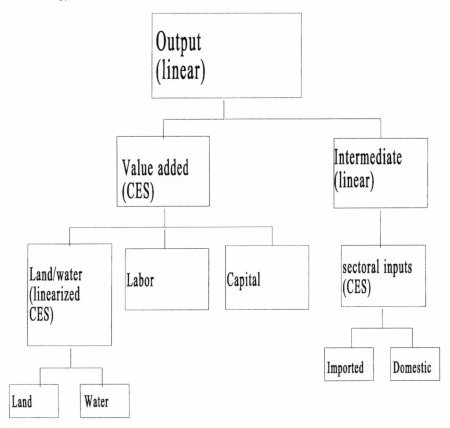

understand the impact on rural development from Morocco's partnership agreement with the EU.

Production Activities

Producers are assumed to maximize profits given their technology and the prices of inputs and outputs. As shown in Figure 4.1, the technology of the production activities is specified as a Leontief function of aggregate value-added and an aggregate intermediate input. Value-added is produced by a CES function (of primary factors), and a Leontief function of intermediate input use. In order to permit technique change in response to significant price changes for inputs, the intermediate coefficients are flexible inside agriculture but fixed for other sectors. For irrigated crop agriculture, an aggregate land-water factor is among the arguments in the CES function.

This aggregate factor is produced by a set of alternative factor-aggregation activities based on Leontief technology that specifies substitution possibilities between land and water along a linearized CES isoquant. This Leontief representation is preferred to a continuous CES function to allow for the possibility of water or land being in excess supply, with a corresponding price of zero for the nonscarce factor.

The income of each factor is allocated to domestic institutions (the households and the government) in fixed shares, after adjustments for factor payments to and from the rest of the world (both of which are fixed in foreign currency).

Institutions

Both rural and urban *households* receive the bulk of their incomes from factor earnings in their respective regions. Compared to the nonpoor, the poor in both regions depend more heavily on labor incomes in general and unskilled labor incomes in particular. In addition to factor income, households receive transfers from the government (the transfer received by each household is a fixed GDP share) and the rest of the world (fixed in foreign currency). Total household income is used to pay direct taxes, save, and consume. Direct taxes and savings are fixed shares of household income. Consumption demand is determined by the linear expenditure system (LES).

Besides factor incomes, *government* revenue consists of taxes—direct taxes from households, indirect taxes from domestic activities, domestic sales taxes, and import tariffs (with different rates applying to EU and non-EU goods' imports). All taxes are *ad valorem*. Apart from the above-mentioned transfers to households, the government uses its income to buy a fixed quantity of consumption goods, transfers to the rest of the world (fixed in foreign currency), and consumer subsidies (a fixed share of the consumption value for manufactured goods, representing food items).

The *rest of the world* interacts with Morocco through commodity trade and the above-mentioned transfers (which add to or deduct from the incomes of factors and domestic institutions).

System Constraints

System constraints, or "closure rules," are those constraints that have to be satisfied by the economic system, but that are not considered in the decisions of any microagent (Robinson 1989, pp. 907–908). They consist of the markets for commodities and factors as well as a set of macroaggregates. We will here present the system constraints of the basic model version; alternative configurations, described later, are used in a subset of the model simulations.

Commodity Markets

Commodities are supplied by domestic production activities and imports. On the other side of the market, we find domestic demand and exports. Imperfect substitutability is assumed for commodities from different sources (different domestic activities, different import regions, or the outside world versus domestic producers). Commodities delivered to different destinations (domestic market vs. aggregated export market or different export markets) are imperfectly transformable.

The commodity flows that underlie the market for a commodity that is produced by two activities and is traded in both directions, both with the EU and with the rest of the outside world, are summarized as follows, with a separate price associated with each commodity flow.

Production from the two activities combine to form aggregate output that, in turn, is transformed to domestic sales and aggregate exports. In the next stage, the latter are further transformed into exports to the EU and the rest of the world. On the domestic supply side, imports from the EU and the rest of the world generate aggregate imports that, together with domestic sales, are aggregated to give domestic composite commodity supply. On the other side of the composite commodity market, demand is made up of household and government consumption, investment, and intermediate input use. The process is simplified for commodities that enter international trade in a less complete fashion (or not at all for nontraded commodities) and/or are supplied by a single domestic activity. Moreover, for imported service commodities, the first step in the aggregation is eliminated since imports are not disaggregated by source.

The functional forms for transformation and aggregation are, respectively, Constant-Elasticity-of-Substitution (CES) and Constant-Elasticity-of-Transformation (CET) functions. At each stage, the shares of commodities from different sources or to different destinations are sensitive to relative prices. These assumptions embodied in these functions—imperfect substitutability and transformability—grant the domestic price system a certain degree of independence from international prices and dampen responses of imports, exports, and domestic sales to price changes.

With the partial exception of export and import markets, price performs the role of clearing the markets—the quantities supplied and demanded are, respectively, positively and inversely related to the price. For imports, the supply side clears the market: it is assumed that Morocco is a small country facing infinitely elastic supplies at exogenous world prices.

For most exports, it is similarly assumed that Morocco is a small country facing infinitely elastic demands at an exogenous world price: in this setting, the demand side clears the market. The only exception is for agricultural exports to the EU. A dual-regime formulation is used according to which an increase in Morocco's supply price will give rise to reduced exports along a constant-elasticity demand curve. However, a decrease in the Moroccan price will not give rise to a corresponding increase in demand. The EU will purchase the base-year quantity at the (lower) price, in the process capturing the rent produced by the constraint. As a result, the EU pays exactly the price needed to induce Morocco to export the fixed quantities.

Factor Markets

The treatment of factor markets in the basic model version is summarized in Table 4.1. Among the *agricultural resources*, it is assumed that rain-fed land and pasture-fallow are mobile across activities, and fully utilized with a market-clearing price. The only exception is tree crops, for which, given the short-run nature of the analysis, land use is fixed.

In irrigated agriculture, land is used in conjunction with irrigation water. Both water and irrigated land are mobile across activities, once again with the exception of tree crop land use. For this sector, the model allows for the fact that flexibility in technique choice may not be sufficient to assure that both factors always are scarce. Hence, for each factor, two regimes are possible: full employment with a market-clearing price or unemployment with the utilization level as the clearing variable. However, in practice at most one of the two factors would be unemployed at any given time.

Both the rain-fed and the irrigated *capital* factors are mobile and fully utilized with a market-clearing price. Given the short-run perspective of the model, the capital use of each livestock activity (primarily represented by the animals themselves) is fixed at base level. For agricultural activities that are not classified as irrigated or rain-fed (other animal, fishing, and forestry) and all nonagricultural sectors (both rural and urban), the treatment of capital is uniform: capital stocks are activity-specific, and fully utilized with a market-clearing price.

For the *labor* market, two alternative formulations are used, a "rigid" alternative that is more relevant for a shorter time frame and a "flexible" alternative that is more applicable over a longer time frame, in particular if complementary measures that enhance flexibility are put in place. For the "rigid" alternative, the rural labor market is divided into three segments (agricultural, rural unskilled, and rural skilled) while the urban market consists of two segments (unskilled and skilled). In each segment, the wage (price) clears the market in a setting with fixed (full) employment. For the "flexible" alternative, migration is permitted within each skill group, in effect creating an integrated national market segmented by skill. For both alternatives, demand changes within a labor segment give rise to wage changes, not changes in employment. When migration is permitted, it performs the role of maintaining base-year relative wage gaps. Hence, *ceteris paribus*, upward wage pressure in the urban unskilled labor market will induce an inflow of labor from the other two segments to which it is linked (agricultural unskilled and rural unskilled labor) up to the point where the relative wage rates are retained.

Macroconstraints

These constraints determine the manner in which the balance is generated for the macroaggregates, associated with the accounts for the government, the rest of the world, and savings-investment. Government savings—the difference between the government's *current* revenues and *current* spending—are fixed. Proportional adjustments in the direct tax rates of urban and rural nonpoor households assure that the savings target is met. The real exchange rate (an index of the ratio between the prices of traded commodities and domestic outputs sold domestically) clears the balance of the rest of the world while foreign savings are fixed. On the spending side of the savings-investment balance, aggregate investment is fixed in real quantity terms. On the savings side, the savings rate of the nonpoor urban household is assumed to be flexible, varying to generate a level of total savings needed to finance aggregate investment.[5]

Database

The model data are based on a disaggregated Social Accounting Matrix (SAM; a 108 × 108 matrix) for 1994, to which the model parameters are calibrated. The SAM was constructed on the basis of data from various sources, most importantly: (i) disaggregated agricultural information from the Moroccan government, the World Bank, and the FAO, primarily for 1990/91;[6] (ii) a disaggregated economy-wide framework represented by SAMs for 1990 and 1994, an input-output table for 1990, as well as data on the 1994 policy regime—taxes, subsidies, and nontariff barriers (Bussolo and Roland-Holst 1993; Roland-Holst, 1996); (iii) 1994 macro and trade data from Royaume du Maroc (1997), the RMSM data base (World Bank, 1997a), and United Nations (1998); and (iv) disaggregated population, consumption, and labor force data from Royaume du Maroc (1993, 1995, 1996, 1997), World Bank (1994, 1995, 1997a, 1997b), International Monetary Fund (1997), and Karshenas (1994). It should be emphasized that in areas where detailed information was lacking (for example regarding wage gaps across different activities), some simplifying assumptions had to be imposed. In doing so, we were guided by the underlying premise of the analysis: the impact of trade policy on the rural economy cannot be properly assessed without a model structure that captures the salient characteristics that are related to the urban-rural divide, including large skill and wage gaps, labor market segmentation, and differences in sectoral structure.

Available information was brought together in one matrix, the disaggre-

Table 4.1
Factor Markets in Basic Model Version

Factor	Mobile across activities	Utilization	Market-clearing variable
Agricultural Resources			
Rain-fed land	Yes*	Full	Price
Pasture-fallow	Yes	Full	Price
Irrigated land	Yes*	Full/unemployment**	Price/utilization
Water	Yes	Full/unemployment**	Price/utilization
Capital			
Rain-fed crops	Yes	Full	Price
Irrigated crops	Yes	Full	Price

60

Livestock	No	Full	Price
Other agriculture***	No	Full	Price
Nonagriculture (urban and rural)	No	Full	Price
Labor			
Rigid alternative			
Separate market for each category (5 markets)****	Yes	Full	Price
Flexible alternative			
Integrated markets for each skill level (2 markets)*****	Yes	Full	Price

Note: *Except for tree crops, for which land is activity-specific (fixed quantities for each tree crop), both for irrigated and rain-fed land.

  **Dual regime with full employment and a flexible price or unemployment with price at zero.

  ***Other agriculture = other animal, forestry, fish.

  ****The five labor markets are agricultural unskilled, other rural unskilled, urban unskilled, rural skilled, urban skilled.

  ****The two labor markets are unskilled and skilled.

gation of which parallels the disaggregation of the current model. Underlying the construction of such a SAM is an attempt to make the best possible use of available scattered data. Inevitably imbalances appear when data from different sources and years are integrated in one framework; cross-entropy method was used to generate a balanced model SAM that uses all the information contained in the original data set (Robinson et al. 1998). A macroversion of the model SAM—identical to the disaggregated SAM except for the aggregated depiction of factors, household, activities, and commodities—is shown in Table 4.2. A variety of other studies of Morocco were consulted for estimates of elasticities for the Armington, CET, CES (production), LES (household consumption), and export-demand functions.[7]

Solution Approach and Time Frame

The current model is solved as a mixed-complementarity problem (MCP), consisting of a set of simultaneous equations that are a mix of strict equalities and inequalities but without an objective function. This approach, made feasible by the recent development of solvers, makes it possible to formulate a model that combines desired features of mathematical programming models (in particular by permitting excess supplies of agricultural resources, such as water) while allowing the full range of assumptions for consumer demand, government policies, and foreign trade that appear in standard CGE models. The GAMS modeling software is used both to generate the database and to implement the model. The model is solved with PATH, a solver for mixed complementarity problems.[8]

The base solution of the model is calibrated to exactly replicate the disaggregated 1994 SAM. In the different simulations, the model is run in a comparative static mode. The results indicate the short-run equilibrium responses to changes in policies and exogenous shocks, comparing a new solution to the base solution. Each new solution represents a new equilibrium since agents (producers and consumers) have fully adjusted themselves to new prices and incomes. It refers to the short run since capital stocks outside crop agriculture are fixed by activity: the time span is too short for current investment to lead to changes in installed capital or for capital to move between noncrop sectors (cf. Hazell and Norton 1986, p. 300).

SIMULATIONS

The simulations, based on the CGE model presented in the preceding section, explore the impact of removing border protection with a focus on disaggregated household welfare and the rural economy. As shown in Table 4.3, we will cumulatively introduce 25 percent cuts in the different import barriers that affect agriculture and industry. The simulations will be im-

Table 4.2
Macro SAM for Morocco, 1994 (billion current Dh.)

	Factors	Institutions			S-I	Activity	Commodity	Tax/Sub/Tariff				Total
	1.	2a.	2b.	2c.	3.	4.	5.	6a.	6b.	6c.	6d.	7.
1. Factors						238.35						238.35
2. Institutions												
2a. Household	232.92		7.74	21.42								262.07
2b. Government	5.38	2.02						15.21	23.70		20.47	66.78
2c. Rest of World	0.06	5.55	7.04				86.21					98.85
3. Savings-Investment		45.05	8.03	6.69								59.77
4. Activities							639.75					639.75
5. Commodities		194.24	40.78	70.75	59.77	392.12	7.97			3.20		768.81
6.Tax/Sub/Tariff												
6a. Direct Taxes		15.21										15.21
6b. Indirect Taxes						9.28	14.42					23.70
6c. Subsidies			3.20									3.20
6d. Import Tariffs							20.47					20.47
7. Total	238.35	262.07	66.78	98.85	59.77	639.75	768.81	15.214	23.70	3.20	20.47	

Table 4.3
Simulation Assumptions*

		AG-LIB1	AG-LIB2	AG-IND-LIB1	AG-IND-LIB2
Agricultural tariffs		-25%	-25%	-25%	-25%
Agricultural NTBs			-25%	-25%	-25%
Industrial tariffs					
	EU			-25%	-25%
	RoW				-25%

Note: *−25 percent means that, after the change, the rates for relevant commodity tariffs or nontariff barriers are three-quarters of the initial rate. (For example, if the initial import tariff for an agricultural commodity is 200 percent, it is reduced to 150 percent under AGLIB-1.)

plemented with two alternative sets of assumptions regarding the flexibility with which labor can be reallocated between different activities (see Table 4.1). We will also investigate the role for complementary policies that in a relatively nondistorting manner counteract negative effects of reduced border protection on the rain-fed sector. Throughout the simulations, proportional variations in the direct tax rates of nonpoor households (urban and rural) assure that government savings are fixed in real (CPI-indexed) terms. Given that reduced tariff rates have a negative impact on the government balance, this mechanism for balancing the government budget is propoor.

The results for the first set of simulations are displayed in Table 4.4. In the first simulation (AGLIB-1), the tariff cut will, *ceteris paribus*, boost imports, reducing demand, prices, and factor returns for domestic agriculture. Lower agricultural prices benefit consumers and sectors that use intermediate inputs from agriculture. An increase in agricultural imports generates a slight current-account deficit and a depreciation in the real exchange rate, boosting exports and reducing imports throughout the economy. Welfare changes for any household group primarily depend on the combined effects of changes in the prices of factors it controls and commodities it consumes.

As expected, the incomes of agricultural labor and resources decline significantly, especially in rain-fed areas since these depend most heavily on livestock production—initially the most highly protected sector. All other factor incomes increase. On the aggregate level, urban factors gain whereas rural factors face a significant decline.

The results on the household level are driven by these changes in factor incomes. Rural households, especially the poor, who depend the most on rain-fed agriculture and labor, lose, while both urban household groups gain. The aggregate welfare effect is mildly positive. There is only a slight decline in tariff revenue relative to GDP, reflecting the fact that tariffs from agricultural imports represent only a small part of total tariff revenue and the trade expansion that takes place. As a result of the assumed rigidity of the labor market (inter alia keeping the agricultural labor force inside agriculture), less than 0.1 percent of the labor force moves between activities.[9]

As nontariff barriers (initially very high for wheat and livestock products) are cut by a quarter in the second simulation (AGLIB-2), the results from the first simulation are reinforced. Changes in factor incomes are further accentuated, with an additional decline in aggregate rural incomes, driven by a drastic fall in the incomes of rain-fed resources and unskilled labor. Rural welfare declines while urban households gain, with a significant boost in aggregate household welfare. Since, in this simulation, imports expand without any additional tariff cut, tariff revenue is boosted, approximately returning to the base level.

In the following two simulations, industrial tariffs are cut by a quarter, starting with imports from the EU (AGINDLIB-1) and then extending the

Table 4.4
Simulation Results: Trade Deprotection with Rigid Labor Market

	1994	AG LIB-1	AG LIB-2	AG-IND-LIB1	AG-IND -LIB2
Real disposable household income (bn. 1994 Dh.)				% change	
All households	9.4	0.5	1.3	1.1	1.1
Poor Urban household	3.0	1.6	5.0	6.6	7.6
Nonpoor Urban household	13.6	1.1	3.2	3.2	3.3
Poor Rural household	2.7	-2.7	-9.2	-9.0	-8.5
Nonpoor rural	6.5	-1.0	-3.1	-4.0	-4.1
Real factor income (bn 1994 Dh.)					
Rural	71.4	-1.9	-6.3	-6.5	-6.1
Urban	158.8	1.8	5.7	7.2	8.0
Irrigated resources	7.6	-2.2	-10.4	-12.2	-12.3
Rain-fed resources	22.0	-4.6	-15.6	-15.5	-15.0
Other agriculture	2.1	-0.4	1.7	2.9	3.8
Rural nonagriculture capital	12.3	1.2	4.2	4.0	4.5
Urban Capital	70.0	1.7	5.6	6.9	7.4

Agriculture unskilled labor	10.8	-4.4	-14.1	-14.7	-14.4
Rural nonagricultural unskilled labor	6.5	1.0	4.2	4.6	5.3
Rural nonagricultural skilled labor	10.1	1.2	4.2	4.2	4.8
Urban unskilled labor	-14.8	1.8	5.9	7.4	8.5
Urban skilled labor	74.1	1.8	5.9	7.4	8.5
Job Shift (% of labor force)		0.1	0.2	0.4	0.5
Real trade quantities (bn 1994 Dh.)					
Exports	70.8	0.2	0.9	3.1	4.2
Agriculture exports	5.7	1.4	4.7	5.1	5.2
Industrial exports	36.3	0.2	1.5	5.1	6.9
Imports	86.3	0.1	0.7	2.3	3.1
Agriculture imports	4.9	3.2	6.2	4.0	3.3
Industrial imports	65.3	-0.2	-0.2	2.7	4.1
Real exchange rate (index 1994 = 100)	100.0	0.8	1.8	3.1	3.7
			(% of GDP)		
Direct tax	5.4	5.6	5.7	6.7	7.3
Tariffs	7.3	7.2	7.3	6.5	6.0

reduction to industrial imports from other parts of the world (AGINDLIB-2). Compared to the preceding scenario, import tariffs decline significantly (by 1.3 percent of GDP for AGINDLIB-2) and, to maintain the fixed current account deficit, the currency depreciates (by 3.7 percent). There is a compensating increase in direct taxes with a negative impact on the welfare of the nonpoor. Urban factor incomes are boosted while rural incomes are largely unchanged. The increase in job shifts implies a growing pressure for labor-market restructuring. Among the households, the urban poor gain significantly whereas others are relatively unaffected. The fact that there is a slight decline in aggregate welfare reflects that the tariff cuts are introduced in a second-best world with significant policy-induced price distortions and severe rigidities, limiting resource mobility and agricultural export expansion.[10] In sum, this first set of simulations demonstrates that, in a rigid short-run equilibrium setting, agricultural deprotection involves a tradeoff between significant gains in aggregate and urban welfare and significant losses in rural welfare. Among the four household categories, it is the poor who are most strongly affected, negatively in rural areas and positively in urban areas.

The first set of simulations assumes a rigid labor market. In the second set of simulations the labor market is more flexible as rural and urban labor markets, disaggregated into skilled and unskilled, are linked via migration. Migration assures that relative wage differences are fixed at the initial ratios, bringing about migration from (to) labor segments that, in the absence of migration, would face a wage decrease (increase) relative to other segments. In this new setting, the income change for any worker depends on the impact of the policy changes in his or her broader labor market (skilled or unskilled) as opposed to the more disaggregated markets (for skilled workers, rural or urban; for unskilled workers, agricultural, rural, or urban) that were in operation in the first set of simulations.

The results, shown in Table 4.5, bring to the fore the important role of the functioning of the labor market. A simulation-by-simulation comparison between Tables 4.5 and 4.4 shows that the aggregate welfare gain is uniformly stronger when the labor market is more flexible. The major migration flow is from the agricultural unskilled market (losing 1 to 5 percent of its labor force) to the rural and urban markets for unskilled nonagricultural labor (whose relative gains in labor force are of similar magnitude). Income changes in each disaggregated segment of the labor market are less extreme, a reflection of the fact that labor demand is inelastic: as migration increases (decreases) the supply in any segment, labor income in that segment decreases (increases). From another perspective, the adjustment cost in the labor market is much larger: the share of the labor force that shifts jobs is 1.5 to 2 percent for the simulations that include reduced tariffs and nontariff barriers for agriculture, i.e., 4 to 6 times as large as for the corresponding simulations with a rigid labor market. Less extreme changes in labor returns engender smaller shocks in household spending patterns and less pronounced discrepancies in gains and losses for nonlabor factors throughout the economy. Among the agricultural factors, rain-fed resources and unskilled labor continue to incur significant losses, albeit on a smaller scale. Other agricultural resources are only affected marginally. On the household level, the net effect is that both rural households gain strongly whereas the urban poor lose equally strongly as migration into the urban unskilled labor market drives down wages.

Otherwise, the pattern of change is similar to that of the simulations in Table 4.4. Agricultural deprotection raises aggregate welfare but the decline in factor incomes within rain-fed agriculture is significant and the rural poor lose. Additional industrial deprotection has a minor negative aggregate impact but improves the welfare of the poor in both regions. This distributional pattern is in part due to the fact that only nonpoor households carry the burden of financing a decline in government savings with higher direct tax payments.

In light of these results—significant pros and cons of trade deprotection—a third set of simulations investigates the potential impact of complementary policies aimed at protecting the vulnerable groups that would be affected most severely without undoing the economy-wide gains from deprotection. In these simulations, three alternative changes are introduced in the context of the scenario AGINDLIB-1 with a flexible labor market: (i) a transfer program that compensates owners of (nonlabor) rain-fed resources for lost factor income due to reduced trade barriers, with direct taxes from the nonpoor covering the need for financing (TRANSFER); (ii) skill upgrading where 1 percent of the unskilled labor in agricultural and other rural activities move to the skilled rural labor force (SKILL UPGRADE); and (iii) a 3 percent increase in total factor productivity (TFP) for all rural nonagricultural activities (RURNAG TFP).

Table 4.6 summarizes the results, for the sake of comparison also including the AGINDLIB-1 scenario under the same assumption of a flexible labor market. The impact of compensatory transfer payments is almost exclusively distributional. In this specific setting, the cost of the scheme amounts to 0.8 percent of GDP. (The cost would be higher if the administrative costs of the program were accounted for.) Since the indirect effects are small, the tax increase is of the same magnitude. The recipients, primarily rural households, gain significantly. The relative gain is larger for the poor (5% versus 1.5% for the nonpoor), since rain-fed resources represent a larger share of their incomes and they do not share in covering the cost. On the other hand, the rural nonpoor, who finance the program and receive only a minor share of the resulting payments, lose 0.7 percent in real welfare. After the transfer, the different households quite evenly share the gains from trade liberalization.

The upgrading of rural skills has stronger economy-wide effects, raising

Table 4.5
Simulation Results: Trade Deprotection with Flexible Labor Market

	1994	AG LIB-1	AG LIB-2	AG-IND-LIB1	AG-IND-LIB2
			(% change)		
Real disposable household income (bn. 1994 Dh.)					
All households	9.4	0.5	1.5	1.4	1.4
Poor urban household	3.0	-0.1	-0.2	0.6	1.3
Nonpoor urban household	13.6	0.8	2.3	2.3	2.3
Poor rural household	2.7	-1.2	-4.2	-3.6	-2.9
Nonpoor rural	6.5	-0.1	-0.2	-0.6	-0.6
Real factor income (bn 1994 Dh.)					
Rural	71.4	-1.0	-3.3	-3.3	-2.7
Urban	158.8	1.2	4.0	5.2	6.0
Irrigated resources	7.6	0.6	-0.7	-2.0	-1.9
Rain-fed resources	22.0	-3.1	-10.6	-10.2	-9.6
Other agriculture	2.1	-1.1	-0.8	0.2	1.0
Rural nonagriculture capital	12.3	0.8	2.8	2.6	3.2
Urban Capital	70.0	1.4	4.3	5.5	6.0

70

Agriculture unskilled labor	10.8	-2.0	-6.4	-6.4	-6.0
Rural nonagricultural unskilled labor	6.5	0.1	1.0	1.4	2.1
Rural nonagricultural skilled labor	10.1	0.9	3.0	3.4	4.1
Urban unskilled labor	14.8	0.5	1.8	2.9	3.8
Urban skilled labor	74.1	1.3	4.1	5.4	6.4
Job Shift (% of labor force)		0.5	1.6	1.7	1.8
Real trade quantities (bn 1994 Dh.)					
Exports	70.8	0.3	1.3	3.6	4.7
Agriculture exports	5.7	1.0	3.1	3.2	3.2
Industrial exports	36.3	0.2	1.5	5.1	6.9
Imports	86.3	0.1	0.8	2.4	3.2
Agriculture imports	4.9	4.7	11.6	9.8	9.2
Industrial imports	65.3	-0.0	0.3	3.3	4.7
Real exchange rate (index 1994 = 100)	100.0	0.9	2.3	3.6	4.3
(% of GDP)					
Direct tax	5.4	5.5	5.4	6.3	6.9
Tariffs	7.3	7.3	7.4	6.5	6.1

71

Table 4.6
Simulation Results: Trade Deprotection and Complementary Changes with Flexible Labor Market

	1994	AG-IND-LIB1	TRANS-FER	SKILL UPGRADE	RURNAG TFP
		% change			
Real disposable household income (bn. 1994 Dh.)					
All-households		9.4	1.4	1.4	2.02.5
Poor urban household	3.0	0.6	0.7	2.1	2.4
Nonpoor urban household	13.6	2.3	1.5	1.6	2.2
Poor rural household	2.7	-3.6	1.2	2.4	2.6
Nonpoor rural	6.5	-0.6	0.9	2.8	2.8
Real factor income (bn 1994 Dh.)					
Rural	71.4	-3.3	-3.0	-1.0	0.0
Urban	158.8	5.2	5.1	4.4	4.9
Irrigated resources	7.6	-2.0	-1.8	3.2	9.6
Rainfed resources	22.0	-10.2	-10.0	-7.2	-2.9
Other agriculture	2.1	0.2	-0.3	2.8	6.5
Rural nonagriculture capital	12.3	2.6	3.4	3.3	-2.5
Urban capital	70.0	5.5	5.3	5.4	5.5

Agriculture unskilled labor	10.8	-6.4	-6.2	-2.9	1.3
Rural nonagricultural unskilled labor	6.5	1.4	1.7	2.8	0.7
Rural nonagricultural skilled labor	10.1	3.4	3.9	2.5	-0.8
Urban unskilled labor	14.8	2.9	2.8	3.6	4.0
Urban skilled labor	74.1	5.4	5.3	3.7	4.5
Job Shift (% of labor force)		1.7	1.7	1.5	1.3
Real trade quantities (bn 1994 Dh.)					
Exports	70.8	3.6	3.6	4.5	5.2
Agriculture exports	5.7	3.2	3.1	2.9	3.4
Industrial exports	36.3	5.1	5.1	5.9	8.0
Imports	86.3	2.4	2.4	2.9	3.6
Agriculture imports	4.9	9.8	10.2	13.6	16.2
Industrial imports	65.3	3.3	3.4	4.1	4.1
Real exchange rate (index 1994 = 100)	100.0	3.6	3.6	3.9	4.2
(% of GDP)					
Direct tax	5.4	6.3	7.1	6.0	6.1
Tariffs		7.3	6.5	6.6	6.66.6
Government transfer to owners of rain-fed factors			0.8		

Note: TRANSFER = AG-IND-LIBI + government transfer to owners of rain-fed (nonlabor) resources; SKILL UPGRADE = AG-IND-LIBI + 1 percent of the labor force in the unskilled rural labor categories (agricultural and other rural) change status to skilled rural labor; RURNAG TFP = AG-IND-LIBI + 3 percent TFP increase for all rural nonagricultural activities.

aggregate welfare by 0.6 percent. Both rural households gain significantly and, compared to the situation in 1994, more than their urban counterparts. In urban areas, the poor gain while the nonpoor lose. These effects are driven by events in the labor markets. The incomes of the rural households increase since part of their labor force now collects significantly higher wages. Downward wage pressure in the skilled labor segment drives down wages and incomes for the urban nonpoor households who control most of the initial skilled labor stock. The urban poor gain since they earn the bulk of their incomes from unskilled labor, the supply of which declines as a result of the skill upgrade. Domestic expansion boosts imports, which, in turn, bring about depreciation of the real exchange rate to keep the current-account deficit in check, in the process raising the degree of economic openness.

Finally, we simulate an increase in the TFP of the rural nonagricultural activities. If the price elasticity of demand is high (for example for the manufactured sector, which is well integrated with the world economy), TFP growth is likely to benefit the owners of scarce activity-specific inputs; on the other hand, if the elasticity is lower (for example for rural services), the gain is most likely to accrue to consumers and activities demanding intermediate inputs. The results indicate that the latter situation predominates. A decline in the rent income of rural nonagricultural capital shows that the aggregate demand elasticity is relatively low (cf. Binswanger 1980, pp. 201–203). Agricultural resource incomes and rural household welfare increase drastically, as producers and consumers benefit from lower prices, especially for rural services. Compared to the other simulations, this scenario gives rise to the largest economy-wide boost in household welfare. Apart from the urban poor, who are relatively unaffected, all household groups gain, especially the rural households.

CONCLUSION

In this paper, a CGE model with a relatively detailed treatment of the rural economy has been used to address the short-run equilibrium effects of agricultural and industrial deprotection in Morocco. The contribution of this study stems from its focus on the impact of trade policies and complementary policies on the rural world, using a model that captures salient characteristics of Morocco's rural-urban divide, including large skill and wage gaps, labor market segmentation, and difference in sectoral structure. The analysis is exploratory—it does not try to mimic any specific liberalization scheme. Rather, it tries to further our understanding of the relative importance of some of the factors that condition the impact of trade liberalization in Morocco.

Three sets of simulations are carried out. The results from the two first sets indicate that reduced agricultural border protection would generate significant aggregate welfare gains at the same time as a large part of the disadvantaged rural population would lose. The impact of industrial tariff cuts is small, a reflection of the fact that these tariffs have a relatively limited impact on domestic price distortions. The results also suggest that, over a slightly longer time frame where migration is feasible, the outcome would be more favorable for the rural households. Nevertheless, for policymakers concerned with both aggregate and rural well-being, the results present a dilemma.

The third and last set of simulations suggests that this dilemma may be overcome if reduced border protection can be introduced in the context of a policy package that includes some combination of government transfers to owners of rain-fed agricultural resources, and government investments in education and infrastructure. Significant time lags are involved before some of these compensatory measures can be implemented or make their effects felt. Hence, if the government wants to reduce agricultural protection while protecting the rural population, it is urgent to start putting compensatory policies in place immediately. A gradualist approach to deprotection would also make it easier to manage the tradeoff between aggregate and rural welfare.

Finally, on the methodological level, the analysis suggests that an economy-wide approach adds to the understanding of the welfare effects of agricultural policy change: the results are strongly influenced by links between agriculture and the rest of the economy in markets for commodities, factors, and foreign exchange, as well as via the government budget.

NOTES

This is a revised version of a paper presented at the Conference of Earnings Inequality, Unemployment, and Poverty in the Middle East and North Africa at the School of Business, Lebanese American University, Byblos, Lebanon, November 5–7, 1998.

I would like to thank Marc Gehlhar for very kind help with trade data and Moataz El-Said, Rebecca Harris, and Marcelle Thomas for valuable research assistance.

1. Unprocessed agricultural products represent around 8 percent of exports and 6 percent of imports.

2. With few exceptions, Morocco already enjoys unrestrained access to the EU for industrial commodities.

3. A mathematical statement of the static module of the Morocco Rural-Urban CGE model is available upon request from the author. This study reports the simulation results.

4. There is one exception to this: the public administration activity uses a combination of urban and rural labor.

5. Savings from the other sources—government, the rest of the world, and other households—are not free to equilibrate aggregate savings-investment. Government

and rest-of-the-world savings are fixed while savings of other households are a fixed share of income after direct taxes.

6. The Moroccan government sources include MAMVA (DPAE/Division des Statistiques and DPV, AGER, DPA, and ORMVA), Ministère des Incitations à l'Economie (Direction de la Statistique), Ministère des Finances, Ministère de l'Industrie, Ministère des Travaux Publics, and Caisse de Compensation.

7. In summary, the values used include: (1) elasticity of substitution for CES value-added functions: 0.8 for all activities except public administration (0.19); (2) elasticity of substitution for CES intermediate-input aggregation functions for agricultural activities: 0.5 for all activities except vegetables (2.0); (3) CES (Armington) function elasticities for aggregation of imports from different regions and of imports and domestic output: between 2 and 5 for all commodities; (4) CET function elasticities for transformation of domestic output to aggregate exports and domestic sales and of aggregate exports to exports disaggregated by region: between 2 and 5 for all commodities; (5) elasticities for constant-elasticity export demand functions for agricultural exports to the EU and for service exports:-1.5.

8. For GAMS, see Brooke et al. (1988). Rutherford (1995) provides more information on PATH.

9. For this indicator, a job shift is defined as a move from one activity to another. All activities are defined at the most disaggregated level except for crop and livestock agriculture, which is defined as a single aggregate activity. Hence, unless migration is permitted, the agricultural labor force cannot change jobs, as here defined.

10. It may also be noted that because of its relatively aggregate representation of industry, the model implicitly exaggerates the initial unity of tariff rates across sectors and, in consequence, understates the efficiency gains from across-the-board tariff cuts.

REFERENCES

Alonso-Gamo, Patricia, Susan Fennell, and Khaled Sakr (1997). "Adjusting to New Realities: MENA, The Uruguay Round, and the EU-Mediterranean Initiative." Washington, DC: IMF working paper.

Binswanger, Hans P. (1980). "Income Distribution Effects of Technical Change: Some Analytical Issues," *South East Asian Economic Review* 1 (3): 179–218.

Brooke, A., D. Kendrick, and A. Meeraus (1988). *GAMS: A User's Guide.* Redwood, CA:The Scientific Press.

Bussolo, Maurizio and David Roland-Holst (1993). *A Detailed Input-Output Table for Morocco, 1990.* OECD Development Centre, Technical Paper no. 90, November.

EIU (Economist Intelligence Unit) (1998). *Morocco: Country Report.* 2nd quarter.

Hazell, Peter B. R. and Roger D. Norton (1986). *Mathematical Programming for Economic Analysis in Agriculture.* New York: Macmillan.

International Monetary Fund (1997). *Morocco—Selected Issues.* Staff Country Report no. 97/6. Washington, DC: IMF.

Karshenas, Massoud (1994). "Structural Adjustment and Employment in the Middle East and North Africa." Economic Research Forum for the Arab Countries, Iran and Turkey, Cairo, Egypt. Working paper 9420.

Löfgren, Hans, Rachid Doukkali, Hassan Serghini, and Sherman Robinson (1997). "Rural Development in Morocco: Alternative Scenarios to the Year 2000," Discussion paper 17, Trade and Macroeconomics Division, IFPRI, February.

Page, John and John Underwood (1997). "Growth, the Maghreb, and Free Trade with the European Union," in Ahmed Galal and Bernard Hoekman, eds. *Regional Partners in Global Markets: Limits and Possibilities of the Euro-Med Agreements.* Cairo: Centre for Economic Policy Research, London, and Egyptian Center for Economic Studies, pp. 98–126.

Robinson, Sherman (1989). "Multisectoral Models," in H. Chenery and T. N. Srinivasan, eds. *Handbook of Development Economics.* Volume 2. Amsterdam, North Holland: Elsevier Science Publishers.

Robinson, Sherman, Andrea Catteneo, and Moataz El-Said (1998). *Estimating a Social Accounting Matrix Using Cross Entropy Methods.* Discussion paper 33, Trade and Macroeconomics Division, International Food Policy Research Institute.

Roland-Holst, David (1996). "SAM for Morocco, 1990 and 1994" (in electronic form).

Roland-Holst, David and Sâad Belghazi (1996). "Morocco: An Economywide Analysis of Selected Policy Reforms," December (mimeo).

Royaume du Maroc (1993). *Niveau de Vie des Menages 1990/91.* Various volumes. Rabat: Direction de la Statistique.

———(1995). *Annuaire Statistique.* Rabat: Direction de la Statistique.

———(1996). *Les Indicateurs Sociaux.* Rabat: Direction de la Statistique.

———(1997). *Annuaire Statistique.* Rabat: Direction de la Statistique.

Rutherford, T. (1995). "Extensions of GAMS for Complementarity Problems Arising in Applied Economic Analysis," *Journal of Economic Dynamics and Control* 19 (8): 1299–1324.

Rutherford, Thomas F., E. E. Rutström, and David Tarr (1993). "Morocco's Free Trade Agreement with the European Community: A Quantitative Assessment," Policy Research Department, WPS 1173, The World Bank, September.

United Nations (1998). *COMTRADE Database.* New York: UN Statistical Division.

World Bank (1994). *Kingdom of Morocco: Poverty, Adjustment, and Growth.* Volumes I–II. Report 11918-MOR. Washington, DC.

——— (1995). *Kingdom of Morocco: Towards Higher Growth and Employment.* Volumes I–II. Report 14155-MOR. Washington, DC.

———(1996). *World Development Report.* Washington, DC.

———(1997a). "RMSM Simulation Data" (mimeo).

———(1997b). "World Development Indicators" (CD-ROM).

———(1997c). *Kingdom of Morocco: Rural Development Strategy. Integrating the Two Moroccos (1997–2010). Synthesis Report.* Volumes II–III. Report 16303-MOR. Washington, DC.

5

Earning Profiles of Women Workers and Education in the Middle East

E. Mine Cinar

INTRODUCTION

Women earn less than men in both industrialized and developing countries, including the Middle East and North Africa (MENA). Earnings differentials, whether by gender or race, have been studied for the last 25 years in labor economics. There is abundant empirical literature on several theories that explain differences in earnings in formal labor markets. One of these, the human capital theory, postulates that earnings differentials are determined by human capital accumulation differences between individuals, and workers in low-wage jobs are primarily low-productivity workers. Here, human capital is a loosely defined term to denote education, training, and experience. Another theory, that of dual markets (Doeringer and Piore 1971; Dickens and Lang 1985), states that there are secondary jobs (low pay, unstable employment, and little opportunity for advancement) versus primary jobs (high pay, advancement into higher wages, and so forth), the latter of which are actually rationed and therefore are very hard to enter by minorities and women. Women will earn less if they are channeled into segregated occupations and tasks with lower pay. Comparing the two, human capital theory emphasizes the quality differences in factors of production whereas dual market theory emphasizes demand restrictions in explaining earning differentials in labor markets. As for policy conclusions, human capital theory suggests training the individuals to have more skills whereas dual labor market theory suggests income supports, minimizing secondary sector jobs, and providing a "fair" rationing system.

One can find evidence to validate both of these theories with respect to labor markets and earnings of women in the Middle East. The educational attainment of women in the area on average is considerably low and the institutional, sociological, and political infrastructure creates job segregation by gender, race, and nationality. The Middle East itself is not monolithic and the area has great diversity. Among the different countries in the region, there are differences in the political systems (monarchy, dictatorship, and democracy), and in the institutional/constitutional setting (religious or secular),[1] in the number of major religions within countries, and in diverse civil rights for women with respect to divorce, inheritance, clothing, education, and careers. Some of the countries in the region are rich in surplus natural energy resources and import labor from the other countries in the region.

As for labor markets, three groups, including the informal sector, microenterprises, and small-scale family firms, provide the bulk of employment in the urban markets in many countries in the Middle East. There is no consensus as to what constitutes informal and formal sector differences.[2] Whatever the different studies use as definitions, there are some characteristics common to all these sectors. Entry-exit rate to the sectors is high and the life span of the industry as well as the enterprise may be short. Bankruptcies are as high as 38 percent in the small-scale textile firms in the formal sector measured during a four-year period (see Cinar 1995).

The situation of women in the formal labor markets in the Middle East depends[3] on the institutional structures imposed on the labor markets as well as the educational endowments and socioeconomic backgrounds of the women. This chapter examines life-cycle labor force participation of unskilled women in formal labor markets in MENA. The next section discusses the earnings stream of women over time. The following section examines human capital development and related proxy indexes. The last section gives conclusions.

GENDER EARNINGS DIFFERENTIALS IN FORMAL MARKETS AND LIFE-CYCLE LABOR FORCE PARTICIPATION

The human capital approach analyzes labor markets in terms of demand for workers by firms and voluntary supply decisions by workers. The former is a derived demand from the demand for output and also depends on the productivity of the workers. The supply of labor is formed by individuals' decision of a choice between labor and leisure, with wage rate determining the opportunity cost of leisure. The demand and supply determine the market wage and, therefore, labor earnings are determined by the human capital stock of the individuals. Mincer and Polachek's (1974) pioneering work on gender earnings gap showed that the gap would decrease by 45 percent if the women had the same experience as men, based on their regressed logarithm of U.S. earnings on years of education and square of years of experience.

Demand for Unskilled Urban Women Workers

The demand for skilled professional urban women in large urban centers in developing countries resembles the demand for their counterparts in developed countries. Yet demand for unskilled female labor is different in MENA, for it is predominantly for the young and the single in the formal sector. Formal sector employers prefer single females over married ones for several reasons. A young, single, unskilled woman's work horizon is limited; almost all of them live at home and one of the primary reasons for work is to accumulate household assets and durable goods during the premarital state (i.e., to prepare a trousseau) and to help out with the household budget. Therefore, she is willing to take entry-level jobs at minimum wage and does not necessarily ask for benefits or promotions. On the average, she is in the workforce for about three to five years. This cost advantage is especially an important factor of demand for labor in export-oriented industries such as textiles, which face very competitive markets abroad.

Single, young women also give the employer flexibility for overtime production. They are also cheaper, for there are no paid maternity leaves or payment for erratic attendance due to sick children. Hence, for the formal sector employer, married women are costlier, less flexible, and therefore less desirable workers (Cinar 1994).

Expected Wages for Women for Intermittent Work in Formal Markets

What is the expected wage gap for an unskilled female laborer in urban areas if she actually did find a formal sector job? Figure 5.1 shows the hypothetical time-earnings profile of unskilled women in formal markets in large urban centers.

Let (a) be the logarithm of minimum wages. Let line (ab) be the hypothetical path of earnings of unskilled male laborers. The earnings path shows an increase over time due to skills gained on the job and work experience. If females start at the same entry-level minimum wages, their hypothetical path should also be (ab). However, they may have a lower earnings path (ac) if they are segregated into jobs in lower-paying sectors. These happen by laws that define where they can or cannot work (Iran, Saudi Arabia) or by convention and social pressures. Both lines (ab) and (ac) show full-time long-term work commitments by males and females, respectively.

Figure 5.1
**Time-Earnings Profile of Unskilled Married Women in Urban Formal Labor
Markets**

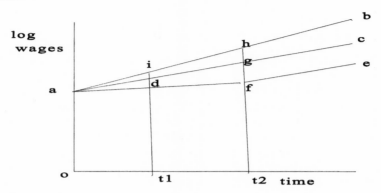

t1 = premarital work
t2 = time of reentry into the labor market
hf = total loss in wages due to reentry into labor market after taking (t2-t1) time off
df = depreciation of skills due to atrophy
fg = lost wages due to losses in seniority
gh = lost wages due to job segregation

If the women work only in the premarital stage and then take on household, childbearing, and childrearing duties and leave work at time t1, their
earnings profile are cut off at segment (ad). When they reenter work at time
t2, perhaps after the children have grown, they again enter at level (a),
which is equal to (f), and (assuming constant minimum wages over time)
face the earnings segment (fe). At the reentry time, they face a wage gap
of (h-a) in the market compared to men in other sectors and a wage gap
of (g-a) due to their intermittent work. Hence, a woman going back to
work after a time faces different wage losses. Using Figure 5.1, she loses
the amount (ag) because she has lost her past accumulated seniority and
work experience of her initial work years. She may lose (gh) if she is segregated into lower wage industries. An approximation, using data collected
in a 1989 survey (Cinar 1994), gave the following estimates for the earnings
losses in Istanbul, Turkey; the total gender earnings gap of (h-a) is 0.52; it
is decomposed of the pure gender earnings gap (h-g) of 0.34 and the intermittent work gap (g-a) of 0.18. Women lost a total of 52 percent of
their earnings with respect to men if they took time out of work and
therefore lost human capital and seniority. Therefore, there is little incentive
(as well as little demand) for married women who have taken time off of
work to reenter the formal job markets. If they do, their further work will
tend to be in the informal markets.

While Figure 5.1 shows the typical earnings pattern of unskilled or semi-

Figure 5.2
Earning-Time Profile of Unskilled Men and Women in Labor-Exporting
Countries

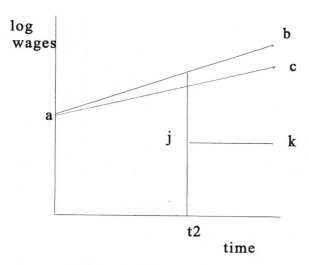

skilled women in typical markets, Figure 5.2 shows the same profile for
women in the large-population, labor-exporting countries in the Middle
East such as Egypt and Turkey. High unemployment rates and the higher
"cost" of married women usually mean that the option to reenter work
after taking time off to raise a family may not be there unless there is a
family business. Lack of part-time jobs and the stiff competition for jobs
with benefits puts the older woman returning to the labor force at a distinct
disadvantage. Therefore, the path of earnings over time (afe from Figure
5.1) is not open to older women returning to work in those countries in
MENA. The earnings path will be either (ac) or a lower-than-minimum-
wage job (jk) in the informal markets.

Why are these jobs almost nonexistent for older women? Not only is
there substitution of labor between single and married women, but there
is also substitution between adult labor and child apprentices in most of
the large countries in the Middle East (Cinar 1996). The minimum wage
for the apprentices is set below the minimum wage of adults. Figure 5.3
explains the budget constraint facing the producers in terms of different
labor inputs into the production process. The costliest input is the adult
male, who is either scarce (with respect to capital inputs) in the oil-
exporting countries or has higher opportunity costs (due to intrafirm mobility, self-employment, internal and foreign migration) in labor-exporting
ones. If we assume that the marginal productivity differences between adult
men, adult single women, and adult married women are comparable and
are all greater than that of child apprentices, an employer will maximize

Figure 5.3
Preference for Industrial Labor in Labor-Exporting Countries

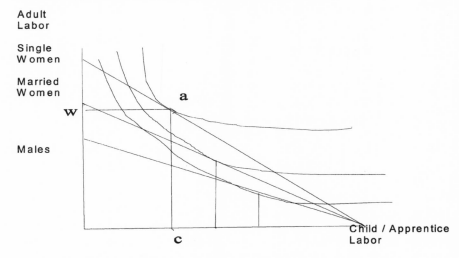

production and minimize costs by using a combination of child apprentices (c) and single women (w) in the workplace (such as point a).

If, however, the marginal productivity rates of adults and children are either the same or very close to each other for a particular type of production, the employer will opt for the corner solution where only children will be employed in the workplace. We see some of the latter in workshops for export goods in Egypt and Morocco (Figure 5.4).

There are no reliable data for the comparative earnings of apprentices. However, we do have some cross-country information on proxies of female welfare in the Middle East and North Africa. Table 5.1 reports the Human Development Index (HDI) ranking of countries in the region. The index is calculated by using three components: life expectancy at birth, educational attainment (composed of adult literacy rate and primary, secondary, and tertiary school enrollment ratios), and real GDP per capita. Based on these criteria, the world rankings of the countries in the Middle East range from 22nd (Israel) to 151st (Yemen).

The female labor force participation rates are also reported in the table. The world average of female labor force participation is 41 percent and the MENA region has a low average of 28 percent, which is one of the lowest in the world. Hypotheses differ as to the cause of the low rates. Some argue that this is due to the socioreligious makeup of the region (Moskoff 1982), or due to protected high wages for resident men in labor-importing countries (and therefore only-one-wage-earner families), or due to the large informal sector that goes undetected from statistics.

Among family workers in the region, we would expect a large percentage

Figure 5.4
Preference for Industrial Labor in Labor-Exporting Countries when Marginal
Productivities Are Equal-Apprentice Workshops

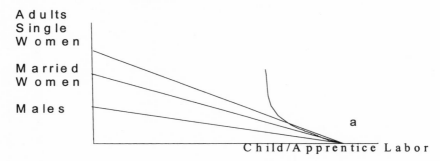

to be women. We find this to be true for a large number of countries in
the region. However, for Bahrain, Kuwait, UAE, Syria, Algeria, and Jordan,
the reported statistics show that less than 10 percent of family businesses
employ women (see Table 5.1, col. 5). Women's share of earned income
for the region (24 percent) is not that divergent from the female labor force
participation rate (28 percent).

THE HUMAN CAPITAL: EDUCATION IN THE
MIDDLE EAST

Studies about economic growth show that education is one of the major
determinants of growth and development. Education has immediate externalities, increases productivity in the long run, and has numerous multiplier
effects with respect to population growth, quality of life, and the social
institutions of the country. Robert Barro (1994) states that growth depends
directly on the quantity of human capital in the form of education and
health and inversely on the percentage of government spending to GDP,
market interventions, and political instability.

Illiteracy rates are high in the MENA. Real spending for public education
also has been declining in some countries. High energy costs (for energy-
importing states), inefficient state economic enterprises, massive government bureaucracies, and military spending have resulted in large budget
deficits, leading to declines in real public education spending. The same
pattern is observed whether the countries are energy-exporting and labor-
importing or energy-importing and labor-exporting. Middle Eastern economies are defined by the large role of government in the economy, increased
public consumption at the expense of private savings, high defense and
internal security expenditures, bloated civil and bureaucratic employment,
overvalued exchange rates, and in labor-importing countries, dual labor
markets biased in favor of residents. Along with the economic woes, vari-

Earnings Inequality, Unemployment, and Poverty

Table 5.1
Female Earnings, 1995

Country	HDI	% Population in Labor Force**	% Women in Earned Income	% Female Share in Family Workers*	% Female Unpaid
Israel	22	42	40	33	72
Bahrain	43	44	19	NA	8
UAE 48	50		13	10	9
Kuwait	54	37	31	25	4
Qatar	57	57	13	NA	4
Libya	64	29	21	NA	NA
Lebanon	66	33	28	NA	NA
Turkey	69	46	36	36	69
S. Arabia	70	33	13	NA	NA
Oman	71	27	14	NA	NA
Iran	78	30	24	19	43
Syria	81	30	25	20	5
Algeria	82	31	24	19	6
Tunisia	83	37	30	25	49
Jordan	87	28	21	19	4
Egypt	112	36	29	25	62
Morocco	125	39	34	28	31
Iraq	127	27	18	NA	50
Yemen	151	32	27	NA	69
Averages					
World		48	41	33	58
Industrial		49	44	37	75
LDC'S (LEAST)		47	48	NA	41
Developing (ALL)		48	41	32	48
Middle East		36	28***	24***	32

Note: *As percentage of total unpaid family workers, 1990.
      **As percentage of workers aged 15 or above, 1995.
      ***Average of 11 observations in the column.

Source: UNDP, Human Development Report, 1998.

ous military conflicts, lack of peace, and lack of long-term sustainable growth characterize the region.

Central government expenditures expressed as a percentage of GDP are high for MENA. For 1980, the ratio of government expenditure to GDP was as high as the following: Morocco, 34 percent; Iran, 36 percent; Oman, 43 percent; Syria, 48 percent; Egypt, 53 percent; and Israel, 72 percent. Table 5.2 reports the central government expenditures as a percentage of GDP for 1985 and 1996. The average expenditure, when data are available, is 39 percent. Government expenditures in industrial countries averaged about 33 percent of their GDP in 1995 (UNDP 1995, p. 183). Large bureaucracies, lack of a viable private sector, and high military expenditures result in high central government expenditures in MENA.

Public education has not been successful in the Middle East. Illiteracy is high for both men and women. The discrepancy between male and female illiteracy rates is especially high for the region. Part of this could be because

Table 5.2
Percentage Allocation of Government Budgets, 1985 and 1995 (countries ranked by HDI Index)

Country	HDI	Defense % of 1985	GDP 1996	Defense $ Per Capita 1985	Defense $ Per Capita 1996	Defense as % of Health and Education 1960	Defense as % of Health and Education 1990-1991	Central Gov. as % of GDP
Israel	22	21	12	1,630	1,620	85	106	45
Bahrain	43	4	6	494	476	NA	41	NA
UAE	48	8	5	1,993	830	NA	44	NA
Kuwait	54	9	13	1,434	2,218	NA	88	51
Qatar	57	6	10	1,301	1,334	NA	192	NA
Libya	64	6	5	490	227	29	71	NA
Lebanon	66	9	4	102	116	NA	NA	26
Turkey	69	5	4	62	110	153	87	27
Saudi Arabia	70	20	13	2,125	1,030	150	151	NA
Oman	71	21	16	1,841	955	NA	293	43
Iran	78	36	5	435	49	141	38	NA
Syria	81	16	5	453	105	329	373	27
Algeria	82	2	4	59	62	31	11	NA
Tunisia	83	5	2	80	42	45	31	NA
Jordan	87	16	6	235	85	464	138	31
Egypt	112	7	5	73	43	117	52	43
Morocco	125	5	4	40	54	49	72	NA
Iraq	127	26	8	1,105	56	128	271	NA
Yemen	151	10	4	66	24	NA	197	39
Averages								
World		5	3	182	137	109	38	
Industrial		4	3	728	493	110	33	33
LDC'S (LEAST)		4	3	13	10	NA	72	
Developing		7	4	51	39	102	63	
Middle East		12	7	738	497	143	125	39

Note: N.A.: Not available. 1985 Defense expenditures are in 1995 U.S. dollars.

Source: UNDP, *Human Development Report*, 1998.

of the rural concept that women do not need to be educated as much as men because rural women have no positive economic incentives to be educated. On the supply side, lack of public school funding has driven the best and the most talented teachers out of the teaching profession in countries such as Egypt and Turkey, most of whom have either migrated abroad or changed professions.

One hypothesis as to why education has lagged behind is that the high military expenditures crowd out educational spending. Educational expenditures and defense expenditures as a percentage of the government budget are given in Table 5.2 for those MENA countries for which data exist. Adjusted for inflation, a large group of the countries in the region allocated far more to defense budgets than to the education and health budgets in 1995. From 1985 to 1996, however, the percentage GDP spent on defense has decreased (with the exception of Bahrain and Kuwait). Therefore, based on expenditure shares, the crowding out (of education by defense) hypothesis does not find strong support in the data over the last 10-year period.

Another hypothesis is that the governments are unable to keep up with the population growth. Per capita expenditures on education are reported on Table 5.3, which show that expenditures per capita are small. These numbers are also biased upward since they also include tertiary education of students on government scholarships abroad (using foreign exchange). For both the 1980s and 1990s, Israel has the highest educational expenditure per capita in the region ($666 and $948), followed by the energy-exporting countries of the region.[4]

Data for the 1990s show that most per capita educational spending is either stationary or declining in nominal terms, giving support to the hypothesis that governments have not been able to keep up with population growth. Regression models on the determinants of female illiteracy in the region produced mixed results (Cinar 1997, pp. 60–61). Calculations of elasticities showed that female illiteracy in the region was inelastic with respect to both GDP per capita and education expenditures per capita. A 1 percent increase in education expenditures per capita decreased female illiteracy by about 1/10th of 1 percent (0.13) and a 1 percent increase in GDP per capita decreased it by ¼th of 1 percent (0.24). Hence, institutional and social factors, as well as expenditures, have to be reevaluated to solve the illiteracy problem in the region.

Table 5.4 reports the HDI index as well as the Gender Development Index (GDI) for the region for 1995. GDI is developed with the same variables as HDI "but captures inequalities in achievement between women and men. . . . The greater the gender disparity in basic human development, the lower the country's GDI compared to its HDI" (UNDP 1998, p. 15). GDI measures the discrepancy between female and male life expectancy at birth, female and male adult literacy rate, female and male enrollment ratio, and earned income shares. With the exception of Israel, Lebanon, and

Table 5.3
Education Expenditures Per Capita in the Middle East, 1992

Country	GNP $ 1992 Billions	Education Per Capita in Dollars		Literacy Rate (15+)	
		1992	1980	Female	Male
Egypt	35	NA	27.84	35	66
Sudan	10	NA	7.40	13	45
Morocco	27	55.86	60.96	40	64
Jordan	4	60.25	NA	72	91
Tunisia	14	98.73	95.03	59	72
Turkey	116	116.43	73.95	72	91
Iran	131	94.05	166.82	45	67
Syria	15	27.78	31.54	53	82
Oman	10	341.43	134.06	NA	NA
Israel	67	666.21	947.56	93*	95
UAE	37	NA	298.86	56	NA

Note: Average Female Literacy: 47 percent.

Countries are ranked by GNP per capita, from the poorest to the richest.

*Israel's literacy rates are for 1985 (World Bank, *World Development Report 1990*).

Source: Cinar 1997, p. 59.

Table 5.4
Human Development Index (HDI) and Gender Development Index (GDI), 1995

Country	Rank HDI	GDI	HDI-GDR Rank		GDP-HDI Rank	GEM
Israel	22	0.913	0.873	0	6	0.484
Bahrain	43	0.872	0.746	-19	-16	NA
UAE	48	0.855	0.718	-20	-24	0.247
Kuwait	54	0.848	0.773	0	-49	0.470
Qatar	57	0.840	0.714	-16	-38	NA
Libya	64	0.806	0.664	-22	-6	NA
Lebanon	66	0.796	0.707	-9	7	NA
Turkey	69	0.782	0.753	7	-2	0.281
Saudi Arabia	70	0.778	0.589	-39	-24	NA
Oman	71	0.771	0.580	-40	-27	NA
Iran	78	0.758	0.643	-21	-10	0.458
Syria	81	0.749	0.638	-20	-10	0.319
Algeria	82	0.746	0.627	-21	-17	0.241
Tunisia	83	0.744	0.670	0	-11	0.345
Jordan	87	0.729	0.647	-10	-6	0.211
Egypt	112	0.612	0.555	-7	-20	0.258
Morocco	125	0.557	0.511	-1	-27	0.302
Iraq	127	0.538	0.443	-10	-25	NA
Yemen	151	0.356	0.336	-2	12	NA
Averages						
World		0.772	0.736			
Industrial		0.911	0.888			
LDC'S (LEAST)		0.344	0.332			
Developing (All)		0.586	0.564			
Middle East		0.740	0.640	-13.16	-15.11	

Note: Rank is based on the value of the HDI Index, where 1 is the highest of 100 (Canada with 0.96) and 174 the least (Sierra Leone, 0.18) Middle East figures are calculated from the data.

Source: UNDP, *Human Development Report* 1998.

Yemen, the negative discrepancies in the ranks of HDI and GDI in the region show gender disparities. The largest gender disparities in the area are in the oil-exporting countries.

UNDP also develops a Gender Empowerment ratio (GEM), reported in Table 5.4, which reveals whether women can take active part in political and economic life. This index is also low for the region. The highest value for the index, reported for Scandinavian countries, is 0.79.

As with all data, especially macroeconomic data, and index numbers, one has to interpret these numbers with caution. The value of the indexes can be questionable for some countries in MENA. However, it is apparent that women in the Middle East do not fare as well as women in the rest of the world when one compares these index numbers.

CONCLUSION

The available international statistics show that the Middle East is still lagging behind the rest of the world in terms of gender development and gender disparity. Even if the intercountry comparison data are questionable, there is enough disparity between the Middle East and the rest of the world to warrant more studies in this topic. For the energy-exporting countries, excess revenues from oil exports have allowed the countries to go with huge economic inefficiencies in their labor markets. Sooner or later, when natural gas and oil revenues run out, these countries have to make amends for these disparities. As for labor-exporting countries in the region, the huge size of the informal markets in which women have low earnings and no social guarantees is cause for concern. Earning disparities and lack of formal sector jobs for older women both point to dual career paths. Yet the lack of human capital, especially when it comes to women in a great many countries in the region, is the biggest stumbling block that has to be overcome before gender disparities can become smaller.

NOTES

This is a revised version of a paper presented at the Conference on Earnings Inequality, Unemployment, and Poverty in the Middle East and North Africa at the School of Business, Lebanese American University, Byblos, Lebanon, November 5–7, 1998.

1. In this study, secular means separation of "church" and state in executive and legislative powers.

2. Formal sector can be defined by tax or registration status of the enterprise or as mainstream production. Informal sector can also be taken as the "politically disfranchised" or "economically marginal" sector as well as an invisible (from statistics) sector. Microenterprises are usually defined either with respect to labor (such as one- or two-people enterprises) or with respect to start-up capital (usually $1,000 or less, depending on the country). Informal sector or microenterprises may

require little or no human and physical capital. Given the amount of rural-urban migration, this sector is the employment depot of most of the urban immigrants in the Middle East. Street vendors of food and goods are the visible part of the informal sector. What is invisible is work done among the homes, usually by taking in homework or household help. Cinar (1994) estimates that a minimum of 23 percent of the immigrant women in Istanbul took homework and were completely disguised in employment statistics.

3. There is direct and indirect evidence of the duality in labor markets facing women. In oil-exporting countries, resident men are favored and protected by high wages and set-asides. In labor-exporting countries, the large size of the informal markets and the use of children in production show the degree of substitution women face for the more competitive formal sector jobs.

4. United Arab Emirates (UAE) had the second highest per capita expenditure at $299 per person, yet has a female literacy rate of only 56 percent. Twenty-five percent of all tertiary students of UAE are educated abroad, so the country may be spending the monies overseas subsidizing tertiary education rather than developing basic literacy skills at home. Oman and Iran, both oil-exporting countries, also have educational expenditures per capita that are greater than $100.

REFERENCES

Barro, R. (1994). "Recent Research on Economic Growth," *National Bureau of Economic Research Reporter* (Summer): 6–10.

Borjas, G. J. (1987). "Self-Selection and Earnings of Migrants," *American Economic Review* 77 (4): 531.

Cain, G. (1966). *Married Women in the Labor Force.* Chicago: University of Chicago Press.

Cinar, E. Mine (1994). "Unskilled Urban Immigrant Women and Disguised Employment: Home Working Women in Contemporary Turkey," *World Development.* 22 (3): 369–380.

———. (1996). "Substitution between Unskilled Females, Males and Apprentices in Small Scale Textile Firms," *METU Studies in Development* 23 (3): 329–340.

Cinar, M. (1987). "Disguised Employment in the Third World," in *IFDA Dossier.* Geneva: United Nations.

———. (1995). "Determinants of Small Scale Family Firm Failure in a Developing Economy with Neural Networks." Chicago: Loyola University School of Business.

———. (1997). "Privatization of Education, Educational Spending and the Case of the 'Missing Girls' in Grade Schools," *Critique* (Fall): 53–64.

Cinar, M., M. Kaytaz, and G. Evcimen (1988). "The Present Status of Small Scale Industries (Sanatkar) in Bursa, Turkey," *International Journal of Middle East Studies* 20 (3): 287–301.

Dickens, W. T. and K. Lang (1985). "A Test of Dual Market Theory," *American Economic Review* 75 (4): 792.

Doeringer, P. B. and Piore, M. J. (1971). *International Labor Markets and Manpower Analysis.* Lexington, MA: Lexington Books.

Esim, S. (1996). "Gender Based Factors Affecting the Earnings of Women Entrepreneurs in Turkey," Ph.D. thesis, American University, Washington, DC.

Hani, A. B. (1996). "Determinants of Agricultural Labor Wage in Jordan: A Comparative Study of Expatriate versus Local Labor," *Economic Development and Cultural Change* 44 (2): 405–448.

Hansen, L. (1961). "The Cyclical Sensitivity of Labor Supply," *American Economic Review* 51: 299–309.

Heckman, J. and T. Macurdy (1980). "A Life Cycle Model of Female Labor Supply," *Review of Economic Studies* 47: 47–74.

——— (1982). "Corrigendum on a Life Cycle Model of Female Labor Supply," *Review of Economic Studies* 49: 659–660.

Kazgan, G. (1978). "Turk Ekonomisinde Kadinlarin Isgucune Katilmasi, Mesleki Dagilimi, Egitim Duzeyi ve Sosyo-Ekonomik Statusu," in N. Abadan-Unat, ed. *Turk Toplumunda Kadin*, Ankara: Turk Sosyal Bilimler Dernegi.

Lehrer, E. and M. Nerlove (1979). "Female Labor Supply Behavior over the Life Cycle: An Econometric Study," *MEDS Discussion paper* no. 382, Northwestern University, Evanston, IL.

Lundberg, S. (1985). "The Added Worker Effect," *Journal of Labor Economics* 3 (1): 11–37.

Mincer, J. (1962). "Labor Force Participation of Married Women: A Study of Labor Supply," in H. G. Lewis, ed., *Aspects of Labor Economics*. Princeton: NBER, Princeton University Press.

Mincer, J. and S. Polachek, (1974). "Family Investments in Human Capital: Earnings of Women," *Journal of Political Economy* 82 (3): 76–108.

Moskoff, W. (1982). "Women and Work in Israel and the Islamic Middle East," *Quarterly Review of Economics and Business* 22 (4): 89.

Richards, A. and P. L. Martin, (1983). "The Laissez-Faire Approach to International Labor Migration: The Case of the Arab Middle East," *Economic Development and Cultural Change* 31 (3): 455–474.

Schultz, Theodore W. (1961). "Investment in Human Capital," *American Economic Review*, March 1961 and in T. Morgan, G. W. Betz, and N. K. Choudry, eds., *Readings in Economic Development*. Belmont, CA: Wadsworth Publishing Co., 1963, pp. 186–200.

Scoville, J. G. (1985). "The Labor Market in Prerevolutionary Iran," *Economic Development and Cultural Change* 34 (1): 543–555.

UNDP. *Human Development Report* 1994, 1995, 1998, published for the United Nations Development Program by Oxford University Press, New York.

World Bank. *World Development Reports* 1990, 1994, 1998, published for the World Bank by Oxford University Press, New York.

Youssef, N. H. (1972). "Differential Labor Force Participation of Women in Latin American and Middle Eastern Countries: The Influence of Family Characteristics," *Social Forces* 51: 135–153.

6

Fiscal Policy and Social Welfare in Selected MENA Countries

Muhammad Q. Islam

INTRODUCTION

Public sector economists have long recognized that fiscal policy, in addition to stabilization, can be utilized over the long term to redistribute income and alleviate poverty. Stewart (1995) identifies three ways that fiscal choices can impact the economically disadvantaged: direct taxes and transfers can change the disposable income of individuals; government can change the prices of basic goods and services through indirect taxes and subsidies; and governments, through level of expenditures, can affect the availability of certain publicly provided goods. In the more developed countries, numerous studies have been conducted to examine the incidence of both government expenditure and taxation. Through these studies, analysts have tried to determine the impact of fiscal policy on the overall distribution of income, and the impact on the income and consumption of those who are in the lower-income groups. Conclusions were that fiscal policy can reduce differences in income among various groups and reduce the incidence of poverty; however, its effectiveness has also been questioned because of the explicit and implicit cost associated with such measures. A simple example can illustrate the basic tension: one way to close the gap between the rich and the poor would be to use a progressive income tax system to collect revenue, and redistribute that revenue through cash and in-kind transfers to individuals in the lower-income groups. Critics could argue that such a policy would result in prolonging the persistence of poverty because of the detrimental effect the policy would have on work and saving effort, and hence, long-term economic growth.

The proposed objective of this study is modest. While detailed analysis of fiscal policies have been carried out for a number of developed countries, for many countries in the developing world, such analysis is still in the formative stages. In this chapter, I put together a description of the various fiscal instruments in use in the MENA countries. These instruments include the various types of taxes that are used to collect revenue. From earlier studies we know the basic impacts of different types of taxes on the distribution of income. Application of this knowledge would provide a general understanding of what impact fiscal instruments might have had on the distribution of income and the incidence of poverty in MENA countries. It is now well established that certain forms of government expenditures can be successfully used as instruments to promote distributional equity and to ameliorate poverty. Therefore, I look at the structure of government expenditures.

POVERTY AND INCOME DISTRIBUTION IN MENA COUNTRIES

Study of fiscal policy in the context of poverty alleviation would be of interest only if there is evidence of poverty in the countries in the region. In this section, I present some data on the extent of poverty in MENA countries. One, however, has to keep in mind that different governments and institutions utilize very different measures of poverty. For example, Van Eeghan (1998), using revised World Bank data, reports poverty levels substantially different than those reported below. Therefore, the extent of poverty documented will vary with the type of measure used to study poverty. Poverty statistics by regions show low figures for MENA countries compared to Asia and Africa. In 1990, the percent of the population living below poverty stood at 47.8 percent for sub-Saharan Africa, 11.3 for East Asia, 49 percent for South Asia, 33.1 for MENA countries, and 25.5 percent for Latin America.[1]

However, despite improvements in per capita income, significant poverty levels still exist in varying degrees in MENA countries. There is substantial variation in the incidence of poverty among the various MENA countries. Poverty and income distribution data for various countries as presented in Table 6.1 remain a substantial problem.

The income and distribution of income figures show that there is substantial disparity in the income of those who are at the bottom of the income scale, both in absolute terms and in income shares. For example, the income of those in the upper 20 percent in Jordan and Tunisia is approximately eight times the income of the poorest 20 percent. Further, in these same countries, less than 2.5 percent of national income accrues to the poorest 20 percent of the population, while the richest 20 percent receive 50 percent of national income. The figures are similar in the other countries listed above. These large disparities result in the high value of the Gini coefficient reported for these countries, and contribute to the poverty reported above for many of them.

Though the incidence of poverty in many of the MENA countries is high, it is also true that poverty has actually declined in some of them. The poverty trend figures show that poverty declined substantially in Morocco and Tunisia, while it may have increased in Egypt and Jordan.

The World Bank, along with UNDP, publishes indicators of human development (HDI:Human Development Index) and deprivation (HPI: Human Poverty Index). The HDI is designed to measure the progress that countries have made towards achieving a better life for their citizens with higher HDI values reflecting improved living conditions. The HPI measures the gaps that remain in the struggle against alleviating poverty and its effects. The two indices are presented below along with selected indicators of human development.

It is clear from Table 6.2 that the oil-exporting economies, fueled by increases in per capita income, have done well in human development. It is apparent from the basic indicators that these countries have been able to raise longevity, reduce infant mortality, and raise the literacy of their people. The non-oil-exporting economies have not done as well, with countries like Egypt and Morocco having higher-than-average infant mortality and lower-than-average life span and literacy, resulting in higher-than-average HPI. But the data presented above also indicate that it is possible to alleviate poverty and improve living conditions. Tunisia, for example, has been able to successfully reduce poverty, decrease child mortality, and improve literacy. It is due to these improvements that HDI is higher than average and HPI lower than average in Tunisia.

FISCAL POLICY TO ALLEVIATE POVERTY

Danziger and Portnoy (1988) define distributional impact studies as "those which investigate the distribution of actual benefits or burdens to various groups or persons in some specified population . . . or focus on alternative policy interventions or implementation schemes as a means of achieving a desired distribution of benefits and burdens. . . . Or they compare the distribution of some characteristic of the population (such as income, health, and educational status) before the adoption/implementation of a policy, to the distribution of that characteristic after the policy has been in effect" (Danziger and Portnoy 1988, pp. 1–2). One approach to measuring the impact of fiscal policy is to use the very broad group benefits method suggested by Cranmer (1988). Cranmer identifies competing interest groups in a society, and identifies the impact of fiscal policy on these

Table 6.1
Income Distribution in Selected MENA Countries

	Per Cap. Income, PPP		Gini	Distribution of Income (%)			
	Poorest 20%	Richest 20%		Bottom 10%	Bottom 20%	Highest 20%	Highest 10%
Algeria	1922	12839	.387	2.8	6.9	46.1	31.5
Egypt	1653	7809	.32	3.9	8.7	41.1	26.7
Iran	1191	8357	.435	1.7	5.0	48.8	33.6
Jordan	1292	10972	.434	2.4	5.9	50.1	34.7
Morocco	1079	7570	.392	2.8	6.6	46.3	30.5
Qatar			.379	2.0	5.7	43.8	27.1
Tunisia	1460	11459	.402	2.3	5.9	46.3	30.7

Source: UNDP, *Human Development Report 1997*; World Bank, *World Development Report, 1997*.

Table 6.2
Trends in Human Development in Selected MENA Countries

	HDI	HDI 1994	HPI 1996	Life Exp. 1960	Life Exp. 1994	Inf. Mort. 1960	Inf. Mort. 1994	Adult Lit. 1970	Adult Lit. 1994	Gross Enr. 1980	Gross Enr. 1994
Bahrain		.870		55.5	72.0	130	20			58	85
UAE	.719	.866	.149	53	73.2	145	17		78	44	82
Kuwait		.844		59.5	75.2	89	17	54	75		
Libya		.801	.188	46.7	63.8	160	64	37	92		
Lebanon		.794		59.6	69	68	32	69	69	67	75
Iran	.406	.780	.226	49.5	68.2	169	40	29	62	46	68
SA	.511	.774		44.4	70.3	170	27	9	70	36	56
Syria	.658	.755	.217	49.8	67.8	135	37	40	65	60	64
Tunisia	.440	.755	.244	48.3	68.4	159	41	31	59	50	67
Algeria	.323	.748	.286	47	67.8	168	51	25	86	52	66
Jordan	.405	.737	.109	46.9	68.5	135	33	47	51	51	69
Egypt	.269	.614	.348	46.1	64.3	179	63	35	42	38	46
Morocco	.282	.566	.417	47.6	65.3	163	58	22	57	67	53
Iraq	.452	.531	.307	48.5	57.0	139	146	34			
MENA			.34								
Dev	.576										

Source: UNDP, *Human Development Report 1997*.

broadly defined interest groups. Cranmer defines two economic class interest groups, upper and lower, and identifies categories of fiscal initiatives
that would benefit each group. Fiscal initiatives include both public expenditures and taxes. Data for MENA countries reveal that they use the usual
assortment of tax instruments, namely: direct taxes on income and profits
of individuals and corporations, and social security taxes; indirect taxes
like domestic value-added taxes (VAT), excise and sales; and imports and
exports duties to collect revenue. For non-oil-exporting countries, these
taxes together account for anywhere between 65 and 80 percent of tax
revenue, while for the oil-exporting countries these taxes account for a
relatively small 30 percent of all revenue. Studies of tax incidence in developed countries (Pechman 1985) have clearly demonstrated that the impact of taxes on the distribution of income depends on the type of tax
instrument used. Specifically, they have shown that the burden of direct
income and profit taxes falls proportionally more on upper-income groups,
and that the burden of social security and indirect taxes falls more on the
wage earners and those who spend a proportionally large part of their
income on consumption. Since economically disadvantaged groups are
largely wage earners spending all of their income on consumption, the economic burden of these taxes is likely to be borne by individuals who are
disadvantaged. Similar patterns for the distribution of direct and indirect
tax burden is reported by Foxley et. al. (1979) for Chile, Devarajan and
Hossain (1995) for the Phillipines, and Tseng and Mao (1994) for Taiwan.
Interestingly, because the two sets of taxes have countervailing effects, all
of the authors above report that the tax system, in general, is distribution-
ally neutral or slightly regressive. This means that the overall tax burdens
are distributed approximately equally across income groups. Commenting
on the distributional property of the tax system, the *World Development
Report* (1988) comments, "Even in terms of vertical equity, tax systems in
developing countries are not notably successful, despite the fact that they
would generally be highly progressive if their rate structures are fully applied. But that is rarely so" (p. 85). For the MENA countries in our sample,
revenues are generated very differently by the oil-exporting and non-oil-
exporting countries. The sources of government revenue are identified in
Table 6.3. For obvious reasons, the three oil-exporting countries in our
sample, Bahrain, Oman, and the UAE, depend on nontax sources for almost 75 percent of their revenue. It should be noted, however, that there
are significant differences in tax policy among the three countries. Oman,
for example, raises a significant portion of its revenues from direct taxes,
and the total revenues collected from direct taxes is almost two to three
times larger than indirect and social security taxes combined. In contrast,
the UAE has no direct taxes, and Bahrain's direct taxes are about 20 percent of the combined social security and indirect taxes.

It is widely believed that social security taxes are passed on to workers

Table 6.3
Sources of Revenue (as % of revenue), Selected Oil-Exporting Countries

	Bahrain		Oman		UAE		Egypt		Jordan		Syria		Yemen		Morocco		Tunisia	
	1986-90	1991-95	1986-90	1991-95	1986-90	1991-5	1986-90	1991-95	1986-90	1991-95	1986-90	1991-95	1986-90	1991-95	1986-90	1991-95	1986-90	1991-95
Income & Profits	4.65	5.08	21.24	19.9		2.1	15.37	20.6	11.13	11.1	29.37	27.4	17.73	22.8	19.97	22.6	13.25	13.6
Social Security	8.76	9.4			2.18		13.76	10.5							4.23	3.8	9.71	12.3
Domestic Goods/ Services	3.94	4.21	0.86	1.0	17.48	26.0	11.24	12.8	17.28	20.6	20.67	34.0	11.28	10.8	43.31	39.9	20.87	23.2
International Trade	8.64	9.17	2.85	3.2			12.91	10.4	30.18	31.6	6.56	11.5	27.45	19.1	15.59	18.0	26.5	28.4
Non-Tax Revenue	72.96	70.14	73.91	74.9	71.66	71.9	33.22	36.0	33.01	26.9	31.87	19.9	33.18	42.9	11.122	12.0	24.53	17.8
SS + Indirect	21.34	22.79	3.71	4.2	19.66	28.1	37.90	33.7	47.46	52.2	27.22	45.5	30.98	26.24	63.13	61.70	57.09	63.90
99/05/05D/SS +1	0.22	0.22	6.14	4.74			0.40	0.61	0.24	0.21	1.35	0.60	0.57	0.87	0.32	0.37	0.23	0.21

Source: IMF, *Government Finance Statistics Yearbook*, various years.

in the form of lower wages and indirect taxes are passed on to consumers in the form of higher prices. Lessons from incidence studies suggest the classification cited in Van der Hoeven (1995): indirect taxes are regressive, social security taxes are slightly regressive, and direct taxes on income and profits are progressive. The last two rows of Table 6.3 show the percentage of revenue collected from indirect and social security taxes (likely to be paid disproportionately by the poor), and the ratio of direct to indirect taxes (as an indicator of the proportion of tax revenue whose incidence is likely to be on upper-income groups). The particular way these tax instruments have been used in the oil-exporting economies suggests that the tax system is quite progressive in Oman and likely to be somewhat regressive in Bahrain and the UAE.

The non-oil-exporting countries, in contrast, depend on taxes for almost three-fourths of their revenue. Further, among these countries, Jordan, Morocco, and Tunisia generate approximately 50 to 70 percent of their revenues from social security and indirect taxes. This is considerably higher than what is seen in developed country figures, but quite consistent with the experience of similarly situated developing countries. Egypt, Syria, and Yemen generate anywhere between 30 and 45 percent of their revenues from indirect and social security taxes. The use of direct income and profit taxes is sparse, accounting for less than 20 percent of revenue. Syria, the only exception, uses direct taxes more extensively compared to the other non-oil-exporting countries. For example, the ratio of direct to combined indirect and social security taxes was 1.35 for the 1986–90 time period. For the same time period, this ratio was 0.40 for Egypt, 0.22 for Jordan, 0.32 for Morocco, 0.23 for Tunisia, and 0.57 for Yemen. Using the same criteria as above, the tax system in the non-oil-exporting countries would seem to be regressive in Jordan, Morocco, and Tunisia, and at least somewhat regressive in Egypt and Yemen. The tax system, on surface, is detrimental to the goal of achieving a more equal distribution of income. Syria is the exception in this group, with the tax system being neutral or mildly progressive. In summary, it would be fair to say that the tax system is not being utilized to redistribute income or as an instrument of poverty alleviation. This is quite consistent with the experience of other developing countries.

The countries that rely disproportionately on social security and indirect taxes could improve the distributive balance by improving the effort to increase direct tax revenue. But as many have documented (Goode 1984), the presence of large informal sectors coupled with the lack of administrative capacity makes collection of direct taxes difficult and administratively costly. Further, direct taxes on income and profits have the potential of distorting both the labor leisure choice and the consumption saving decision, and imposing large costs to society. Therefore, if allocational efficiency is deemed highly desirable, indirect taxes might actually be preferable. This, however, means that the fiscal measures designed to improve the distribution of income and alleviate poverty will have to rely mostly on the structure of government expenditures. The *World Development Report* (1988) explicitly recognizes this viewpoint: "In practice it seems taxes do little to change the overall distribution of income. Their important role in the pursuit of equity is to raise the revenue needed to pay for distributive spending, particularly to alleviate poverty" (WDR 1988, p. 85).

The *World Development Report* (1990) addresses what it calls "the most pressing issue now facing the development community: how to reduce poverty" (p. iii). The *Report* cites evidence that "suggests that rapid and politically sustainable progress on poverty has been achieved by pursuing a strategy that has two equally important elements. The first element is to promote the productive use of the poor's most important asset—labor. . . . The second is to provide basic social services to the poor. Primary health care, family planning, nutrition, and primary education are especially important" (WDR 1990, p. 3). This important role of public expenditure is now a significant part of the discussion surrounding structural adjustment (Structural Adjustment Facility [SAF], Enhanced Structural Adjustment Facility [ESAF]), and a number of studies have tried to determine whether structural adjustment has had detrimental effects on expenditures on health and education (see, for example, Gupta et al. 1998). The fiscal strategy outlined by the World Bank implies that a larger share of national income and government spending should go to the poor. The *Report* cautions that even with the adoption of this two-part strategy many of the poor will continue to be deprived. Therefore, the *Report* suggests the use of transfers and safety nets to complement the basic strategy. The fiscal strategy thus outlined is compatible with the group benefit method of Cranmer. Cranmer identifies high rural expenditures and high expenditures on social welfare, public health, and education as those favoring the economically disadvantaged, with expenditures in support of private enterprise and expenditures on security as those favoring the upper economic groups. The *World Development Report* (1990) implicitly recognizes the problem with excessive defense spending, stating, "Reigning in defense spending in developing countries should also be a priority over the coming decade" (p. 17, Box 1.3). The message is quite clear: to reduce poverty, countries must be able to make institutional and structural changes to mobilize domestic resources, but must also commit themselves to use the government budget to reallocate resources to enhance human capital while at the same time providing a social safety net.

Obviously, any discussion of poverty alleviation through the judicious use of government expenditures would be useless unless it can be demonstrated that certain expenditures do alleviate poverty. Evidence has now been collected to suggest that certain programs in general and others that are well targeted are quite effective in alleviating poverty. Van de Walle (1995) reviews some of the literature on this topic. Summarizing results from incidence studies of education, health, social transfers, and expenditures to improve nutrition, Van de Walle concludes that these expenditures are "mildly progressive"; that is, the proportion of the benefit received by the poor is higher as a percentage of their initial income. However, there is considerable within-sector variation in the distribution of benefits from public expenditure. For example, education expenditures on primary and secondary schooling provide significant benefit to the poor (who have a larger number of younger children whose education ends with either primary or secondary) while expenditures on tertiary education tend to benefit the affluent (see, e.g., Hammer et al. 1995 and Grosh 1990). Health care expenditures benefit the economically disadvantaged to a greater extent in societies where private alternatives to socialized medicine exist. In those communities the benefit from government health expenditures accrues primarily to the less advantaged because they tend to use the public health care facilities more intensively. Further, expenditures on primary care tend to help the poor most. Similarly, food subsidies targeted toward the poor and social security expenditures on social safety net programs tend to improve the lot of the economically disadvantaged. How can the distribution of public spending be improved? Van de Walle writes: "First, governments should invest and reallocate budgets towards basic services. . . . But, above all, services such as primary education and basic health care are found to be among the best ways to reach the poor. Among other categories of public spending—including food subsidy schemes, social security and cash transfers, there have been both successes and failures" (1995, p. 25). Given this evidence, it is apparent that social expenditures are likely to result in improving the capabilities of the poor and alleviating poverty, while expenditures on defense and in support of private industry might be detrimental to the interests of the disadvantaged. Further, though benefits are likely to be disbursed, fairly broad targeting of social expenditures might be optimal. Fine targeting might impose both high economic (design and administrative) and political costs (lack of support). It is against this backdrop that we examine government expenditures in MENA countries.

We look at government expenditures by function primarily because this tells us something about the budgetary priorities of a particular government. Expenditures for the oil-exporting GCC countries and other selected MENA countries are reported in Table 6.4.

It is immediately noticeable that budgetary priorities are different in many of the MENA countries. The MENA countries as a group spend a larger share of their income on defense. Jordan, Oman, Syria, the UAE, and Yemen are countries that allocate at least a quarter of the central government budget to defense. Kuwait, Oman, and the UAE allocate over 40 percent to defense. This is a cause for concern, because "evidence in-

Table 6.4
Functional Expenditures (as % of expenditures), Selected MENA Countries

	Bahrain		Tunisia		Oman		UAE		Egypt		Jordan		Syria		Yemen		Morocco	
	1986-90	1991-95	1986-90	1991-95	1986-90	1991-5	1986-90	1991-95	1986-90	1991-95	1986-90	1991-95	1986-90	1991-95	1986-90	1991-95	1986-90	1991-95
Defense	14.85	16.44	6.15	5.5	40.23	35.61	42.67	40.095	12.99	9.36	25.51	23.25	35.40	37.56	28.49	30.31	13.42	14.3
Social Security	2.33	2.82	12.96	14.1	12.65	13.24	3.07	3.4	11.95	10.41	9.914	14.67	3.36	1.97			6.07	6.1
Education	13.15	13.37	15.7	17.5	10.62	11.88	14.64	16.23	12.53	12.03	14.24	14.5	8.94	9.05	19.29	19.70	17.33	17.8
Health	7.43	8.92	6.04	6.5	4.86	5.96	6.9	7.06	2.57	2.43	4.93	6.17	1.49	2.17	3.99	4.40	2.90	3.0
Housing	4.87	2.26	4.56		4.19	8.42	0.42	1.38	5.48	5.96	1.96	1.33	1.01	-2.21	0.24	2.46	0.52	
Mining/Manuf.	1.54	0.36	3.01		1.20	0.18	0.08	0.17	0.20	0.13	3.26	0.11	1.25	1.20	2.41	0.38	0.53	
Fuel/Energy	8.80	6.03	0.58		5.57	5.81	2.95	4.68	0.66	0.19	2.12	1.48	4.79	4.39	0.18	0.59	0.87	
Agriculture	1.01	0.16	8.02		1.82	2.10	0.76	0.76	4.43	4.06	3.62	2.86	8.78	9.17	2.05	2.43	5.24	
Trans/Comm.	11.02	11.21	4.4		2.72	2.01			3.22	2.67	4.73	5.81	2.54	3.42	1.73	2.17	7.36	
H+E	20.57	22.30	21.74	24.0	15.48	17.84	12.92	23.29	15.10	14.47	19.17	20.67	10.43	11.22	23.28	24.09	20.23	20.8
Social	22.91	25.11	34.70	38.1	23.07	31.08	14.77	26.69	27.06	24.87	29.09	35.34	13.79	13.19	23.28	24.09	26.29	26.9
H+E/D	1.39	1.36	3.53	4.36	0.39	0.50	0.30	0.58	1.16	1.55	0.75	0.89	0.29	0.30	0.82	0.79	1.51	1.45

Source: IMF, *Government Finance Statistics Yearbook*, various years.

creasingly points to high military spending as contributing to fiscal and debt crises, complicating stabilization and adjustment, and negatively affecting economic growth and development" (WDR 1988, p. 107). Defense expenditures are a more moderate 15 percent in Bahrain, Egypt, and Morocco. Tunisia, in contrast, spends less than 10 percent on national defense. Except for Egypt, Syria, and Oman, expenditures on education and health hover slightly above 20 percent for most of the countries. Of the GCC countries in our sample, UAE has seen a substantial increase while Kuwait has seen a substantial decrease in health and education expenditures. Egypt, Oman, and Syria spend proportionally less on health and education, around 15 percent for Egypt and Oman, and a considerably lower 10 percent in Syria. Social expenditures, which include social security in addition to health and education, are comparable across countries. Tunisia and Jordan allocate most to social expenditures (35 percent in the 1990s). In contrast, Syria allocated the least (about 14 percent) to social expenditures. The other countries allocated approximately 25 percent of their budget to social spending.

The last three rows of Table 6.4 report expenditure on health and education (H+E), social expenditures (health, education, and housing, expenditures likely to be most favorable to the poor), and a measure of resource use imbalance, health and education expenditures as a percentage of defense expenditures (H+E/D), with a smaller percent indicating that a larger share of government expenditure benefits the wealthy. For some of the countries above, there seems to be strong imbalance between social expenditures and expenditures on defense. It is clear from the ratio of expenditures on health and education as a percentage of defense expenditures that countries that tend to allocate a substantially larger part of their budget to defense are also the countries that allocate a proportionally smaller amount to social sectors. For example, the ratio is smaller than 1 for all the countries in our sample that spend more than a quarter of their budget on defense. For Syria and Oman, this ratio is less than 0.5, meaning that half as much is allocated to health and education compared to defense. On the other hand, the ratio is larger than 1 for all the countries where defense expenditures are less than 15 percent of all expenditures. This apparent tradeoff between social and defense expenditures is troubling, particularly for Jordan, Syria, and Yemen, where the incidence of poverty is high. The highest ratio of social to defense spending is found in Tunisia, where defense expenditures are also lowest. Perhaps due to the deliberate decision to devote resources to health and education, the incidence of poverty has decreased rapidly and dramatically in Tunisia.

Many of the authors cited point out that while expenditures on education and health help the disadvantaged in general, what is most helpful is the expenditure to support primary and secondary, as opposed to tertiary, ed-

Table 6.5
Human Expenditure Ratio, Selected MENA Countries

Country	Year	HER	Alternative HER		Remark	HPI
Bahrain	1991	4.23			Medium	
Egypt	1993	3.36			Medium	.348
Iran	1994	3.58			Medium	.226
Jordan	1993	5.23	1988	5.5	High	.109
Kuwait			1988	4.0	Medium	
Morocco	1992	4.67	1988	6.3	Medium/High	.417
Oman	1994	6.79			High	
Syria	1993	1.85			Low	.217
Tunisia	1992	4.49			Medium	.244

Source: Primary health expenditure data: WHOSIS, World Health Organization; primary/
secondary education data: UNDP, *Human Development Report* 1997; World Bank expenditure data: IMF, *Government Finance Statistics Yearbook*; Alternative HER: UNDP,
Human Development Report 1991.

ucation, and expenditure on primary health care. The human expenditure
ratio, calculated as

$$HER = E/Y * S/E * P/S$$

computes the percentage of national income *(Y)* that is devoted to human
priorities *(P)*. The human expenditure ratio can be made larger by (i) increasing the share of national income used to undertake public expenditure
(E/Y), (ii) increasing the social expenditure share of public expenditure *(S/
E)*, or (iii) increasing the priority share of social expenditure *(P/S)*. Stewart
(1995) identifies favorable policies as the following:

1. During periods of economic growth, countries increase the share of expenditure
   on health and education. This can be done by earmarking new revenues to these
   sectors.
2. During periods of negative growth, the budget is reallocated to maintain or
   increase the share of expenditure devoted to the social sectors. The latter would
   require action to reduce the share of the budget devoted to other sectors of the
   economy.

Table 6.5 reports the HER for MENA countries for which expenditure
on primary education and primary health care is publicly available.

It was observed that for many of the MENA countries with high defense
expenditures, the social expenditure share of public expenditure (S/E) is
quite low. For HER to be high in these countries, either the public sector
has to be quite large, or more of government social expenditure has to be
devoted to priority activities like primary education, primary health care,
and provision of social safety nets. Egypt, Jordan, and Morocco have com-

parably sized public sectors at approximately 35 percent, 32 percent, and 30 percent, respectively, of GDP. The social expenditure ratio in these countries is 15 percent, 23 percent, and 19 percent, respectively. The corresponding priority ratio is 64 percent, 69 percent, and 75 percent, respectively. Despite having the highest expenditure ratio, Egypt has the lowest HER of the three countries, explained by the low social priority ratio and social expenditure. In contrast, both Jordan and Morocco have larger social expenditure and priority ratios, which offset the lower expenditure ratio, resulting in larger HERs. Good policy would seem to suggest that countries with high HPI would also adopt fiscal policies resulting in high HER. Jordan, Tunisia, and, to some extent, Morocco seemed to have followed this path, but Egypt has lagged behind. For example, Egypt spends approximately 40 percent of its education budget on tertiary education (by far the highest among the sample countries), though it is well known that social returns to education in MENA countries are the highest at the primary level (15.5 percent), followed by the return at the secondary level (11.2 percent). The point here is that it is possible to improve the way countries conduct fiscal policy: that there is room to shift resources to the social sectors, and to improve the allocation of these resources within the social sector.

Care must be exercised, however, in deriving conclusions from such aggregate data. Van Eeghan (1998) discusses the impact of the outcomes from fiscal initiatives and various poverty-reducing programs. It is immediately noticeable that public expenditures on health, education, and social welfare may have large overall impact but, at the same time, may not be very efficient. The leakage, meaning the proportion of benefits accruing to people not necessarily disadvantaged, is indeed large for many of the programs undertaken. This occurs because the programs are not necessarily targeted to the poor, or, when targeted, are poorly administered. Narrow targeting may also be problematic because of the political necessity to include broader, but less needy, segments of society.

CONCLUSION

Fiscal policy, or the use of the power of the government, to raise revenue and spend those revenues were studied for selected MENA countries. It is now recognized that this policy can be successfully utilized to improve the capabilities of the economically disadvantaged and, thereby, reduce poverty. However, policy has to be well designed and targeted. Tax policy in MENA countries is very similar to that in other developing countries. This involves reliance on indirect taxes on production, consumption, and trade to raise government revenue. Since these taxes, along with social security taxes, are likely to be regressive, it is safe to conclude that tax policy in MENA countries is mostly regressive, and at best neutral. Therefore, taxation is not an effective tool for the redistribution of income. The other instrument available to alleviate poverty is government expenditure. Since social expenditures, those on health, education, social security, and welfare, seem to help the cause of the poor, those expenditures and the imbalance between social expenditures and defense expenditures were examined. It was determined that for many of the countries, there seems to be a tradeoff between military and social expenditures, with the former coming at the expense of the latter. This imbalance can be offset if governments prioritize expenditures so that the benefit to the poor is the greatest. To that end, expenditures on primary health care and primary and secondary education were examined. For the countries for which these data are publicly available, countries like Jordan, Morocco, and Oman seem to have done better in targeting their expenditures toward the poor compared to Bahrain, Kuwait, and Tunisia. Egypt, on the other hand, has lagged behind in its efforts, despite the fact that the incidence of poverty and deprivation is quite high.

NOTES

This is a revised version of a paper presented at the Conference on Earnings Inequality, Unemployment, and Poverty in the Middle East and North Africa at the School of Business, Lebanese American University, Byblos, Lebanon, November 5–7, 1998.

1. World Bank, cited in Tabatabai 1996.

REFERENCES

Cranmer, William H. (1988). "The Group Benefit Method: A New Methodology for Distributional Analysis of Fiscal Policies in Developing Nations," in Sheldon Danziger and Kent Portnoy, eds. *The Distributional Impacts of Public Policies*. New York: St. Martins Press, pp. 219–238.

Danziger, Sheldon and Kent Portnoy (1988). "Introduction," in Sheldon Danziger and Kent Portnoy, eds. *The Distributional Impacts of Public Policies*, New York: St. Martins Press, pp. 1–12.

Devarajan, S. and Shaikh Hossain (1995). "The Combined Effect of Taxes and Public Expenditure in the Phillipines." Washington, DC.: World Bank, WPS no. 1543.

Foxley, A. et al. (1979). *Redistributive Effects of Government Programmes: The Chilean Case*. New York: Pergamon Press.

Goode, Richard (1984). *Government Finance in Developing Countries*. Washington, DC: The Brookings Institution.

Grosh, Margaret (1990). "Social Spending in Latin America: The Story of the 80's." Washington DC: World Bank Discussion paper no. 106.

Gupta, S. et al. (1998). "Public Spending on Human Development," *Finance and Development*, 35 (3): 10–13.

Hammer, Jeffrey et al. (1995). "Distributional Effects of Social Sector Expenditure in Malaysia," in Dominique Van de Walle and Kimberly Nead, eds. *Public Spending and the Poor*. Baltimore: Johns Hopkins Press.

IMF. *Government Finance Statistics Yearbook*, various issues.

Pechman, J. (1985). *Who Paid the Taxes, 1966–85*. Washington, DC: Brookings Institution.

Richards, Alan and John Waterbury (1996). *A Political Economy of the Middle East*. Boulder, CO: Westview Press.

Stewart, Frances (1995). *Adjustment and Poverty: Options and Choices*. London: Routledge.

Tabatabai, Hamid (1996). *Statistics on Poverty and Income Distribution: An ILO Compendium of Data*. Geneva: ILO.

Tseng, Chu-Wei and Wei-Lin Mao (1994). "Fiscal Policy and Economic Development in Taiwan: A Digression on the Effects of Taxation of Income Distribution," in Joel Auerbach et al., eds. *The Role of the State in Taiwan's Development*. New York: M. E. Sharpe, pp. 254–274.

UNDP. *Human Development Report*, various issues.

Van der Hoeven, Rolph (1995). "Structural Adjustment, Poverty, and Macroeconomic Policy," in Gerry Rodgers and Rolph Van der Hoeven, eds. *New Approaches to Poverty Analysis and Policy—III*. Geneva: ILO, pp. 177–205.

Van de Walle, Dominique (1995). "Public Spending and the Poor: What We Know, What We Need to Know." Washington, DC: Policy Research Dept. World Bank, WPS no. 1476.

Van Eeghan, Willem (1998). "Poverty in the Middle East and North Africa," in Nemat Shafik, ed. *Prospects for Middle Eastern and North African Economies*. New York: St. Martin's Press.

World Bank. *World Development Report*. Washington, DC: World Bank, various issues.

World Health Organization. *WHOSIS Database*. Internet access.

7

Does Structural Adjustment Spell Relief from Unemployment?: A Comparison of Four IMF "Success Stories" in the Middle East and North Africa

Karen Pfeifer

Structural Adjustment Programs (SAPs) promoted by the International Monetary Fund (IMF) are geared toward converting developing countries to the universal path of free trade and private property as the motivators of economic life. SAPs have provided more or less the same formula for economic salvation to every country to which they have been given access. Here is an example of the mantra on the benefits of trade liberalization for MENA countries in general: "Closer integration, specifically through trade reform, leads to a higher level of economic growth as a result of improved resource allocation and economic efficiency. . . . Other spillover effects from trade—higher productivity levels that stem from technology transfers from the industrial countries and the interaction between trade and the stock of foreign research and development capital—are also clear" (Handy 1998, pp. 66–67).[1]

Thus are the benefits of Western capitalism transmitted with the opening of these economies under the auspices of SAPs. The costs are either ignored or downplayed, costs such as periodic danger of capital flight, net outflow of profits from foreign investment, the failure of foreign firms in pursuit of cheap labor to transfer up-to-date technology, and the bankrupting of local firms with concomitant disemployment of workers.

Ironically, a careful examination of the evidence from 1980 to 1995 for four IMF-denominated "success stories" in the Arab World, namely Egypt, Jordan, Morocco, and Tunisia, suggests that structural adjustment programs at best returned these economies to their 1980 (precrisis) levels of investment, economic growth, debt, and debt-service burdens. What they do not do is address market-related social problems like unemployment, poverty, and stagnant living standards. These problems, while not solved, had at least been on the agenda in the precrisis era. The major change is, instead, the shift from public to private centrality in investment decisions and the shift from inward orientation to outward orientation, characterized by a disproportionate growth in financial and trade activity relative to real production.

From a historical perspective, and from a close reading of IMF staff studies of the four countries, it appears that one relatively successful stage of public-investment-led growth, lasting approximately 25 to 30 years, gradually succumbed in the mid-to-late 1980s to a combination of external pressures and internal contradictions. The external pressures included rising real interest rates and a simultaneous decline in the demand, and the terms of trade, for primary exports, such as oil and phosphates, the prices of which fell precipitously. The internal contradictions included declining productivity growth,[2] inequality in income distribution, and rising public deficits. The interaction between these two culminated in the debt crises of the late 1980s.

An alternative model of IMF-supervised and private-investment-led, export-oriented growth arose out of the crisis and was applied in the Middle East as elsewhere. While its promoters seem to think this one-path-fits-all free-market model will last indefinitely, it is questionable, given extant domestic social problems and intense international pressures, such as the Asian financial crisis, whether the model can facilitate its own 25-year-long period of growth and development in MENA and elsewhere around the globe.

This chapter first examines how well the sample countries hewed to their structural adjustment programs, comparing the five-year periods from 1980 to 1995. The year 1995 was the most recent year for which systematic data were available and was also an ending date that gave the SAPs a long enough time to prove themselves. The chapter then examines how well these countries performed on the expected dimensions of "success," international and domestic. The data used in Tables 7.A1, 7.A2a–d, and 7.A3a–d come primarily from the IMF's annual publication, the *International Financial Statistics Yearbook*, and secondarily from the *World Development Report* when particular items are not available in the *IFS*.[3] This information is supplemented with additional statistical material and qualitative summation and analysis from recent IMF case studies of the four countries. The last section of the chapter, deconstructing the domestic dimensions of "success," focuses on unemployment and social development.

THE IMF VISION OF SUCCESSFUL "STRUCTURAL ADJUSTMENT" FOR EGYPT, JORDAN, MOROCCO, AND TUNISIA

The four "occasional papers" (case studies) generated by the staff of the International Monetary Fund on our four countries were published over five years: Tunisia in 1993, Morocco in 1995, Jordan in 1996, and Egypt in 1998. Even their titles are suffused with confidence and optimism about the success of structural adjustment and the renewed commitment to market-based development (e.g., "toward a dynamic economy," "resilience and growth through structural adjustment"). In many ways the studies are similar to one another, in writing style, in structure of argumentation, and in the premises governing both evaluation of and proposals for development strategy. In other ways, they reveal (often inadvertently) important differences among the countries that tend to undermine the overt analysis and policy recommendations and bring the model's assumptions into question.

Ironically, these studies describe investment and economic growth during the period from 1970 to about 1985 as relatively strong. Egypt experienced its most rapid economic growth, 8.4 percent per year, from 1974/75 to 1984/85. While growth in Egypt in the periods immediately before and after that was 3 percent or more, growth fell to 1 percent annually during the first phase of structural adjustment, 1989–90, jumping to 5 percent in 1996–97, a boom year, but still much below the peak decade (Handy 1998, p. 5). Furthermore, total factor productivity growth in Egypt was comparatively high, at 5 percent per year, during the 1970/71–1985/86 period (Handy 1998, pp. 7–8).[4]

Jordan's economy grew at the rate of 7.8 percent per year from 1976 to 1985 and gross fixed investment was about one-third of GDP (Maciejewski and Mansur, 1996, p. 14). Morocco's real GDP grew at an annual average of 5.7 percent during 1970–1979. It fell in the early 1980s (to 2.8 percent) but gross domestic investment as a percent of GDP averaged 26.7 percent from 1975 to 1985, higher than it had been before or since (Nsouli et al. 1993, pp. 3–7, including Table 1). Tunisia's economy, especially manufacturing, grew at an average annual rate of 7.4 percent from 1970 to 1980 (Nsouli et al. 1993, p. 3).

Be that as it may, each study begins with a mantra composed of two parts. The first part bemoans the crisis conditions that existed prior to the advent of structural adjustment in the second half of the 1980s. The crisis is presented as the fault of heavy-handed government intervention in the economy held over from the previous era. The second part of the mantra celebrates the policy changes that took place since reform began, changes focusing on the shift from government-led investment to private-sector-led investment, even if the latter remains small in scale, and from an inward-looking development strategy to an outward-looking development strategy (Nsouli et al. 1993, pp. 1–2; Nsouli et al. 1995, pp. 1–3; Maciejewski and Mansur 1996, pp. 2, 8–9). An example from the Egypt study: "By the standards of recent experience with economic stabilization, Egypt in the 1990s [actually 1994–1996] is a remarkable success story" (Handy 1998, p. 1).

The mantra is repeated frequently throughout the studies, e.g., for Tunisia in the chapter on monetary policy (Nsouli et al. 1993, pp. 15, 21–22) and the chapter on structural reforms (Nsouli et al. 1993, p. 23). For Morocco, see the "Outstanding Issues" section of Chapter 4 on fiscal policy (Nsouli et al. 1995, pp. 20–21) or Chapter 7 on convertibility (Nsouli et al. 1995, pp. 37–41). For Jordan, see the sections on "economic crisis" and "economic recovery" (Maciejewski and Mansur 1996, pp. 1–15). Continuing the Egypt example from above: "A sustained reinvigoration of Egypt's structural reform effort is essential to strengthen investment and growth, in the context of integrated global capital and goods markets" (Handy 1998, p. 3).

Ultimately, the single most important goal, toward which all the various policies and adjustments aim, is the opening up (*infitah*) of these economies to private capital, foreign and domestic, real and financial. This goal is considered essential to attract investment capital to sustain growth and, in the long run, raise living standards and create jobs. Free markets in international capital will send investment to the most deserving countries, those with the most attractive tax and currency convertibility policies, the most favorable investment laws. These laws include the freedom of foreign capital to repatriate not only profits but also proceeds from sale of vested capital, as well as "flexible labor markets," the freedom of employers to hire and fire and to negotiate variable remuneration with employees (for Tunisia, for example, see Nsouli et al. 1993, pp. 28–29; for Morocco, Nsouli et al. 1995, pp. 37–41; for Jordan, Maciejewski and Mansur 1996, pp. 11–12; and for Egypt, Handy 1998, p. 15).

The faith that these policies will lead to the best economic outcomes allows the authors to dismiss or marginalize evidence of mediocre or unsatisfactory income growth and unemployment. "Successful" structural adjustment is a sociological and political construct as much as a set of purely economic outcomes, of which the treatment of unemployment in these studies is a critical example.

IMPLEMENTATION OF A STRUCTURAL ADJUSTMENT PROGRAM

Objectives

The structural adjustment paradigm advises a country in fiscal and trade difficulties to devalue or float its currency in order to make its exports more competitive on the world market, earn more foreign exchange, and pay down its external debt. For example, Egypt is credited with managing the currency so as to keep the pound pegged to within 3 percent of the U.S. dollar (Handy 1998, p. 34), and Jordan is praised for the ease of convertibility of external current account transactions (Maciejewski and Mansur 1996, pp. 11–12).

The program calls for either setting interest rates higher or allowing them to rise to levels comparable in real terms to other countries' interest rates, on the argument that this will encourage increased domestic savings, prevent capital flight, and attract foreign financial capital. The program calls for slowing the rate of growth of the money supply to combat inflation, and for curbing government budget deficits so as not to crowd private borrowers out of the loanable funds market.

Implementation Measures

Several indicators that demonstrate to what extent our four countries applied these SAP tools from 1985 to 1995 (the latest date for which consistent IMF data were available) are presented in Table 7.A1.

Currency. The one variable in which all four countries consistently show movement in the expected direction is in the value of the currency, which fell from 1980 (the base year) through 1995 in all cases.

Discount Rate. Evidence on the second variable, the discount rate, is more mixed. Jordan raised it and kept it raised, while Egypt, Morocco, and Tunisia all saw slippage in the 1990s.

Money Supply. The third variable, rate of growth of the money supply, moves more consistently in the expected direction, especially if M2 is used as the definition of the money supply rather than M1. While the others show a slowing of the growth of M1, at least after 1990, Tunisia shows a speeding up. In all cases, M2's growth slows, except for Morocco's blip between 1985 and 1990.

Budget Balance. The fourth variable, budget balance, indicates continuing deficits for the four countries in 1985 and 1990, but with all but Egypt showing shrinkage between these years. Morocco and Tunisia show still-shrinking deficits in 1992, but Egypt shows a surplus for 1993 (the latest year for which figures were available) as did Jordan for 1995. Accordingly, in all cases the deficit shrinks as a percent of GDP or disappears into a small surplus as a percent of GDP, a clear sign of successful budget cutting prescribed by the SAP.

Grants. Fifth, grants to the government of Jordan decreased dramatically as a percent of revenue, while Egypt showed a slight decrease from 1990 to 1993 and Tunisia showed a slight increase from 1985 to 1990 and then held constant in 1992 (data for Morocco are missing). This signifies that donors are providing less, or very little in Tunisia's case, in the way of direct budgetary support to these governments, another sign of success. Aid

Table 7.A1
Indicators of Implementation of Structural Adjustment Program

	EGYPT			JORDAN			MOROCCO			TUNISIA		
	1985	1990	1995	1985	1990	1995	1985	1990	1995	1985	1990	1995
Value of Currency relative to value in 1980 (SDRs)	0.86	0.31	0.18	1.0	0.41	0.37	0.52	0.48	0.44	0.64	0.45	0.38
Discount Rate (%)[1]	13	14	13.5	6.25	8.5	8.5	8.50	-	1994 7.00	9.25	11.88	8.88
Average Annual Rate of Growth of M1[2]	80-85 16.8%	85-90 12.3%	90-95 9.7%	80-85 7.9%	85-90 10.9%	90-95 4.1%	80-85 9.7%	85-90 17.6%	90-95 8.4%	80-85 16.7%	85-90 5.4%	90-95 6.3%
Growth of M2[3]	24.2%	21.9%	1993 14.6%	13.9%	13.3%	6.4%	13.7%	15.1%	10.2%	17.0%	12.0%	7.0%
Budget Surplus/Deficit, after grants, local currency	-3439	-5494	1993 +2681	-112	-94	+60	-9424	-4760	1992 -3368	-354	-586	1992 -349
as % of Expenditures	-23%	-21%	+5%	-16%	-9%	+4%	-24%	-8%	-5%	-14%	-16%	-8%
as % of nominal GDP	-9%	-6%	+2%	-6%	-3%	+1%	-7%	-2%	-1%	-5%	-5%	-3%
Grants as % of Revenue	2%	6%	1993 5%	43%	22%	12%	-	-	-	0%	2%	1992 2%

Note: [1] A market-based rate such as the lending rate would have been preferable, but the data series for these four countries were incomplete.
[2] M1 = currency and demand deposits (excluding government).
[3] M2 = M1 + time, savings, and foreign currency deposits (excluding government).

Source: International Monetary Fund, *International Financial Statistics Yearbook*, 1996; Egypt, pp. 336–339; Jordan, pp. 462–465; Morocco, pp. 550–553; Tunisia, pp. 760–763. Budget data are given for Egypt through 1993 and for Morocco and Tunisia through 1992; the "grants" line, number 81z, is missing from the accounts for Morocco.

is being superseded by other means of deficit finance, for example government bonds, if needed.

The results from Table 7.A1 are summarized here in Table 7.1. With a group score of 83 percent, it appears that the "ayes" have it: these four countries adhered relatively closely to the SAP prescription through 1995, and it is that for which they are praised most highly in International Monetary Fund publications examined below. It is noteworthy that the country that apparently seemed to stray from its SAP the most is Tunisia, with three yes and three no, although it is considered by the IMF and the World Bank to be the most stellar of economic reformers among Arab countries.

Case Studies Commentary on Government Budgets

The four country case studies present the IMF staff researchers' interpretation of the evidence, sometimes putting an unwarranted spin on them. The study on Jordan, for example, portrays fiscal policy in the best light, even when the evidence is mixed. While Jordan's central government expenditures average 43 percent of GDP over the whole of the 1972–94 period, Jordan is credited with keeping them under 40 percent for 1991–94 (Maciejewski and Mansur 1996, p. 21). Similarly, while grants to the central government equal more than 50 percent of the fiscal deficit from 1986 on, as compared to less than half in the 1976–85 era, it is said to be a positive sign that direct aid to the central government has declined as a percent of GDP over the whole period 1976–1994 (Maciejewski and Mansur 1996, p. 14, Tables 3.1 and 3.2).

Other examples are found in Table 7.2, which includes Israel for comparative purposes. It appears that structural adjustment stars Tunisia and Jordan have expenditures significantly above the average and that Tunisia has the largest deficit (relative to GDP). Israel, the paragon of the thriving developed market economy in the Middle East, has not only a central government that weighs as heavily as any Western European welfare state in terms of revenues and expenditures but also, like Tunisia, a significant deficit. Tunisia's failure to reduce its deficit runs contrary to SAP logic, but fits with Keynesian logic and may well have Keynesian results, as discussed below.

In contrast, Egypt's central government revenues and expenditures are below average, challenging stereotypes of its burdensome state sector. Furthermore, the details of the table (not included here) indicate that Egypt's payments of wages and salaries to central government employees (6.1 percent of GDP) and transfers and subsidies (1.9 percent of GDP) are also below the regional averages of 7.6 and 6.6 percent, respectively. Perhaps the IMF credits structural adjustment as the force that drove the Egyptian government to pare its budget down to this size. But, central government budgets have been cut in large measure by shrinking public investment. The

Table 7.1
Summary of Structural Adjustment Program Implementation, 1985–1995

Tools	Egypt	Jordan	Morocco	Tunisia	Total
Devalue Currency	yes	yes	yes	yes	4 yes
Raise interest rates	yes	yes	no	no	2 yes, 2 no
Slow growth M1 (cash + checking deposits)	yes	yes	yes	no	3 yes, 1 no
Slow growth M2 (M1 + savings)	yes	yes	yes	yes	4 yes
Reduce budget deficit	yes	yes	NA	yes	4 yes
Reduce budget grants	yes	yes	NA	no	2 yes, 1 no
Total	6 yes	6 yes	4 yes, 1 no	3 yes, 3 no	**19 yes, 4 no**

GROUP SCORE: 19 YES/23 ENTRIES = 83%

Source: Table 7.A1.

118

Table 7.2
Central Government Budgets, 1996, in % of GDP

	Egypt 1996	Jordan 1996	Morocco 1996	Tunisia 1996	Israel 1995	Region-wide average[1]
Revenue	25.7	29.2	23.0	24.8	40.8	26.0
Expenditure[2]	26.6	33.8	26.7	34.5	47.8	29.8
------- interest	6.2	4.6	5.5	4.4	6.5	4.9
Balance= Rev-Exp	-0.9	-4.6	-3.8	-9.7	-7.0	-3.8

Note: [1] Besides the five in this table, countries included in the region are Algeria, Pakistan, Turkey, Syria, and Iran.
[2] Expenditure includes interest.

Source: Handy 1998, p. 13, Table 3.

problem with this scenario, aside from the human costs of cuts in subsidies, for example, is that the shrinkage of public investment has not been compensated by sufficient expansion of private domestic and foreign investment, putting a permanent crimp in the basis for sustained economic growth.

EVALUATING THE RESULTS OF STRUCTURAL ADJUSTMENT

Indicators of Success in International Transactions

Table 7.A2, parts a, b, c, and d, uses International Monetary Fund data to judge the impact of the SAP on economic performance in international economic transactions. While each country shows some areas in which its performance has improved as expected, no country has a consistently good performance and the evidence on the four as a group is decidedly mixed, even negative on balance. These results stand in contrast to the SAP implementation results discussed above.

Exports. For the rate of growth of exports of goods and services (EGS), Egypt and Morocco register a decrease, Tunisia remains the same at a reasonably good rate of 5.6 percent, and Jordan shows a sharp improvement to 8.2 percent. For comparison's sake, the world pacesetters in export growth, China, Indonesia, Thailand, and Malaysia, all had rates in excess of 10 percent in the first half of the 1990s (*World Development Report 1997*, Table 11, pp. 234–235). This constituted a lofty competitive challenge to our four stars in the Arab world.

Debt Service. Not shown in Table 7.A2a–d is that debt service rose in the 1980s and fell in the 1990s for all four countries. However, our four countries continue to be under pressure to earn greater quantities of foreign exchange, as shown by the second indicator, debt service as a percent of exports of goods and services. The figure is higher in 1995 than in 1980 for Egypt, Jordan, and Tunisia, while Morocco shows no difference between these two years.

Trade and Current Account Balances. Similarly, the trade balance shows no change for Egypt and Jordan and is, on balance, worse for Morocco and Tunisia. But the current account balance shows improvement for all except Jordan. The difference between the trade and current account balances comes in services, such as Suez Canal fees and tourism, and also in net remittances, which are strongly positive. The main detraction is in net income, such as profits to foreign investors, which remains negative and which seems in Tunisia's case to have totally canceled out remittances in 1994. How much of this improvement in the current account balance is due to structural reform and how much to the strong world economy through 1995 is a worthy question that cannot be answered here. One can

Table 7.A2a
Indicators of International Success, 1980–1995: Egypt

	1980–90	1980	Average 1985–89	1985	1990	Average 1990–94	1994	1990–95	1995
Current Account									
Average Annual Rate of Growth of Exports of Goods & Services[1]	5.2%							4.2%	
Debt Service as % Exports Goods & Serv[2]		13.4%							14.6%
Trade Balance ($ mns)[3]				-5215	-6379		-5953		
Remittances (net)				4007	5403		4343		
Income (net)				-793	-1022		-784		
Current Account Balance				-2166	185		31		
Current Acct Balance as % Nominal GDP				-4%	0		0		-2%[5]
Capital Account									
Foreign Direct Investment ($ mns)[3]			1157	1178	734	639	1256		
External Debt as %GDP[2]		89.2%							73.3%
Multilateral Debt as % Total External Debt[2]		13.7%							12.4%
Aid as % GNP[4]		6.5%					6.4%		

Source: [1,3,4,5]*World Development Report,* 1997; [2]*International Financial Statistics Yearbook,* 1996.

Table 7.A2b
Indicators of International Success, 1980–1995: Jordan

Current Account					
Average Annual Rate of Growth of Exports Goods & Services[1]			1980-90 5.9%		1990-95 8.2%
Debt Service as % Exports Goods & Serv[2]	1980 8.4%				1995 12.6%
Trade Balance ($ mns)[3]		1985 -1638	1990 -1237	1994 -1579	
Remittances (net)		1585	1045	1326	
Income (net)		-89	-215	-315	
Current Account Balance		-261	-227	-398	
Current Account Balance as % Nominal GDP		-5%	-6%	-7%	-9%[5]
Capital Account					
Foreign Direct Investment ($ mns)[3]		25 (average 1985-89 23)	38	3	average 1990-94 7
External Debt as %GDP[2]	1980 NA				1995 126%
Multilateral Debt as % Total External Debt[2]	8%				15%
Aid as % GNP[4]	NA				7%

Source: See Table 7.A2a.

122

Table 7.A2c
Indicators of International Success, 1980–1995: Morocco

Current Account

Indicator	1980–90				1990–95
Average Annual Rate of Growth of Exports of Goods & Services[1]	6.8%				3.1%
Debt Service as % Exports Goods & Serv[2]	1980 — 33.4%				1995 — 32.1%
Trade Balance ($ mns)[3]		1985 — -1353	1990 — -2108	1992 — -2463	
Remittances (net)		1074	2336	2533	
Income (net)		-766	-988	-1057	
Current Account Balance		-891	-196	-433	
Current Acct Balance as % Nominal GDP		-7%	-1%	-2%	1995 — -5%[5]

Capital Account

Indicator	Average 1985-89	Average 1990-94	1985	1990	1994	1980	1995
Foreign Direct Investment ($ mns)[3]	67	399	20	165	601		
External Debt as %GDP[2]						51%	71%
Multilateral Debt as % Total External Debt[2]						7.8%	30.8%
Aid as % GNP[4]						4.9%	2.2%

Source: See Table 7.A2a.

Table 7.A2d
Indicators of International Success, 1980–1995: Tunisia

Current Account	1980-90	1980	1985	1990	1994	1990-95	1995
Average Annual Rate of Growth of Exports of Goods & Services[1]	5.6%					5.6%	
Debt Service as % Exports Goods & Serv[2]		14.8%					17.0%
Trade Balance ($ mns)[3]			-886	-1685	-1574		
Remittances (net)			312	823	798		
Income (net)			-360	-496	-781		
Current Account Balance			-581	-469	-304		
Current Account Balance as % Nominal GDP			-6%	-4%	-2%		-4%[5]
Capital Account							
Foreign Direct Investment ($ mns)[3] — Average 1985-89: 81, Average 1990-94: 201			108	76	194		
External Debt as %GDP[2]		41.6%					57.3%
Multilateral Debt as % Total External Debt[2]		12.3%					37.5%
Aid as % GNP[4]		2.7%			0.7%		

Source: See Table 7.A2a.

only observe that a recession in the world economy could well weaken services payments for all four of our countries and thus damage the current account showing.

Foreign Direct Investment. Foreign direct investment shows improvement in Morocco and Tunisia, no change in Egypt, and a worsening in Jordan. Egypt's situation is not surprising, given that it is still considered relatively high risk because of the sometimes violent conflict between the government and the Islamic movement. However, the last bit of evidence on Jordan is surprising given the new economic status of Jordan in its relationship with Israel. It is possible that Arab capital, unhappy with Jordan's peace treaty with Israel, is pulling out, while Western and Israeli capital have not yet decided to go in (see the discussion on capital markets below).

External Debt. Not shown in Table 7.A2a–d is that external debt rose in the 1980s and fell in the 1990s for all four countries. But still, Egypt is the sole case in which debt as a percent of GDP is lower in 1995 than in 1980, although 73 percent is not "low." One of the main contributing factors to this reduction had little directly to do with economic programs: rather, the United States wrote off the military portion of Egypt's debt (about half) after Egypt's participation in the alliance against Iraq in 1991. In contrast, Jordan's debt-to-GDP level was 126 percent in 1995, at the high end of the range for lower-middle-and upper-middle-income countries. This is a consequence of the profound economic malaise that struck Jordan in the late 1980s, compounded by the immediate aftermath of the Gulf War, when Jordan lost most of its trade with Iraq and aid from the Arab world. But Morocco and Tunisia also show debt to be larger relative to GDP in 1995 than in 1980. This is partly due to the shift on the part of the world financial system from donating aid to lending to these two countries in the 1990s. This was one of their rewards for being classified as successful economic reformers by the IMF.

The ratio of multilateral debt to total debt is similar to the evidence on total debt. Multilateral debt is incurred by the government of one country from international agencies and organizations. Egypt shows a slight decrease, due to the post-Gulf War writing off of part of the outstanding economic debt Egypt had incurred with European agencies (another reward for Gulf War participation). Jordan shows a near doubling of the multilateral proportion of its debt, reflecting the help it received as it introduced economic reform and made its peace treaty with Israel. Morocco and Tunisia both show large increases, reflecting the shift from multilateral aid to multilateral lending by international and European agencies.

Aid Relative to GNP. Finally, if we designate 5 percent as the border between higher and lower ratios of aid to GNP, Egypt's shows no change but remains higher (mostly due to the annual provision of aid from the United States). Jordan shows a higher rate, much of the aid coming fresh from Europe and the United States after its agreement to economic reform and peace with Israel. And Morocco and Tunisia show a decrease to lower rates, in tandem with the switch from donations to lending by the international financial community.

These results are summarized in Table 7.3. The picture is one of partial success, with a collective score of 31 percent (10 yes out of 32 entries) and no one country having a score above 37 percent (3 yes out of 8 entries). Such a mixed showing on the international dimensions gives the impression that the standards for successful structural adjustment may be either low or flexible, as the following examination of external financial support also suggests.

External Financial Support

Successful adjustment may require thorough relief from external pressures and a certain amount of political indulgence by the IMF and other donors. For example, such support relieves pressures on central government budgets, as well as domestic opposition pressures, by paying for services or programs to alleviate the worst recessionary effects of the stabilization phase of the adjustment process. It also reduces current account deficits by shrinking the debt service burden, freeing up more foreign exchange for the purchase of imports.

All four of our countries have been the beneficiaries of frequent and generous financial support. This support includes: multilateral aid from the OECD or EU, bilateral aid from the United States or other individual countries, loans with long durations and low interest rates, rescheduling of outstanding loans by private creditors or the Paris Club, World Bank sectoral adjustment loans, and, not to be forgotten, financial assistance or guarantees from the International Monetary Fund via standby arrangements and extended fund facilities.

The most dramatic of the financial rescues of these countries has clearly been based on political, not economic, considerations. Egypt has been the beneficiary of U.S. aid since 1979, and was rewarded for its participation in the Gulf War by the writing-off of half its debt by the United States and by debt-reduction actions by other Gulf War allies. It has been the beneficiary as well of a string of IMF stabilization and structural adjustment facilities, in addition to World Bank sectoral development loans, and concessionary loans and grants from other multilateral sources.

Jordan has been the beneficiary of external financial support in the form of two standby arrangements (1989, 1992), an Extended Fund Facility for three years starting in 1994, several World Bank sectoral adjustment loans, aid from the European Union, and debt rescheduling from the Paris Club, for total debt relief of $1.4 billion (Maciejewski and Mansur 1996, p. 51). "Receipts of exceptional assistance from the Gulf Crisis Financial Coordi-

Table 7.3
Summary of Indicators of International Success, 1980–1995

Objective	Egypt	Jordan	Morocco	Tunisia	Total
Increase rate growth of exports of goods and services (EGS)	no	yes	no	no	1 yes,3 no
Reduce debt service as %EGS	no	no	no	no	0 yes,4 no
Improve trade balance	no	no	no	no	0 yes,4 no
Improve curr acct balance	yes	no	yes	yes	3 yes,1 no
Increase FDI	no	no	yes	yes	2 yes,2 no
Reduce external debt	yes	no	no	no	1 yes,3 no
Reduce multilateral debt	yes	no	no	no	1 yes,3 no
Reduce aid as %GNP	no	no	yes	yes	2 yes,2 no
Total	3 yes 5 no	1 yes 7 no	3 yes 5 no	3 yes 5 no	10 yes, 22 no

GROUP SCORE: 10 YES/32 ENTRIES = 31%

Source: Table 7.A2a–d.

nation Group" in 1992 ($800 million in debt reduction, of which $702 million was from the United States) were critical to the reestablishment of economic growth during the adjustment period (Maciejewski and Mansur 1996, pp. 11, 52).[5] Foreign grants, mainly used for investment in public goods, have always been critical to Jordan's long-term growth: if there had been no grants over the whole period 1976–94, economic growth would have been lower by 5 percentage points (7 points in the 1976–80 subperiod, 2 points in the 1991–94 subperiod). Grants from the Arab states approximated 12 percent of GDP from 1975 to 1988, with debt finance running second at 10 percent of GDP (Maciejewski and Mansur 1996, pp. 16–17, 21). Jordan's signing of the Euromed agreement is expected to stimulate another round of aid from the EU (Maciejewski and Mansur 1996, pp. 53–57).

Tunisia was the recipient of five years of IMF support (a standby agreement in 1986 and then a four-year Extended Fund Facility) and six World Bank structural adjustment loans from 1986 through 1989, and thus never had to seek rescheduling of its debt with private creditors nor fell behind in its debt-service payments (Nsouli et al. 1993, p. 2). An examination of the composition of Tunisia's external debt in 1992 (Nsouli et al. 1993, p. 67, Table A33) indicates that more than half of it is owed to the OECD countries, about a third to multilateral and other organizations, and only 2 percent to financial markets. Tunisia reentered the international financial markets in 1992 for the first time since 1986 (Nsouli et al. 1993, p. 41).

In the case of Morocco, "massive financing was required over a prolonged period," including three reschedulings by private international banks, six by the Paris Club, several World Bank loans, and nine arrangements with the IMF between 1980 and 1992 (Nsouli et al. 1995, pp. 1, 9). The otherwise stern IMF presents an avuncular tolerance of Morocco's delinquency in meeting SAP objectives: "Morocco's approach to adjustment can be characterized as gradual, as the authorities considered it politically more acceptable and hence more sustainable. . . . [Furthermore] in terms of strength and policy mix, the implementation of policies diverged somewhat from the programs" (Nsouli et al. 1995, p. 9).

For example, although civil servants' wages were frozen in 1992 (and thus fell in real terms for two years thereafter),[6] real minimum wages for the labor force as a whole rose gradually from 1989 to 1993 in both the agricultural and nonagricultural sectors (Nsouli et al. 1995, pp. 78, 82, 96). This is contrary to the typical falling real wage pattern during the first part of an SAP. In another example, Morocco had even more public sector companies in 1993 (700) than it had in 1985 (620), operating in key sectors, producing 50 percent of the value added in mining, energy, water, transportation, and communications, and supplying 50 percent of merchandise exports. The privatization program that had been announced in 1985 only got under way in 1993 (Nsouli et al. 1995, pp. 30–31).

Case Study Commentary on International Success

The case study authors suggest that one of the defects in Egypt's structural adjustment was slow progress in trade liberalization.[7] This led Egypt to fall behind in world trade: Egypt's share of world exports and imports decreased in the 1985–96 decade and its share of the European Union market fell from 1 percent to 0.5 percent. However, Egypt is commended, as are Israel, Jordan, Morocco, and Tunisia, for moving to rectify this situation by signing trade agreements with the European Union. The authors suggest that, due to its relatively low wages, Egypt would be "a natural assembler of consumer goods for the EU" (Handy 1998, pp. 3, 69), but whether that would provide a net increase in the number of jobs is not mentioned.

Jordan is commended by its case study authors for its many reform achievements on the international side. Its currency and exchange rate policies were credited for attracting increased remittances and repatriation of workers' savings. Jordan experienced growth in tourism and in nontraditional exports such as manufactured goods and chemicals, and reduced concentration on exports of raw materials and fertilizer. Debt decreased from 193 percent of GDP in 1990 to 110 percent in 1994, and debt service was reduced from 45 percent of goods and services exports in 1990 to 25 percent in 1994 (Maciejewski and Mansur 1996, pp. 9–11, 52). According to the authors, these all led to an improvement in the balance of payments (Maciejewski and Mansur, 1996, p. 21). However, a close look at the tables accompanying the commentary shows the current account deficit to be significantly worse in the 1991–1994 period than it had been at any time previous, minus 12.5 percent of GDP, versus an average of minus 4.8 percent for the entire 1976–1994 period (Maciejewski and Mansur 1996, p. 14, Tables 3.1 and 3.2).

Morocco is commended for a modest increase in manufactured exports, an improvement in the trade and current account balances (though both remain negative), and a decrease in the external debt and debt-service burdens (Nsouli et al. 1995, pp. 42–52).

Tunisia is credited for strengthening its balance of payments (mainly in services and income flows), and for reducing its external debt/GDP and debt service/current receipts ratios. While import share was nearly constant, Tunisia's share of world exports rose from 0.14 percent in 1990/91 to 0.9 percent in 1995/96 (Handy 1998, pp. 65–66). Agriculture and manufacturing grew fastest of economic sectors and manufactures went from 35 percent of total exports in 1985 to 61 percent in 1992, with 75 percent of total exports going to the European Community (Nsouli et al. 1993, pp. 33–41). Tunisia is the best and most consistent performer, but does not conform to the SAP rules on tariffs as seen in Handy (1998), with Egypt and, surprisingly, star economic adjuster Tunisia having weighted average tariffs much higher than Jordan, Morocco, East Asia, and other developing countries. All of that group are drastically higher than the world as a whole. Once again Tunisia defies the logic of the SAP. It keeps higher tariffs even as its export performance appears to be relatively good, as seen here in Table 7.A2d and text Table 7.3, as well as in the case study discussion.

Indicators of Success in Domestic Variables

Measures of domestic economic success expected from a structural adjustment program are presented in Table 7.A3, a through d, for each of the four countries.

Inflation. The first measure is the rate of inflation as indicated by the consumer price index (CPI) itself and then the rate of increase of the CPI. While the price level continued to rise from 1980 through 1990 to 1995, the rate of increase slowed for three of the four countries, Egypt, Jordan, and Tunisia. This is what the SAP predicts will happen when the rate of growth of the money supply is curbed and when government deficits are reduced.

Case Study Commentary on Inflation. Jordan is credited with the adoption of indirect money-supply controls (Maciejewski and Mansur 1996, pp. 11–12) and the decrease in the rate of inflation in both Morocco and Tunisia is praised (Nsouli et al. 1995, pp. 42–52; Nsouli et al. 1993, pp. 33–41). The comment for Egypt favorably compares the 6 percent rate of inflation in 1996/97 to that of the early 1970s (Handy 1998, p. 19).

Real GDP Growth. Three countries of the four, Egypt, Morocco, and Tunisia, experienced growth of real GDP from 1985 to 1995. Only Jordan underwent actual contraction in the late 1980s, due largely to the decline in oil revenues in those countries that trade with Jordan and from which Jordanian migrant workers send home remittances. Jordan then recovered and experienced a leap in the average annual rate of economic growth in the 1990s, to 7.1 percent, an excellent showing for an Arab country (albeit from a lowered base due to the previous depressed period). Tunisia showed a less dramatic increase in the rate of GDP growth. Egypt and Morocco showed declines in the rate of growth, a matter of some concern given their relatively successful application of reform policies and given the worldwide economic expansion after 1991. For comparison, the pacesetters in economic growth in the 1990s were Korea with 7.2 percent, Indonesia with 7.6 percent, Malaysia with 8.7 percent, and Thailand with 8.4 percent (*World Development Report* 1997, pp. 234–235, Table 11).

Real GDP Per Capita. Most economists view real GDP per capita as a shorthand indication of the standard of living of a country. As with aggregate real GDP, real GDP per capita rose from 1985 through 1990 to 1995 for Egypt, Morocco, and Tunisia, while Jordan experienced a drop from 1985 to 1990 and a recovery from 1990 to 1995. Jordan's annual rate of

Table 7.A3a
Indicators of Domestic Success, 1980–1995: Egypt

Inflation				
Consumer Price Index		1985: 40.5	1990: 100	1995: 178.7
Average Annual Rate of increase of CPI	1985-90: 19.8%		1990-95: 12.3%	
Economic Growth				
Real GDP, pounds (LE) mns, 1990 prices		1985: 70,785	1990: 96,100	1995: 113,433
Average annual rate of increase of real GDP	1985-90: 6.3%		1990-95: 3.4%	
Population, mns		1985: 46.5	1990: 52.7	1995: 59.2
Real GDP per capita		1523	1824	1916
Average Annual rate of increase of GDP/capita	1985-90: 3.7%		1990-95: 1.0%	
Investment				
Gross Domestic Investment as % GDP	1980: 28%			1995: 17%
Gross Domestic Saving as % GDP	15%			6%
GDS- GDI, % points	-13			-11
Annual Average Rate of Growth of GDI	1980-90: 2.7%		1990-95: -1.5%	
ICOR: Incremental Capital Output Ratio*	5.6			5.0
Employment				

Source: *International Financial Statistics Yearbook*, 1996; *World Development Report*, 1997. The ICOR is calculated by dividing Gross Domestic Investment as a percentage of GDP for the given year by the rate of growth of real GDP for the adjacent period.

Table 7.A3b
Indicators of Domestic Success, 1980–1995: Jordan

Inflation				
Consumer Price Index		1985: 64.3	1990: 100	1995: 124.8
Average Annual Rate of increase of CPI	1985-90: 9.2%		1990-95: 4.5%	
Economic Growth				
Real GDP, dinars mns, 1990 prices		1985: 2,825	1990: 2,668	1995: 3,761
Average annual rate of increase of real GDP	1985-90: -1.1		1990-95: 7.1%	
Population, mns		1985: 3.83	1990: 4.26	1994: 5.2
Real GDP per capita		737.6	626.29	723.3
Average Annual rate of increase of GDP/capita	1985-90: -3.2%		1990-94: 3.7%[6]	
Investment				
Gross Domestic Investment as % GDP	1980: na			1995: 26%
Gross Domestic Saving as % GDP	na			3%
GDS- GDI, % points				-23
Annual Average Rate of Growth of GDI	1980-90: 7.3%		1990-95: 6.5%	
ICOR: Incremental Capital Output Ratio	na			3.66
Employment				

Source: International Financial Statistics Yearbook, 1996; World Development Report, 1997.

Table 7.A3c
Indicators of Domestic Success, 1980–1995: Morocco

Inflation			
Consumer Price Index	1985: 79.3	1990: 100	1995: 134.0
Average Annual Rate of increase of CPI	1985-90: 4.8%	1990-95: 6.0%	
Economic Growth			
Real GDP, dirhams bns, 1990 prices	1985: 172.5	1990: 214.0	1994: 242.3
Average annual rate of increase of real GDP	1985-90: 4.4%	1990-94: 3.2%	
Population, mns	1985: 21.8	1990: 24.5	1994: 26.6
Real GDP per capita	7912.8	8734.7	9109.0
Average Annual rate of increase of GDP/capita	1985-90: 2.0%	1990-95: 1.1%	
Investment			
Gross Domestic Investment as % GDP	1980 24%		1995 21%
Gross Domestic Saving as % GDP	14%		13%
GDS - GDI, % points	-10		-8
Annual Average Rate of Growth of GDI	1980-90: 2.5	1990-95: -2.5	
ICOR: Incremental Capital Output Ratio	5.71		6.56
Employment			

Source: *International Financial Statistics Yearbook, 1996; World Development Report, 1997.*

Table 7.A3d
Indicators of Domestic Success, 1980–1995: Tunisia

Inflation					
Consumer Price Index		1985: 70.7	1990: 100		1995: 132.5
Average Annual Rate of increase of CPI		1985-90: 7.2%		1990-95: 5.8%	
Economic Growth					
Real GDP, dinars mns, 1990 prices		1985: 9,358	1990: 10,816		1995: 13,216
Average annual rate of increase of real GDP		1985-90: 2.9%		1990-95: 4.1%	
Population, mns		1985: 7.26	1990: 8.07		1995: 9.0
Real GDP per capita		1289	1340		1468
Average Annual rate of increase of GDP/capita		1985-90: 0.8%		1990-95:1.8%	
Investment					
Gross Domestic Investment as % GDP	1980 29%				1995 24%
Gross Domestic Saving as % GDP	24%				20%
GDS - GDI, % points	-5				-4
Annual Average Rate of Growth of GDI		1980-90: -1.8		1990-95: 1.4	
ICOR: Incremental Capital Output Ratio	8.79				5.85
Employment					

Source: International Financial Statistics Yearbook, 1996, p. 763; World Development Report, 1997.

increase for the latter five-year period was a strong 3.7 percent. Tunisia also experienced a one-percentage-point increase, to 1.8 percent per year, but Egypt and Morocco showed a drop in the rate of growth of GDP per capita, to 1.0 percent and 1.1 percent, respectively. Of course, these low rates are partly due to large denominators, i.e., fast-growing populations, as well as to small numerators, relatively slowly growing GDP, both of which contribute to slowing improvement in the standard of living. Of the two sister Bretton Woods organizations, the World Bank carries the responsibility to help slow the growth of those denominators with support for family planning programs.

Gross Domestic Investment. Future economic growth is dependent on investment out of current income. In general, gross domestic investment as a percent of GDP is lower in the Arab countries than elsewhere in the world. Looking at the same four Asian tigers again, we see that Korea invests 37 percent of GDP, Indonesia 38 percent, Malaysia 41 percent, and Thailand 43 percent (*World Development Report* 1997, pp. 238–239, Table 13). The highest performer among our four Arab countries was Jordan, weighing in with 26 percent in 1995, 11 percentage points lower than the lowest of the Asian four. Contrary to structural-adjustment expectations, Egypt, Morocco, and Tunisia all showed a lower figure for 1995 than they did back in 1980, in the precrisis, prestructural adjustment days.

Another indicator of a country's success in raising investment is the rate of growth of gross domestic investment. Here the picture is again mixed. Egypt and Morocco showed declines between the 1980–90 and 1990–95 periods, indeed falling into the negative range in the 1990s. These two countries have followed the IMF prescription to cut back on government spending. From the mid-1960s to the mid-1980s era, this "spending" involved public investment on infrastructure, services and public enterprise development. Indeed public investment made up the bulk of total investment. So to cut back on public sector spending in the late 1980s and 1990s meant cutting public investment in the expectation that private investment would grow to fill the gap.

Public sector investment was also important in Tunisia and Jordan; however, these two countries had left greater latitude for private sector investment, and for a longer period of time, stretching back to the 1970s, than did Egypt and Morocco. Tunisia did much of its pruning of public sector investment in the 1980s, and was experiencing the growth of domestic private investment in the 1990s (see the savings rate discussion below), as predicted and approved by the SAP formula. Jordan's high growth rate in the 1980s was related to a belated rush to develop infrastructure and other public investment as Jordan emerged as a distinct economic entity (it was also stimulated by Beirut businesses moving to Amman and by the inflow of investible remittances). Jordan's boom in the 1990s was fed by the return of migrants from the Gulf and Peninsula who brought back savings to invest as well as spend.

Efficiency of Investment. SAPs aim to promote efficiency of investment because, it is said, more efficient producers will be more competitive on world markets (or otherwise put, those firms that compete on the world stage will be forced to become more competitive). A crude, but still instructive, measure of aggregate efficiency is the incremental capital/output ratio (ICOR). This ratio indicates how much capital investment it takes in a given year to produce one dollar of output in that and subsequent years. The lower the figure the better: the less capital it takes to produce a dollar's worth of output, the more efficient the country is. For comparison's sake, these ICORs were calculated for the four Asian tigers in 1995: Korea 5.14, Thailand 5.12, Malaysia 4.71, and Indonesia 5.00 (*World Development Report* 1997, pp. 234–235, 238–239, Tables 11 and 13). By this standard, our four Arab countries measured up well in 1995: Jordan comes in the champion at 3.66, Tunisia shows a marked drop to 5.85, and Egypt shows a slight drop to 5.0. Only Morocco, with a rise to 6.56, is out of step with the international standard.[8]

Gross Domestic Saving. Gross domestic saving compared to gross domestic investment, both expressed as percentages of GDP, indicates the extent to which investment can be financed from local sources. The difference, the resource gap, indicates how much must be financed from abroad, either by borrowing or by attracting foreign capital. All four of our countries had a resource gap, Jordan being the worst case in 1995 (no figures are available for 1980) with a dearth of 23 percentage points of investment to be covered from external sources. Egypt and Morocco showed one or two percentage points' worth of improvement in 1995 as compared with 1980, but their needs for external finance remain significant at 11 and 8 percentage points, respectively. Tunisia is exceptional in that it already had a respectable savings rate prior to IMF-led structural adjustment. Tunisia's resource gap was small in 1980 and, while it was smaller by one percentage point by 1995, an indicator of success that closely fits the SAP prescription, the historical sequence suggests that the SAP is not the main reason for it. In any case, Tunisia's total levels of savings and investment remained low by world pacesetter standards in 1995.

These results are summarized in Table 7.4. The scoreboard suggests that as a group our four countries were still weak in 1995 in terms of factors of domestic success ostensibly brought by a structural adjustment program. The collective score is 40%. Tunisia performed the best, with a score of five positives out of seven indicators (71 percent). Given that Tunisia was different from the other countries as far back as 1980 at least, in terms of room for private investment and a higher savings rate, and given that it was less rigorous in applying the SAP prescription from 1985 to 1995, the part of its domestic-indicator success that can be attributed to the SAP

Table 7.4
Summary of Indicators of Domestic Success, 1980–1995

Objective	Egypt	Jordan	Morocco	Tunisia	Total
Lower price inflation	yes	yes	no	yes	3 yes,1 no
Raise rate of GDP growth	no	yes	no	yes	2 yes,2 no
Raise rate growth GDP/cap	no	yes	no	yes	2 yes,2 no
Raise GDI as % GDP	no	NA	no	no	1 NA,3 no
Raise GDS as % GDP	no	NA	no	no	1 NA, 3 no
Raise rate growth GDI	no	no	no	yes	1 yes,3 no
Lower ICOR	yes	NA	no	yes	2 yes,1 no 1 NA
Total	2 yes 5 no	3 yes 1 no 2 NA	0 yes 7 no	5 yes 2 no	10 yes 15 no 2 NA

GROUP SCORE: 10 YES OUT OF 25 ENTRIES = 40%

Source: Table 7.A3a–d.

seems limited. Tunisia may be the most stellar performer in the Arab world, but the SAP cannot be given full credit.

Case Study Commentary on Investment and Growth

Egypt. The case study on Egypt provides an analysis of the reasons for Egypt's growth record. Investment was at its historical high, 25 percent of GDP, from 1974/75 to 1981/82, falling to 18 percent of GDP from 1982/83 to 1992/93. Public investment led until 1982, then was gradually overtaken by private investment. Private investment accounted for 12 percent of GDP in 1996/97, greater than public investment, but still low as compared to an average of 24 percent in Asia (Handy 1998, pp. 6–7). The analysis suggests that an improvement in living standards (per capita income was relatively stagnant from 1985 to 1995) and in job creation would require an aggregate real growth rate of 7 percent per year, based on an additional six to eight percentage points of investment each year. Furthermore, the efficiency of production would have to increase, with growth of total factor productivity (TFP) rising from an average of 1.8 percent during the last decade to 2.25 percent. This, and the required tandem rise in the savings rate, is a tall order for Egypt, and probably cannot be accomplished, the study advises, without additional foreign savings in the form of foreign direct investment (Handy 1998, pp. 5, 8–10).

Jordan. According to the case study, growth of real GDP in Jordan is due more to the increase of physical capital than to the increase of labor. Investment is said to be stimulated by the inflow of remittances and workers' savings, by the reduction of crowding out due to the public sector deficit, by exchange rate stability, and by the volume of gross official reserves. Indeed, in spite of "high GDP growth" in the mid-1990s, total factor productivity growth was negative (minus 14.2 for 1991–1994) due to the return of 300,000 migrant workers from the Gulf; i.e., capital and labor grew much faster than output (Maciejewski and Mansur 1996, pp. 13, 18–20).

The magnitude of the success of Jordan's economic recovery during the adjustment period (1989–1994) appears to be modest, according to IMF data provided in the case study. In terms of growth and investment, 1991–94 restores the economy to less than pre-1985 performance levels, albeit with lower inflation rates and lower deficits (Maciejewski and Mansur 1996, pp. 14–15 Tables 3.1 and 3.2). Total investment had recovered to 29 percent of GDP by 1992, having reached its nadir of under 20 percent in 1986, but this was down from a peak of over 40 percent in 1982 (Maciejewski and Mansur 1996, p. 15).

Morocco. In Morocco's case, the magnitude of the growth rate of real GDP varies according to the specification of the periods being compared. On page 2 of the case study, the whole period 1981–93 is cited as having a "healthy" rate of growth of real GDP of 3.2% (all references to Nsouli 1995). While more data are available in a table on p. 43, p. 42 cites a growth rate of 4.7% per year for 1986–91. This achievement can be profitably compared to 5.1% for 1971–75, 5.3% for 1976–80 (their table calculations) and 4.2% for 1981–86 (my calculation from their table). However, if the most recent (the "adjustment") period is taken to include 1992 and 1993, the rate of growth for 1987–93 is but 2.29% (my calculation). A real GDP growth rate of 2.29% is only slightly above the approximately 2.2% rate of growth of population (data from Nsouli 1995: 43, Table 7, which includes 1992 and 1993), yielding a per capita GDP growth rate of 0.09% in that period. Including 1992 and 1993 in the adjustment period means that Morocco's growth rates since the SAP was adopted are rather modest.

Other successes listed for Morocco since reform began in 1986 include a gradually, but unevenly, rising per capita income, increasing at an average rate of 0.8% per year (1986–1993), an increase of 2 percentage points in the contribution of manufacturing to GDP, and some closing of the gap between gross national savings and gross domestic investment (Nsouli 1995: 42–52).

Tunisia. Successes claimed from structural adjustment for Tunisia since 1986 include an increase in economic growth and in both private savings and private investment (although total investment decreased as a percentage of GDP), and the fact that manufacturing and agriculture grew faster than other economic sectors, namely services and industry as a whole (Nsouli 1993: 33), again affirming Tunisia as the most successful of these economic reformers.

Other Case Study Commentary on Domestic Success

Privatization. Jordan is commended by the case study authors for its reform of agriculture to favor private farmers and its decontrol of the water and energy sectors, opening them to private firms and market forces. It privatized hotels, the tourism industry in general, and duty-free shops, and it improved the environment for private investment with a new law that treats all investors alike, whether foreign or domestic (Maciejewski and Mansur 1996, pp. 11–12).

Egypt is commended for progress on privatizing the public sector portfolio of productive enterprises since 1996, which "will help raise productivity growth and domestic savings" (Handy 1998, p. 4). The public sector, prior to 1996, had accounted for one-third of total output and employed one-third of the labor force. From 1996 to 1998, sales of public companies, as well as sales of shares in public companies, to the private sector affected 84 companies and 35 percent of the public sector portfolio, the transactions equivalent to 7 percent of GDP (Handy 1998, p. 45). The authors, recognizing that there is such a thing as profitable public sector enterprises, indicate that the companies sold off were the more profitable ones, and predict that it will be more difficult to sell off the less-efficient and loss-making units. Furthermore, they say, compensation to the laid-off workers (about one-third of the total are said to be redundant) is estimated at a daunting $1.7 billion.

While privatization is expected to continue in Egypt, other methods of restructuring are also underway, including public enterprise internal reform (Law 203 of 1991) and sales of some firms to their employees, who have formed Employee Shareholder Association-Held Companies (ESAs) with a fair degree of success (Handy 1998, pp. 48–55). The authors do not point out that these alternatives, some of which are economically viable, are less expensive to undertake because they do not require compensation to laid-off workers, and may be more positive for employment than the straight-out privatization they seem to favor.

Tax Systems. The IMF studies uniformly criticize the prereform tax systems of the four countries as overly complex and unfair, with government spending high and unsustainable. Reforms call for the institution of a Value-Added Tax (VAT) or a consumption tax, the streamlining of corporate and personal income taxes (while broadening the tax base), and the restriction of government investment to just infrastructure and human resource development. Tunisia and Morocco are credited with making significant progress in this regard (Nsouli et al. 1993, pp. 5–9; Nsouli et al. 1995, p. 55). Approved reforms in Jordan include the introduction of a general sales tax, which is effected at the manufacturing and import stages, compensated by rebates on inputs provided to certain favored production enterprises. Jordan also simplified its direct tax structure, reducing tax rates and reducing the number of rates on corporate and personal income (Maciejewski and Mansur 1996, pp. 11–12).

Capital Markets and Capital Flows. Jordan is credited with the foresight to have established the Amman Financial Market (AFM) in 1976, a "re-emerging market" which experienced a renaissance in the 1990s. One case study (Maciejewski and Mansur 1996) provides capital market data for all four of our subject countries. The study indicates that Jordan had the highest market capitalization in both absolute and relative terms in 1994, although it is known that there is little foreign participation in the Jordanian market. The size of Tunisia's capital market, relative to the size of its economy, is surprisingly small, although Tunisia is considered to be one of the most open economies in the Arab World.

The case studies credit structural adjustment for the surge of capital inflows into Jordan and Egypt from 1991 to 1994. The inflows included the remittances and then the savings of emigré workers returning after the Gulf crisis, with inflows of short-term capital and foreign aid also flush. For Egypt, these were boom years, with both the current account and the capital account at peak surplus levels. If this surge were due to structural adjustment, it would be hard to understand why the flows subsequently fell back to pre–Gulf War levels. Of course, the wave had to subside as the sociological consequences of the Gulf War played themselves out.

The case studies authors' hope is that other forms of capital inflow, such as foreign direct investment and portfolio investment, will pick up the slack. Foreign direct investment to Egypt peaked at $US 1.3 billion in 1993/94 and then fell back to 0.6 or 0.7 billion in subsequent years (Handy 1998, p. 27, Table 11). The analysis of the data in our Table 7. A2 (see summary in Table 7.3) did not indicate large flows of foreign direct investment into any of the four countries.

Portfolio investment in Egypt, on the other hand, previously nonexistent, was $U.S. 0.3 billion in 1995/96 and a projected $U.S. 1.5 billion in 1996/97. Egyptian capital markets experienced a burst of activity from 1994 to 1997, with dramatic rises in trading value (a 43-fold rise), market capitalization (from 8 percent of GDP in 1993/94 to 24 percent in 1996/97), a near doubling of transactions, and more than an eightfold rise in new equity issues (Handy 1998, p. 30). While this is a promising record for an "emerging market," not addressed are the issues of the ease of flight of short-term or portfolio capital, not to mention the potential liquidation of real capital assets by foreign direct investors, as happens in emerging markets in times of crisis (Mexico and Thailand are two compelling examples from the mid-1990s).

Case Study Commentary on Unemployment and Human Development

The subject of employment, unemployment, and human development is rarely at the center of the discussion in the case studies. When it is mentioned it is to restate the SAP logic that a decrease in unemployment depends on continuous implementation of privatization and liberalization policies to stimulate private investment, which in turn is said to create economic growth and new job opportunities. Poverty reduction is expected to ultimately follow from the same process.

In Table 7.5, a comparison of educational indicators and spending on education provides some insight into how well these four countries were doing on human resource development at the end of the 1980s. The table was presented in the case study on Jordan, and Jordan comes out ahead in each dimension. That the majority of the Jordanian population is Palestinian, a people who value education very highly in their diaspora, is probably as important as Jordanian public policy in this regard, but Jordan gets the credit for these achievements in this document.

Complementary information dated 1995 appears in Table 7.6. This is the first and only data set in the four country studies to specifically portray

Table 7.5
Educational Indicators and Expenditures

	Illiteracy rate % (ages 15-19) 1990	% Students advancing to final year of primary school 1987	Spending on Education as % GDP, 1990
Egypt	36	95	4.9
Jordan	3	96	5.4
Morocco	21	67	4.8
Tunisia	5	72	5.1

Source: Maciejewski and Mansur 1996, p. 64, Table 8.4.

Table 7.6
Human Development Indicators, 1995

	Egypt	Jordan	Morocco	Tunisia
Population Growth Rate	2.0	5.7	2.0	1.9
Labor Force Growth Rate	2.7	5.3	2.6	3.0
Unemployment[1]	10-22	14.0	23.0	15.0
% in Absolute Poverty[2]	7.6	2.5	1.1	3.9
Life Expectancy at Birth	63	70	65	69
Adult Illiteracy	49	13	56	33

Note: [1] The figures for unemployment are estimates made by the IMF staff.
[2] Absolute poverty is defined as living on less than $US1 per day (purchasing power parity formula).

Source: Handy 1998, p. 43, Table 17.

143

unemployment as an important variable to be considered, now, far into the structural adjustment process. Each country has its weaknesses in one or another of the dimensions shown, but all have high rates of unemployment. The rates at which the labor force is growing and the levels of adult illiteracy combine to make a solution to the problem of unemployment very difficult.

Egypt. For Egypt it is noteworthy that unemployment is not even mentioned in the introductory chapter nor in the case study's Table 7.1, "Key Economic Indicators." Apparently unemployment is no longer a key economic indicator. However, what is mentioned in the first chapter, under poverty alleviation, is that the Social Fund for Development promotes labor-intensive public works projects and microenterprises (Handy 1998, p. 2). There is no direct mention of the impact of privatization on employment, save for a reference to severance payments made to laid-off public sector workers out of the same Social Development Fund.

Egypt is described as a still-low-income country with significant poverty. While, according to our Table 7.6, less than 8 percent of the population are abjectly poor (living on less than $1 per day on the purchasing power parity formula), this definition of poverty is hotly contested. One researcher analyzed data from broad consumption surveys taken in the early and mid-1990s and found that, based on the criterion of ability to purchase nutritious food, the overall poverty rate remained virtually unchanged throughout five years of structural adjustment. He found that 44 percent of the population was unable to spend enough to have a minimally adequate diet (Handy 1998, p. 42).[9]

Egypt's system of general subsidies on consumer necessities was gradually broken down under structural adjustment. Instead, the World Bank helped Egypt establish the Social Fund for Development, a "social safety net," which is supposed to target specific consumer subsidies, social insurance, cash transfers, and income supplements to that part of the population hit hardest during structural adjustment. As of this writing in early 1999, these programs were still underdeveloped.

In addition to antipoverty programs, the Social Fund was assigned to provide support for economic development programs using microcredit schemes and other forms of encouragement to small enterprise (up to 25,000 firms per year). Expansion of community services and cottage industries was also planned, as well as retraining of redundant public sector workers, all of which programs were said to increase employment (although no figures are provided).

However, the case study tells us on page 44 that the job-creating public works projects undertaken in the early part of structural adjustment, and cited above from page 2 of the case study, have been reduced by almost 50 percent, in favor of locally run community development programs assisted by voluntary private organizations (Handy 1998, pp. 42–44). So, in this 1998 study of Egypt (the most recent of the four we have examined), unemployment is addressed explicitly for the first time. However, there is faith (without evidence) that jobs will be created by the new businesses emerging from structural adjustment on the local level, and the one program that did actually create jobs directly, in public works, was drastically cut back.

Jordan. As for Egypt, so for Jordan unemployment and employment are not included in the economic indicator tables in the "overview" chapter but are first mentioned on the tenth page of an 11-page introductory chapter. In the last chapter, on the "social aspects of the adjustment program," where one might expect it, employment is not mentioned at all in the text and no data are provided for it in the relevant tables (Maciejewski and Mansur 1996, pp. 60–61, 64–65). An indirect mention comes under poverty alleviation policies, where UNRWA (an agency for Palestinian refugee relief) is cited as providing income-generating employment projects (Maciejewski and Mansur 1996, p. 61), something UNRWA has been doing for 50 years, long before SAPs were invented.

Be that as it may, it is said that, in the context of structural adjustment, the unemployment rate in Jordan fell from a high of 25 percent in 1990 to 12–15 percent in 1993–94 (Maciejewski and Mansur 1996, pp. 10, 21). Perhaps the more liberal atmosphere of the SAP encouraged business enterprise, but it is also true that emigré workers sent in their earnings and then their savings and built housing at a fast pace during those years, contributing the wherewithal in labor and capital to sustain an economic boom. That is to say, the historic context, not just the SAP, was critical to the improvement in economic activity.

It is well known that Jordan experienced labor shortages in the decade from 1975 to 1985 and imported unskilled and agricultural labor to fill places emptied by emigré workers. The regional crisis precipitated by falling oil prices put an end to this situation around 1986 and unemployment began to rise. While the 1994 rate is certainly better than the rate during the depths of Jordan's economic crisis, whether it is better or worse than the precrisis rate cannot be determined with the data provided, but it is apparent that contextual events, perhaps more than SAP policy, have a strong impact on employment and unemployment in Jordan.

As for the "social aspects of adjustment," the poverty trend does seem to follow the unemployment trend in Jordan. Poverty declined in the precrisis 1980s, from 24 percent in 1980 to 3 percent in 1986–87, then rose to almost 20 percent in 1991 at the start of the SAP, and, the case study suggests, it may have declined since then but no specific figure is given (Maciejewski and Mansur 1996, pp. 58–59). As was described for Egypt, so for Jordan the development of a "social safety net" is intended to help soften the negative impact of some aspects of structural adjustment. Jordan is praised for its development of a set of such programs, and for its social security system, which covers the one-third of the labor force in private sector companies with at least five employees. The public sector retains its own separate system (Maciejewski and Mansur 1996, pp. 58–65).

Morocco. In Morocco's case, employment and unemployment are not mentioned in the chapter on the inward-oriented development strategy (Nsouli et al. 1995, Chapter 2) nor in the chapter describing the adjustment strategy, even though the latter mentioned "domestic resistance" to the SAP policies (Nsouli et al. 1995, Chapter 3). Contrary to the usual pattern of real wage declines during the early years of an SAP, the evidence in the case study Tables A-25, A-29, and A-39 suggests that this "resistance" apparently contributed to a long delay in the fall of real wages in Morocco. This resistance may be one of the considerations that led the Moroccan authorities to take a gradual approach to adjustment, as quoted above in the discussion on external financial support. Two rounds of highly visible demonstrations in September and October 1998 by unemployed graduates demanding jobs from the government are signs of continued "resistance."[10]

The case study asserts that structural reforms contributed to the provision of "substantial employment of a growing population" (Nsouli et al. 1995, pp. 18–19). However, in its Chapter 4 on fiscal policy in Morocco, data on employment and unemployment are presented. There, Table 5, "Social Indicators," shows a population growth rate of over 2 percent per year from 1971 through 1992, but total employment as a percent of the urban population falling from 27.5 in 1990 to 27.4 in 1991 to 27.1 in 1992. This implies that workers are dropping out of the labor force. The assertion is further undermined by Appendix Table A30, "Urban Population by Activity and Profession" (Nsouli et al. 1995, p. 83), showing that unemployment was 14 percent in 1988, 16 percent in 1989, 15 percent in 1990, 17 percent in 1991, and 16 percent in 1992. So during the period of the most intensive structural adjustment, labor force growth slowed and unemployment became worse by 3 percentage points before it finally became better by 1 point. There is no "substantial employment" growth to be found here.

Morocco's achievements under structural adjustment are described in Chapter 8 on performance, where there is no mention whatsoever of employment or unemployment (Nsouli et al. 1995, pp. 42–52). However, unemployment is mentioned in the final chapter on challenges and lessons, which repeats the mantra of liberalization and privatization as the means to alleviate it (Nsouli et al. 1995, pp. 53–55).

Structural adjustment is credited with a 50 percent decline in the proportion of the Moroccan population in poverty (under a more liberal definition than the "$1.00 per person per day" formula), down to 3.3 million people, or 13 percent of the population (Nsouli et al. 1995, p. 18). The recommendation for further poverty reduction is increased private investment and productivity growth and flexible labor markets, with government supporting the private productive process through infrastructure investment (Nsouli et al. 1995, pp. 18–19).

Tunisia. For Tunisia, an unemployment rate of 15 percent in 1986 is said to have been a sign of crisis (Nsouli et al. 1993, p. 1). Table 7.6 indicated that unemployment was 15 percent in 1995, after nine years of structural adjustment, but apparently this was not construed as "a sign of crisis" by the authors. Unemployment is not mentioned at all in the chapter on fiscal policy and reforms thereof, although one trained in the Keynesian tradition, at least, might expect this economic problem to be dealt with there in the sections on "social development" and "outstanding issues" (Nsouli et al. 1993, pp. 12–13). Nor is unemployment mentioned in the chapter on structural reforms, including public enterprise reform, where it would seem most appropriate (Nsouli, et al. 1993, pp. 23–26), nor in the "Performance" chapter where the achievements since the reform are touted (Nsouli, et al. 1993, pp. 30–41). Employment data do not even appear in Appendix Table A13, "Wage and Employment Indicators," despite the title (Nsouli et al. 1993, p. 51).

In the final chapter on "Challenge and Lessons," it is posited that the rate of job creation must have kept up with labor force growth in Tunisia during the adjustment period, since the rate of unemployment remains about the same. The implication is that this is an accomplishment of structural adjustment. The case study authors propose that the actual reduction of unemployment will require higher rates of economic growth and more flexible labor markets that tie pay to productivity (Nsouli et al. 1993, p. 42). This is clearly not a head-on address of the problem of unemployment.

Another publication of the IMF sums up the agency directors' approval of Tunisia's performance in robot-like language, repeating the mantra several times in a four-page "public information notice" (press release) issued in June 1998. Unemployment is mentioned once:

Executive Directors commended the Tunisian authorities for continuing in 1997 prudent fiscal and monetary policies while implementing structural reforms. . . . Directors emphasized, however, that continued high unemployment underscored the need for a shift to a higher growth path, as planned under the IXth Economic Development Plan. Directors stressed that this would require continued prudent macroeconomics and income policies, and an acceleration of structural reforms, to help achieve the needed increases in national savings and investment, and to strengthen the role of the private sector. They placed emphasis on the importance of privatization and price decontrol, the further strengthening of the banking system, and the easing of labor market rigidities to facilitate the movement of labor toward more dynamic sectors. (International Monetary Fund 1998, p. 131)

However, no data on employment and unemployment were included in the table accompanying this press release, "Tunisia: Selected Economic Indicators" (International Monetary Fund 1998, p. 133). But the message that the market will solve the problem, and that otherwise nothing can be done, is again placed at the center of the proposed policy.

ALTERNATIVE VISIONS FOR ECONOMIC REFORM IN THE REGION

Given the slide into debt crisis and recession in the second half of the 1980s, it is clear that the earlier state-led development programs were in deep trouble and needed help. SAPs purport to have provided that help. However, the performance of these four countries as of 1995, after years of structural adjustment programs, is no better than their performance under the precrisis *ancien régime*, and is in some important ways worse. SAPs, and the external funds they brought into the reforming country, may have helped to restore these countries to precrisis levels of debt and debt service, to promote exports, and to encourage foreign investment. But they have not restored the sustained economic growth, high levels of investment, and employment opportunities of the precrisis era.

The evidence discussed here suggests that in spite of nonstellar performance in both the international and domestic dimensions expected by SAPs, Egypt, Jordan, Morocco, and Tunisia won IMF approval by sooner or later implementing most of the formal requirements of their SAPs. They were rewarded with verbal kudos in IMF publications and their efforts were lubricated with external financial support of all types over some years. Of the four countries, Tunisia is the most successful in performance, especially on the domestic criteria and when viewed over a long period of time. Ironically, Tunisia was the weakest on implementation of a number of planks in the SAP, for example, by running a relatively high public deficit and by failing to reduce tariffs to world-competitive levels. Jordan is the second-best performer of the group, yet violates the standard SAP prescription by maintaining a relatively high level of public investment. This evidence suggests that countries that pick and choose which policies to implement—some SAP and some not according to their own vision of their development needs—may perform better than those countries that more fully adopt the SAP policies.

IMF documents on the region as a whole, in which Egypt, Jordan, Morocco, and Tunisia are often favorably cited, are as impoverished and unhelpful on the subject of employment and unemployment as those discussed above (El-Erian 1996; Kanaan 1997; Middle Eastern Department 1996). In contrast, after a period of disinterest in the 1980s, World Bank publications on the Middle East began to grapple with the issues of human development and employment in relation to structural adjustment (e.g., World Bank 1995). The 1998–99 edition of the *World Development Report* shows the data section of the volume to have been reconfigured to highlight human development and environmental issues (World Bank 1998).

The World Bank's encouragement of, and collegial support for the establishment of a regional economic "think tank," the Economic Research Forum for the Arab Countries, Iran, and Turkey (ERF), also suggests serious concern for human development issues. The Economic Research Forum aims to develop regional research capacity, including the cultivation of researchers themselves and the methods of modern economic research. Its members aim explicitly to promote policy to improve labor market outcomes, i.e., employment and wages, alleviate poverty and inequality, and promote human capital development and gender equity (*Forum* 1995). This is a significant improvement over the IMF's total failure to address employment and unemployment as key features of a viable economy.

The World Bank has paid attention to public policy regarding employment and human resource development, for example in the 1995 study "Will Arab Workers Prosper . . . ?" The argument here, as generally among ERF member economists,[11] is that reliance on markets provides the best outcomes, but that market activity has to be encouraged in certain directions or modified around the edges by a clear and strong public policy promoting positive externalities (e.g., the education of women) and reducing or neutralizing negative externalities (e.g., the displacement of redundant workers). As the vice president for the World Bank's Middle East and North Africa Region put it in his foreword: "Policymakers . . . need to articulate a broad vision of a new social contract that is realistic and capable of benefiting most workers, in the context of a world that is changing rapidly and to which the Arab economies must adapt quickly" (World Bank 1995, p. v).

The ERF and the World Bank present a softened version of structural adjustment, the free-market model with a human face. Does this take us far enough beyond the SAP vision to facilitate the birth of coherent institutional frameworks for "sustainable development"? Or is something more required: the placing of human development needs, including work with dignity, at the hub of the development wheel, with markets and the pursuit of profit serving as the spokes put into their service? Global integration and worldwide growth may be more sustainable in the long run if the latter vision prevails.

NOTES

This is a revised version of a paper presented at the conference on Earnings Inequality, Unemployment, and Poverty in the Middle East and North Africa at the School of Business, Lebanese American University, Byblos, Lebanon, November 5–7, 1998.

1. The quotation is from Patricia Alonso-Gamo, Susan Fennell, and Khaled

Sakr 1997, "Adjusting to New Realities: MENA, the Uruguay Round, and the EU-Mediterranean Initiative," IMF Working paper 97/5 (Washington, DC: International Monetary Fund), p. 1.

2. The decline in productivity growth is surmised from rising ICORs and growing deficit problems among publicly owned enterprises. See Handy, for example, on total factor productivity growth in Egypt (1998, pp. 5–10).

3. This liberty seems reasonable insofar as the International Monetary Fund country studies themselves rely on World Bank data.

4. Jordan is considered different from other Arab countries because its public sector, while large, is not involved in direct production. Otherwise its problems are "similar to those of Tunisia and Morocco [and Egypt]": tax and subsidy systems, controlled trade regime, price and quantity controls in agriculture and energy (Maciejewski and Mansur 1996; p. 2).

5. Several European countries provided debt-for-equity and debt-for-nature swaps instead of funds (Maciejewski and Mansur 1996, p. 52).

6. There is an ironic touch here: a future IMF-backed plan proposes civil service reform to "tackle the large share of the wage bill" in the government budget (Nsouli et al. 1995, p. 21) but later says that "Morocco has a highly competent civil service" that implemented recent tax system changes effectively (Nsouli et al. 1995, p. 55).

7. Trade liberalization entails reducing or eliminating import bans and nontariff barriers, as well as reducing and unifying tariffs (Handy 1998, p. 65).

8. Important to remember, however, is that the same ICOR value can be obtained with a lower GDI/GDP divided by a lower rate of GDP growth (the four Arab countries) as it can be by a higher GDI/GDP divided by a higher rate of GDP growth (the four Asian countries). Paying attention to the actual magnitudes in the numerator and denominator is necessary in order to obtain useful information from the comparison of ICORs for one country over time or for a set of countries at any one point in time.

9. This finding is quoted without comment by the author of the chapter on poverty and human development in Handy (1998, p. 42). The analysis, by USAID researcher Patrick Cardiff, stirred some controversy within both the IMF and the World Bank when it was circulated in draft form prior to publication. The bibliographic citation in Handy 1998 is inaccurate. See Cardiff 1997.

10. As reported by Rawhi Abeideh, "Police Beat, Arrest Protesters in Morocco," Reuters Internet dispatch from Rabat, October 26, 1998.

11. Members of the ERF served as commentators on this study.

REFERENCES

Cardiff, Patrick W. (1997). "Poverty and Inequality in Egypt," in Karen Pfeifer, ed., *Research in Middle East Economics*, Volume 2. Stamford CT: JAI Press, Inc., in cooperation with the Middle East Economic Association, pp. 1–38.

El-Erian, Mohamed A., Sena Eken, Susan Fennell, and Jean-Pierre Chauffour (1996). *Growth and Stability in the Middle East and North Africa*. Washington, DC: International Monetary Fund.

Forum (1995). Newsletter of the Economic Research Forum for the Arab Countries, Iran, and Turkey 2 (2): 3.

Handy, Howard and Staff Team (1998). *Egypt: Beyond Stabilization, toward a Dynamic Market Economy.* Washington, DC: International Monetary Fund.

International Monetary Fund (1996). *International Financial Statistics Yearbook 1996.* Washington, DC: International Monetary Fund.

———(1998). "IMF Concludes Article IV Consultation with Tunisia," Press Information Notice (PIN) No. 98/45. *IMF Economic Reviews* 2:130–133.

Kanaan, Taher H., ed. (1997). *The Social Effects of Economic Adjustment on Arab Countries.* Washington, DC: International Monetary Fund.

Maciejewski, Edouard and Ahsan Mansur, eds. (1996). *Jordan: Strategy for Adjustment and Growth.* Washington DC: International Monetary Fund (Occasional Paper 136).

Middle Eastern Department (1996). *Building on Progress: Reform and Growth in the Middle East and North Africa.* Washington, DC: International Monetary Fund.

Nsouli, Saleh M., Sena Eken, Paul Duran, Gerwin Bell, and Zuhtu Yucelik (1993). *The Path to Convertibility and Growth: The Tunisian Experience.* Washington, DC: International Monetary Fund (Occasional Paper 109).

Nsouli, Saleh M., Sena Eken, Klaus Enders, Van-Can Thai, Jorg Decressin, and Filippo Cartiglia (1995). *Resilience and Growth through Sustained Adjustment: The Moroccan Experience.* Washington, DC: International Monetary Fund (Occasional Paper 117).

Shaban, Radwan A., Ragui Assaad, and Sulayman S. Al-Qudsi (1995). "The Challenge of Unemployment in the Arab Region," *International Labour Review* 134 (1):65–81.

World Bank (1995). *Will Arab Workers Prosper or Be Left Out in the Twenty-First Century?* Washington, DC: The World Bank.

———(1997). *World Development Report 1997.* Washington, DC: The World Bank.

———(1998). *World Development Report 1998–99.* Washington, DC: The World Bank.

8

Earnings, Education, Experience, and Gender: Kuwaiti Evidence

Salim Chishti and Badria Khalaf

INTRODUCTION

Education is one form of capital. Investment in education has been claiming a significant proportion of national resources. During the last 50 years it has been expanding rapidly throughout the world. Many key economic issues such as resource allocations, income distribution, and overall economic productivity and growth are tied with the investment in education. Furthermore, it also plays a key role in the social and political development and closely relates with the issues of regional/ethnic/race/gender income inequalities. This pivotal role of investment in education has induced widespread research to evaluate its private and social rates of return and assess its impact on socioeconomic development. Interest in this area has been continually sustained for the last 40 years and perhaps will continue to capture the attention of the profession in the foreseeable future. In Kuwait the relation between human capital and earnings inequality is particularly important. This is because the more conventional monetary and fiscal instruments that are frequently used to adjust income inequalities in other countries are not in place here. On the other hand, the public sector employs about 95 percent of the total Kuwaiti workforce and their salaries/allowances are among the important instruments to distribute the national oil wealth.

Human capital theory implies that the variance in individuals' earnings is largely attributable to their education and experience. The basic theoretical model generally used to explain this variance is some adaptation of the Mincerian function in which log earnings are regressed on schooling, work experience, and experience squared. The interpretation of the estimated coefficient of education in such a model, namely that it measures the direct effect of schooling on earnings, is valid on the presumption that the level of schooling is independent of the amount of work experience. Casual empiricism suggests it to be an implausible assumption. Researchers have generally found it to be not a valid assumption. In order to allow for the interdependence in the rates of return between various levels of education and experience, some researchers, including Psacharopoulos and Layard (1979), have added terms in the regression in which the level of schooling is multiplied by the level of experience and its squared terms. However, this approach arbitrarily imposes a multiplicative structure on the interaction between the two variables. It also makes the interpretation of the estimated coefficients problematic. An alternative approach to allow for the possibility of varying coefficients at various levels of experience, which has been followed, among others, by McNabb and Richardson (1989), is to estimate separate regressions for the returns to schooling at various levels of experience groups and similarly to estimate separate regressions for experience at various levels of schooling groups. However, in order to have reliable estimates for separate schooling groups and estimates for separate experience groups requires a fairly large data set so that every group has a reasonable number of earners. Since we have a large data set consisting of more than 100,000 earners, we have followed both the approaches in this study, namely, estimating the regressions with interaction terms included and estimating separate regressions for various groups of schooling and separate regressions for various experience groups.

Besides estimating returns to education and a life-cycle profile of experience, we have also estimated the proportion of total variance that is attributable to human capital, education, and experience combined. This proportion has been estimated at that level of experience at which the differently sloped earnings profiles intersect. Mincer (1974) called it the "crossover" year. His argument was that at this point of intersection the variance in the earnings, arising from various unmeasured differences in postschooling investments in human capital, is at its minimum. In order to identify this crossover year separate regressions have been estimated within various experience groups. The one that has the minimum residual variance has been identified to correspond to the crossover year.

In order to assess the level of gender inequality in the earnings functions, we have taken advantage of the large data set and have estimated all the above regressions separately for male and female employees and the results have been compared.

SALIENT FEATURES OF KUWAITI EMPLOYMENT

Before we proceed further, let us briefly review the Kuwaiti labor market. This will facilitate a better understanding of the results of this study. Since the focus of the study is Kuwaiti labor, this review has been confined to Kuwaiti employees only.

More than 95 percent of the Kuwaitis are employed in the public sector. Only a few Kuwaitis work in the private sector. The private sector has the majority of expatriates. Of the total public sector employment, a little more than 60 percent consists of Kuwaitis. About half of the Kuwaitis are in clerical jobs and another one-third have professional and technical jobs. The balance accounts for various types of services. Two-thirds of the Kuwaiti labor in the public sector consists of male employees. While female labor has a higher percentage of employment in the professional/technical occupations, all other categories are dominated by male employees. About 45 percent of the Kuwaiti labor in the public sector has less than or equal to an intermediate level of education. Intermediate is equivalent to eight to 11 years of schooling in Kuwait. It is also interesting to note that women account for 57 percent of the university and higher-education graduates. On the other hand, they represent less than 10 percent in the managerial/administrative jobs. The significance of this observation lies in the fact that the average earnings in the managerial/administrative jobs are more than double those of the professional/technical jobs.

The salaries/allowances of the employees are fixed according to the government pay scales. The government pay scales are divided into four categories of jobs. The lowest category, called "supporters jobs," has three scales. The initial basic salary in these three scales ranges between KD (Kuwaiti Dinar) 90 and 160 plus social allowances that range between KD 136 and 165 for single persons and KD 211 and 253 for married employees. The second category, called "assistance technical jobs," has six scales. The initial basic salary in these scales ranges between KD 90 and 225 along with social allowances that range between KD 136 and 189 for singles and KD 211 and 282 for married employees. The third category, called "general jobs," has 10 scales. The initial salary in these scales ranges between KD 110 and 520 along with social allowances that range between KD 141 and 268 for singles and KD 216 and 368 for married employees. The last category, called "leaders jobs," has three scales. The initial salary in these scales ranges between KD 600 and 790 along with social allowances that range between KD 400 and 448 for singles and the same for married employees. The leaders jobs have acting allowances also that range between KD 114 and 231.

DATA, VARIABLES, AND THE MODEL

Data

The data for this study are drawn from the Civil Service Commission database. It comprises 37 ministries and administrations and covers about 80 percent of all public sector employees. Since about 95 percent of the Kuwaiti labor is employed in the public sector, the Civil Service Commission data cover approximately 75 percent of the total Kuwaitis employed. The Civil Service Commission has more than 57,000 male employees and more then 47,000 female employees. We have used the data for the year 1996 for this study.

Variables

In the analysis we have used only three variables. The dependent variable is the log of monthly earnings. It includes the basic salary and various allowances. As described above, the allowances are a significant part of the total earnings. For the lower grades they are more than the basic salary. There are built-in differences in the allowances for married/unmarried and male/female employees. Therefore, an argument could be made in favor of using basic salary as the dependent variable rather than total earnings. However, we chose the total earnings because rates of allowances are tied to various grades and the grades are tied to education and experience. Therefore, we view social allowance as part of the returns to human capital.

Only two independent variables are used in this study, namely, education and experience. The latter has been taken directly from the database without any adjustments. In the database education is reported in terms of academic qualifications rather than years of schooling. However, academic qualifications are given in sufficient detail to convert them into reasonably accurate estimates of years of schooling. In Kuwait there is also provision for a part-time education system; therefore, data in terms of academic qualifications is more appropriate. In the educational system of Kuwait, 8 to 11 years of full-time schooling is termed as intermediate. High school is equivalent to 12 years of schooling. There are a number of post–high school diplomas, which require 12 to 14 years of schooling, and postuniversity diplomas, which require 16 years of schooling. The B.A./B.Sc. degree is equivalent to 16 years, the M.A./M.Sc. degree ranges between 18 and 21 years, and the Ph.D. degree between 22 and 23 years of education. This information, which is available in more detail than reported here, has been used to convert academic qualifications into number of years of schooling.

Model

The basic model of estimation is the following:

$$ln\ Y = \alpha_0 + \alpha_1 S + \alpha_2 X + \alpha_3 X^2 + \upsilon$$

where $ln\ Y$ is the log of monthly earnings in KD. α_0 may be interpreted as the initial earnings at the time of entry in the labor force. α_1 is the rate of return on schooling. α_2 and α_3 are the coefficients tracing the earnings profile over the service years. S is the number of years of schooling and X is the number of years of work experience.

Human capital theory suggests that an increase in education and work experience augments skills and wages and therefore α_1 and α_2 are expected to have positive signs. Work experience is also included in squared terms to see if there is concavity in the earnings profile in the sense that the relative premium to experience falls as the amount of experience increases. Therefore, a priori theoretical conjecture is that the sign of α_3 should be negative.

Subsequent to this basic regression various interaction terms are successively added. For instance, in the next regression we included the interaction between schooling and experience (i.e., $S*X$). The coefficient of this term would indicate whether the slope of the experience-earnings profile depends on the level of education. Human capital theory implies that those employees with higher levels of education are likely to be inclined to seek job opportunities with steeper profiles. Therefore, the interaction term is expected to take a positive sign.

As an alternate to including interaction terms in the same regression, we regressed earnings on experience separately for various schooling groups. Finally, to estimate the proportion of variance in earnings that is attributable to human capital, we regressed separate regressions of earnings on schooling for various experience groups. Following the approach of Mincer (1974) and Psacharopoulos and Layard (1979), we identified the crossover year as the one that corresponds to that experience group for which the residual variance is minimum and hence used the following formula to estimate the fraction of earnings variance explained by human capital:

$$1 - \frac{Var\left(U_{min}\right)}{Var(ln\ Y)}$$

where Var (U_{min}) is the minimum residual variance among various experience groups and Var $(ln\ Y)$ is the variance in the earnings of the whole data.

EMPIRICAL RESULTS

The means and variances of the variables and correlation matrices for male and female employees are reported in Table 8.1. Figures show that

Table 8.1
Summary Statistics for Male and Female Employees

Variables	MALE		FEMALE		TOTAL	
	Mean	Variance	Mean	Variance	Mean	Variance
lnY	6.28	0.18	6.22	0.151	6.25	0.17
S	10.9	17.87	13.0	12.75	11.9	16.68
X	10.2	60.34	8.5	36.66	9.4	50.32

Correlation Matrix (Male)

	lnY	X	S
lnY	1	0.53	0.51
X	0.53	1	-0.134
S	0.51	-0.134	1

Correlation Matrix (Female)

	lnY	X	S
lnY	1	0.41	0.71
X	0.41	1	-0.12
S	0.71	-0.12	1

lnY = log of monthly income.
S = years of schooling.
X = years of experience.

the average earnings of women are lower than those of men, whereas the average years of schooling of women are higher than those of men. It also shows that the variance in earnings is relatively small. The significant differences between the averages of male and female employees' earnings, education, and experience imply that pooling of male and female data would obscure important differences in their effects on return to education. Therefore, we have performed all our analyses separately for male and female employees. Results indicate a negative correlation between education and experience for both groups.

The basic regression results are reported in Table 8.2. Separate regressions are estimated for the male and female employees. In regression 1, the log of monthly earnings of 57,000 male employees is regressed on the number of their schooling years. It shows that the rate of return to schooling is 5.2 percent. The corresponding t value and R^2 are highly significant. In regression 2, reported in Table 8.3, we added the number of years of ex-

Table 8.2
Earnings Function for Kuwait 1996, Dependent Variable: Log Monthly Earnings

	MALE				FEMALE			
	R1	R2	R3	R4	R5	R6	R7	R8
Constant	5.72	5.23	5.144	5.19	5.21	4.86	4.77	4.84
S	0.052	0.060	0.67	0.064	0.07	0.083	0.09	0.085
	(140.5)	(225.8)	(141.2)	(98.9)	(220.4)	(330.5)	(192.3)	(134.5)
X		0.049	0.056	0.095		0.033	0.043	0.115
		(107.3)	(91.07)	(66.2)		(72.81)	(58.20)	(54.2)
X^2		-0.001	-0.0006	-0.002		-0.00007	-0.0008	-0.0035
		(-34.9)	(-37.59)	(-41.7)		(-3.28)	(-3.95)	(-33.9)
Sx			-0.0006	-0.011			-0.0007	-0.017
			(-17.8)	(-44.9)			(-16.24)	(-55.5)
Sx^2				0.0001				0.0007
				(39.8)				(45.2)
S^2x				0.001				0.0008
				(48.2)				(59.1)
S^2x^2				-0.0001				-0.00004
				(-42.9)				(-48.5)
$\bar{R}^2$	0.26	0.62	0.63	0.64	0.51	0.75	0.75	0.77
SEE	0.37	0.27	0.26	0.26	0.27	0.19	0.194	0.18
N	57057	57057	57057	57057	47220	47220	47220	47220

perience and its square term. As a result of the inclusion of experience, the rate of return to schooling substantially increased to 6 percent. This is because experience is negatively correlated with schooling. The explanatory power of the schooling and experience together is 62 percent of the variance in incomes of Kuwaiti male employees. According to this result, the maximum level of earnings is attained after 24 years of experience. Furthermore, the maximum earnings are about 82 percent higher than the initial earnings with no experience. It also shows that the rate of return to experience is 4.9 percent. In regression 3 we included the interaction term, SX, which allows the level of schooling to influence the slope of the log of earnings. The inclusion of the interaction term resulted in a further increase in the rate of return to schooling of up to 6.7 percent. However, although all the coefficients are highly significant and have expected signs, the increase in the explanatory power is only marginal. In regression 4 we included all the terms pertaining to the interactions between schooling and experience. It may be observed that all the interaction terms yield highly significant coefficients. All the signs are as expected. While the rate of return to schooling remained almost at the previous level, the return to experience has now substantially changed.

The other half of Table 8.2 reports the returns to schooling and experience of 47,000 female employees. These results show the same patterns as found for the male employees, namely, that the rate of return on schooling increases when we include their experience in the regression. Again all the coefficients turned out highly significant and with expected signs. The

Table 8.3
Earnings Function for Kuwait, Dependent Variable: Log Monthly Earnings

	Male		Female	
	Coefficient	t-value	Coefficient	t-value
Constant	5.686	-	5.53	-
X	0.009	5.34	-0.009	-3.66
X^2	0.0001	2.911	0.0006	5.85
Sx	0.008	25.2	0.006	13.66
Sx^2	0.0001	-11.01	-0.00003	-1.58
S^2x	-0.0001	-26.27	-0.0002	-10.35
S^2x^2	0.0001	10.55	0.00001	-1.85
D_2	-0.001	-0.118	0.02	2.69
D_3	0.105	15.96	0.103	11.32
D_4	0.390	55.04	0.46	49.91
D_5	0.723	93.71	0.71	78.22
D_6	0.888	90.66	0.85	79.13
D_7	1.366	69.56	1.29	58.11
D_8	1.865	84.23	1.58	64.32
$\overline{R}^2$	0.69	-	.81	-
SEE	0.24	-	.17	-
N	57057	-	47220	-

combined explanatory power of schooling and experience is above 75 percent for female employees. It may also be observed that the rate of return to schooling is consistently higher for the female employees in all the regressions. It ranges between 7 percent and 8.5 percent.

These empirical findings raise several important questions. The results indicate that the rate of return to education in Kuwait is much lower than what has been found in other developing countries but is somewhat closer to, although still lower than, the returns of developed countries. For instance, Psacharopoulos (1985) reported Mincer-type returns to schooling to be 13 percent in Africa and 14 percent in Latin America. Others have found the rates even much higher. On the other hand, most of the studies find the rate of return on education in advanced countries to be close to 10 percent. Psacharopoulos (1985) found it to be 9 percent for advanced countries. Although the majority of researchers report high rates of return to education, many have found them to be as low as 3 to 4 percent. For instance, Guisinger et al. (1984) found these returns for an urban area of

Pakistan to be 3.4 to 7.6 percent. McNabb and Richardson (1989) found them to be 7 percent for Australia. One possible explanation of the relatively lower rates of return to education in Kuwait may be that there is virtually no free market for Kuwaiti labor. More than 95 percent of the Kuwaitis are employed by the public sector. As we observed earlier, the public sector has fairly compressed pay scales tied to various levels of education. Furthermore, a significant part of their earnings is in the form of social allowances. The rate structure of the social allowances is quite regressive. For instance, at the lowest category, the social allowance is more than twice the basic salary, whereas at the highest category, it is only a little more than half of the basic salary. This regressivity in the rate structure of social allowances has compressed the returns to education.

The second important observation is that the rate of return to education is substantially higher for women than men. However, this finding is consistent with the findings of many other researchers (Duncan 1996; O'Neill and Polachek 1993; Bedi and Gaston 1997; Loury 1997). There are several possible explanations for this finding. First, the average education of women in Kuwait is higher than that of men and due to the progressivity in the rate of earnings with various levels of education the return on education of women is higher. This is particularly so because the government pay scales do not provide appropriate signals for more desired areas of study. Initial pay scales are determined largely on the basis of the number of years of schooling with little consideration of the area of specialization.

Interdependence between Schooling and Experience

In order to allow for the possibility that marginal rates of return might be different at various levels of schooling, we introduced separate dummies for various years of schooling. The dummies are defined as follows: $D_1 = 1$ if $S <= 7$, otherwise zero. $D_2 = 1$ if $8 < = S <= 10$, otherwise zero. All other dummies represent two-year groups of schooling. The results for male and female employees are reported in Table 8.5. The omitted schooling dummy is D_1. It may be noted that eight years of schooling is equivalent to "intermediate" degree in Kuwait. Therefore, the reference category is below intermediate. The regression coefficients corresponding to the dummies in both the regressions of male and female employees turned out to be highly significant. The results clearly show the patterns of incremental returns for various levels of schooling. They show that the returns are quite different at various levels of schooling. This is true for both male and female employees. The results indicate that the incremental returns keep increasing with the level of education. The most glaring exception to this pattern is the schooling group of 17 to 18 years for which the incremental returns suddenly take a dip for both male and female employees.

Since we had an exceptionally large data set, we disaggregated the total data into different schooling groups and estimated returns to experience and its square term separately for each schooling group. This ensures that the impact of schooling on the return to experience is not arbitrarily constrained. The results of the corresponding regressions for male employees are reported in Table 8.4. It may be observed that in spite of disaggregation, each group has a large number of observations. Second, all the coefficients in all the schooling groups are highly significant. All the square terms yield negative coefficients, which is consistent with theoretical expectation. A comparison across various schooling groups shows that the return to experience depends on the level of schooling. Also the return to experience increases with the level of schooling, reaches a peak at 11 to 12 years of schooling, and then drops. This group of schooling corresponds to high school level of education in Kuwait. Table 8.5 displays the returns to experience at various levels of schooling for female employees. The pattern of returns to experience for female employees is similar to that of male employees. It also increases with the level of schooling, reaches a maximum, and then drops. This is also borne out from the results that the steeper profiles flatten out relatively more rapidly. This is signified by the fact that the largest negative coefficient of X^2 is associated with the highest positive coefficient of X for both the male and female regressions. However, there are two differences in the results between male and female employees. First, for the female employees the return to experience reaches its peak at 13 to 14 years whereas for males it reaches its peak at 11 to 12 years. Second, the return to experience for women is lower than for men at almost all levels of schooling. This finding is shared with many other researchers. The conventional arguments that have appeared in the literature to explain this gender differential regarding the returns to experience relate to the lower forgone earnings of women; to the fact that the statistical analysis does not account for differences in work efforts and level of commitment that may exist between the two genders; to the preferences of women for certain types of jobs; and to their preferences to mix career with child care, which may result in acquiring less and lower quality of work experience. In Kuwait there may be two additional possible explanations. One relates to the social allowances and the other to the occupational discrimination. In addition to the social allowances there is a child allowance admissible to public sector employees in Kuwait, which is paid at a flat rate of KD 50 per child. This allowance is paid to the father of the child. Therefore, as the number of years of experience of the father increases so does the number of children and consequently his total "earnings," which include the child allowance increase in larger proportion than the earnings of women. Another possible explanation is that the administrative/managerial jobs in Kuwait are largely confined to Kuwaiti men. Women are represented less than 10 percent in these jobs. Administrative/managerial jobs entail faster

Table 8.4
Rate of Return to Experience for Male Employees by Schooling Groups, Dependent Variable: Log
Monthly Earnings

Years of Schooling	Constant	X	X^2	$\overline{R}^2$	SE	F	N
0-7	5.76	0.02 (22.1)	-0.00001 (-0.35)	0.39	0.25	2449	7540
8-10	5.70	0.044 (68.6)	-0.0004 (-15.2)	0.64	0.19	15565	17334
11-12	5.70	0.07 (66.9)	-0.001 (-24.6)	0.61	0.23	8980	11371
13-14	6.04	0.05 (53.8)	-0.0006 (-16.9)	0.63	0.19	8319	9886
15-16	6.55	0.02 (8.9)	-0.0002 (-3.01)	0.15	0.31	733	8490
>=17	6.69	0.027 (371.1)	-0.0001 (-12.8)	0.13	0.34	176	2436

Note: t statistics in parentheses.

Table 8.5
Rate of Return to Experience for Female Employees by Schooling Groups, Dependent Variable: Log Monthly Earnings

Years of Schooling	Constant	X	X^2	$\overline{R}^2$	SE	F	N
0-7	5.56	0.005	0.0007	0.31	0.19	431	1926
		(1.95)	(7.82)				
8-10	5.58	0.023	0.0003	0.59	0.14	6547	8900
		(27.12)	(8.56)				
11-12	5.66	0.028	0.0003	0.65	0.14	4966	5451
		(26.72)	(5.80)				
13-14	5.89	0.052	-0.0006	0.64	0.19	11557	12682
		(66.02)	(-16.92)				
15-16	6.29	0.027	-0.00004	0.44	0.16	6828	17113
		(38.89)	(-1.07)				
>=17	6.34	0.055	-0.001	0.37	0.25	343	1148
		(16.27)	(-8.7)				

Note: t statistics in parentheses.

promotions and the average salaries in these positions are more than double those of technical/professional jobs for comparable qualification and experience.

The Explanatory Power of Human Capital

In order to estimate the proportion of variance in earnings attributable to human capital, we have to identify the crossover year. This is because the variance in the crossover year is minimal. Taking advantage of the large data set we can have reliable regression estimates of the returns to education separately at various levels of experience and hence identify the crossover year. The results of the returns to schooling for male employees within various experience groups are displayed in Table 8.6. The consistently declining coefficient of the schooling variable indicates that with the accumulation of more and more experience returns to education become relatively less important.

The results indicate that there are two possible candidates for the crossover year based on the minimum variance of the residual. It should be taken as either 21 to 23 or 9 to 11 years. It may be mentioned that Psacharopoulos and Layard (1979) found the unexplained variance in earnings at a minimum corresponding to the experience group 12 to 17 years. They believe this to be implausibly late and therefore arbitrarily chose 9 to 11 years as the crossover year. We have at least a discernible trough at 9 to 11 years. Therefore, we shall take 9 to 11 years as the crossover years for Kuwaiti men. Consequently, the proportion of variance in earnings of male employees attributable to human capital is given by:

$$1 - \frac{Var\left(U_{min}\right)}{Var\ (ln\ Y)} = 1 - (0.55/0.18) = 69\%$$

The rates of returns to schooling at various experience groups of women are presented in Table 8.7. These results also confirm the earlier conclusion that returns attributable to education decrease as the level of experience increases. They also confirm that the range of variation is relatively small. There are fewer observations for the last two experience groups making the reliability of the results for those groups suspect. For the rest of the experience groups the return to education ranges from 7.9 to 8.9 percent.

The crossover year for the women employees is quite late at 24 to 26 years, according to the minimum variance criteria. Using the same formula as above, we estimated the proportion of variance in the earnings of women explainable by human capital to be 80 percent. This is quite a high percentage. International evidence indicates that human capital explains 30 to 65 percent of the variance in earnings (Psacharopoulos and Layard, 1979;

Table 8.6
Rate of Return to Schooling for Male Employees by Experience Groups, Dependent Variable: Log
Monthly Earnings

Years of Experience	Constant	S	R^2	SE	N	Var(lnY)	Var(u)
0-2	5.19	0.066	0.36	0.29	10173	0.052	0.089
3-5	5.39	0.064	0.39	0.30	11499	0.058	0.092
6-8	5.52	0.064	0.50	0.25	7007	0.067	0.066
9-11	5.68	0.060	0.53	0.23	6599	0.061	0.054
12-14	5.77	0.058	0.54	0.23	5819	0.063	0.055
15-17	5.87	0.056	0.55	0.24	5219	0.071	0.058
18-20	5.99	0.054	0.58	0.22	3686	0.070	0.050
21-23	6.05	0.054	0.59	0.22	2860	0.070	0.048
24-26	6.05	0.059	0.62	0.23	2421	0.082	0.051
27-29	6.24	0.051	0.51	0.25	1117	0.069	0.065
>=30	6.44	0.045	0.35	0.32	657	0.057	0.107

Table 8.7
Rate of Return to Schooling for Female Employees by Experience Groups, Dependent Variable:
Log Monthly Earnings

Years of Experience	Constant	S	R^2	SE	N	Var(lnY)	Var(u)
0-2	4.82	0.089	0.63	0.20	8987	0.068	0.041
3-5	4.96	0.087	0.68	0.20	10771	0.087	0.041
6-8	5.06	0.084	0.70	0.20	5757	0.093	0.039
9-11	5.21	0.081	0.70	0.19	6975	0.086	0.037
12-14	5.27	0.084	0.75	0.19	6341	0.109	0.036
15-17	5.44	0.079	0.72	0.19	4681	0.092	0.035
18-20	5.53	0.078	0.73	0.18	2040	0.090	0.033
21-23	5.64	0.077	0.70	0.19	784	0.086	0.037
24-26	5.71	0.079	0.74	0.17	628	0.088	0.031
27-29	6.06	0.058	0.48	0.18	185	0.032	0.034
>=30	6.57	0.020	0.16	0.19	71	0.007	0.038

McNabb and Richardson 1989). A possible explanation for this higher percentage may be that there is almost no Kuwaiti labor market in the private sector. Most of the Kuwaitis are employed in the public sector, where the salary fixation is somewhat more mechanical, largely being determined on the basis of education and experience. Factors such as quality, productivity, excellence, entrepreneurship, and so forth, which determine much of the remaining unexplained variance in earnings, are not properly reflected in the earnings.

SUMMARY AND CONCLUSION

The focus of the study has been the estimation of the human capital earnings profile of Kuwaiti labor. Since there are significant differences between the average earnings, average education as well as experience of male and female labor, we have performed the analysis separately for men and women to capture the gender differentials toward the earnings profiles. The analysis is based on the Civil Service Commission database for the year 1996. It covers more than 100,000 Kuwaiti employees. The large data set has allowed us to estimate the regressions for various schooling groups as well as for various experience groups separately. The results indicate the return to education ranges between 5.2 percent and 6.4 percent for male employees and between 7.0 percent and 8.5 percent for female employees. This is explainable in terms of relatively higher level of education of women in Kuwait. The results indicate that the returns to experience are lower for women. Besides other conventional explanations, this finding is explainable in terms of child allowance and a significantly lower representation of women in administrative and managerial positions. Finally the analysis indicates that human capital explains about 70 percent of the variance in earnings of male employees and 80 percent of female employees. This is because in the criteria used in the fixation of salary in the public sector, education and experience overwhelmingly dominate. Other productivity- and excellence-related factors could have played a larger role but there is almost no labor market for the Kuwaitis in the private sector.

REFERENCES

Bedi, A. S. and N. Gaston (1997). "Returns to Endogenous Education: The Case of Hounduras," *Applied Economics* 29 (4): 519–528.

Duncan, K. C. (1996). "Gender Differences in the Effect of Education on the Slope of Experience-Earnings Profiles: National Longitudinal Survey of Youth, 1979–1988," *American Journal of Economics and Sociology* 55 (4): 457–471.

Guisinger, S. E., J. W. Henderson, and G. W. Sculy (1984). "Earnings, Rates of Return to Education and the Earnings Distribution in Pakistan," *Economics of Education Review* 3 (4): 257–267.

Loury, L. D. (1997). "The Gender Earnings Gap among College-Educated Workers," *Industrial and Labor Relations Review* 50 (4): 580–583.

McNabb, R. and S. Richardson (1989). "Earnings, Education and Experience: Is Australia Different?" *Australian Economic Papers* (June): 57–75.

Mincer, J. (1974). *Schooling, Experience and Earnings*. New York: N.B.E.R.

O'Neill, J. and S. Polachek (1993). "Why the Gender Gap in Wages Narrowed in the 1980s," *Journal of Labor Economics* (11): 205–227.

Psacharopoulos G. (1985). "Returns to Education: A Further International Update and Implications," *Journal of Human Resources* XX (4): 583–597.

Psacharopoulos, G. and R. Layard (1979). "Human Capital and Earnings: British Evidence and Critique," *Review of Economic Studies* 46: 485–503.

9

What Accounts for Earnings Inequality in Jordan and How Can Labor Policies Help Reduce Poverty?

Zafiris Tzannatos

INTRODUCTION

This is an empirical chapter that asks a series of questions to examine the potential of reducing poverty through various labor market policies (such as direct transfers, wage interventions, and pensions) and changes in the distribution of labor earnings. The objective is to provide some indication as to whether *poverty reduction via the labor market* is a viable policy option. The chapter uses Jordan as a test case.[1] Though the results are tentative, partly because of data quality and partly because the analysis is primarily static, their magnitude and comparisons with results of other countries suggest that labor market policies cannot reduce poverty to any significant extent. In addition, most such policies would have heavy budgetary implications and the resources required to lift a person out of poverty imply that such measures are simply not cost-effective. This conclusion is amplified by the fact that the chapter assumes conditions of perfect targeting while it ignores any distortionary effects of labor market interventions.

More specifically, the chapter first quantifies "how many would have been poor, if they or other members in their household had no income from employment?" One can examine from the results the contribution of labor incomes to poverty reduction. Indeed, household labor earnings contribute significantly to poverty reduction. In the absence of labor earnings, almost 70 percent of the population would have been poor. With labor earnings, the actual figure is 17 percent. Thus, labor, the poor's most abundant resource, is the single most important contributor to poverty reduction.

Second, the chapter estimates the amount by which labor incomes and other incomes of the working/retired poor should increase to eliminate poverty. It finds that, first, this would require an unrealistic increase in wages of 50 percent. Even an increase in the wages of the poor by 20 percent would reduce poverty by just over one percentage point. Second, the effects of unemployment insurance would be similar in relative terms—too expensive a policy with little effect on poverty reduction. Third, lump sum payments to workers (such as wage subsidies) or increase in existing pensions or the introduction of noncontributory old-age pensions will again require heavy budgetary outlays with marginal effects on poverty. As a comparator, poverty in 1991 figures could be eliminated with perfectly targeted transfers totalling JD 12.2 million a year. Perfect targeting of benefits to the unemployed poor would lift them out of poverty at a total cost of JD 6.3 million a year. This would decrease the share of poor in the total population by less than 2 percentage points compared with 17 percentage points under the previous (equally hypothetical) policy.

Since direct support to the labor force participants and other household members seems to be a limited instrument for increasing the welfare of the poor, an alternative approach is to identify the determinants of earnings and their role in creating inequality in the labor market. The chapter therefore examines whether earnings inequality arises from the demographic composition of workers (for example, age or regional wage differentials), different returns to various education levels, public/private differences, or simply the sex of the worker. Somewhat surprisingly, the chapter finds that the prime determinant of earnings inequality in Jordan is the worker's age rather than a more explicit policy variable such as education. This is in contrast with the dynamic East Asian economies as evidenced from results for Indonesia and Thailand. An explanation for this is that the East Asian economies are more competitive than the Jordanian economy, which is characterized by a large public sector with possible spillover effects on pay determination in the private sector. Another explanation is that education policies in Jordan have been by far more egalitarian than in the other two countries.

In conclusion, direct labor market interventions or distributional policies seem to be poor instruments for poverty reduction. Additional social policies (such as targeted subsidies for health and education services) could be superior alternatives to such policies. However, the most important policies should be those that enhance growth and increase the efficiency of the labor market: the prime determinant of the welfare of poor households is earnings from employment at large. Still, despite the relatively clear-cut nature of our estimates, additional research will be required to establish the robustness of our results for Jordan and their applicability to other countries.

The chapter is organized as follows. The next section presents the results of simulations of various labor market policies on policy reduction. The following section examines inequality in earnings. The final section is a conclusion.

CAN POVERTY BE REDUCED VIA THE LABOR MARKET?

This section examines the effects of alternative labor market policies on poverty. These policies include lump sum payments to workers, wage increases, benefits to unemployed workers, and retirement or old-age pensions.

Given that Jordan does not have an official or widely accepted poverty line, this chapter uses poverty lines calculated with the World Bank methodology. The 1990 *World Development Report* (WDR) of the World Bank used two poverty lines for developing countries based on specific data for several countries (WDR 1990, p. 27). The general poverty line was estimated to be $370 per capita per year at 1985 U.S. prices. The severe poverty line was $275. The lower line is similar to one used in India while the higher one incorporates poverty lines from several other countries, including Egypt and Morocco (Ravallion et al., 1991). While these measures have the advantage of permitting international comparisons, they may not accurately reflect the situation in any particular country especially a middle-income country like Jordan. For example, the poverty line proposed by Al-Saquor (1990) for Jordan implied that 3 percent of the population were poor in 1986/7 compared to 17 percent for 1991 in the present chapter. However, a significant part of the difference can be attributed to the price changes that took place between these two periods, the fall in household expenditures by 27 percent, and the increase in the Gini coefficient of inequality from 0.36 to 0.43 (World Bank 1994, pp. vi–vii, 9).

The present estimates of the poverty line are derived from the Employment, Unemployment, Returnees, and Poverty Survey 1991 (EURPS). On these data and using the World Bank methodology, we estimate that the general poverty line ("the poor") is JD 137 while the severe poverty line ("the poorest") is JD 102. On these two estimates, the head-count index of poverty comes, respectively, to 17 percent and 8 percent of the population (World Bank 1994). The results of policy simulations reported below are for the general poverty line at JD 137.[2] The analysis assumes that incomes from all sources are shared equally within the household irrespective of who is the original recipient.[3] Our analysis ignores second-round effects of policy interventions.

The results refer to all persons in Jordan, citizens and guest workers. There is a little (practically no) difference between the two groups in the sense that the percentages of those below the poverty line for Jordanians and non-Jordanians is the same. This is surprising as non-Jordanians are considered to have lower incomes than Jordanians. If there are no irregularities in the data, our finding has two possible explanations. First, many foreign workers live together—thus, even if they are paid lower wages than Jordanians, they have fewer nonworking members in their households. Second, though foreign workers are considered to be low-paid, they may not be so in practice. More likely they work longer hours than Jordanians at lower hourly wages compared to other Jordanians. For example, Egyptian workers in Amman are paid about JD 100 per month as cleaners. Foreign workers in construction are paid about JD 8 per day. In agriculture Egyptians are paid JD 50 to 150 per month. Domestic workers from the Philippines earn about $150 (JD 100) per month. These rates are not low: a civil servant with secondary education and a wife and two children will start at about JD 91 per month. But to earn these wages foreign workers have to work long hours for seven days a week without sick or annual leave or employment protection. Thus, although non-Jordanians are engaged in jobs that are not attractive to Jordanian workers, these are not low-pay jobs in a strict monetary sense.

To start, we ask, "How many would have been poor, if they or other members in their household had no income from employment?" The answer is 70 percent. Their average annual per capita income from all sources other than employment would have been only JD 26. Introducing income from employment lifts 53 percent above the poverty line. This leaves 17 percent below the poverty line set here at JD 137.

The per capita income of the 17 percent who remained below the poverty line averaged JD 99. The question addressed what the labor market can do for them to reduce poverty. To answer this, we calculate the number of those who cannot be reached through a labor market policy because they do not have a labor force participant, employed or unemployed, in their households. These may be households in which members are too young or too old, unable to work because of a disability, looking after relatives on a full-time basis, and so on. These are 2.5 percent of the population and would require transfers to get above the poverty line. So, even if the labor market could do its best, there would be 2.5 poor Jordanians for every 100.

Next we consider lump sum payments to workers in poverty, increases in their wages, unemployment benefits, and increases in contributory and noncontributory pensions. When applicable, costs for each policy are calculated.

Characteristics of Poor Who Can Be Affected by Labor Market Policies

Of those who live with, or are themselves, labor market participants, 14.7 percent are poor.[4] This consists of 9.5 percent who live only with

Table 9.1
Explained Percentage of the Variance of Log Earnings, Jordan 1992

Variable	% of total variance	% of explained variance
Sex	2.2	7.8
Age	17.9	62.0
Schooling (total effect)	6.2	21.4
Below primary	0.3	0.9
Primary	-0.7	-2.3
Preparatory	-2.2	-7.8
Secondary	0.6	2.1
University	6.1	21.0
Postgraduate	2.9	9.9
Vocational	-0.3	-1.0
Community college	-0.4	-1.5
Public sector	2.7	9.2
Urban	-0.1	-0.3
Total explained (R-sq)	28.8	100.0
Unexplained	71.2	
Total	100.0	

Source: Calculated from the Household Income and Expenditure Survey, 1992.

employed persons(s), 1.5 percent who live with unemployed person(s), and 3.7 percent who live with both employed and unemployed persons.

The average poor household with a labor market participant has about 11 members, of whom approximately 1.3 are employed, 0.5 are unemployed, and 9.2 are outside the labor force. Policies can be targeted to the employed or to the unemployed or to both (obviously, persons living with both employed and unemployed will benefit in either case).

Measures for the Employed

The employed poor cannot rise above the poverty line despite their work. They constitute 10 percent of all workers. They earn on average about JD 42 per month.[5] To eliminate poverty among households with employed members, workers in these households should earn on average an additional JD 250/year (JD 21/month), which amounts to an increase in wages of an average of 50 percent.

Flat-rate transfers can be made to employed workers in households below the poverty line. A payment of JD 10 per month to these workers would reduce poverty by 1.3 percentage points. (The relevant population—those who live with a labor market participant—is 13.2 percent. See Table 9.1.) The cost of lifting one person out of poverty using this measure would be JD 60.5 per annum, and the total transfers would be JD 8.8 million per year.[6] To reduce poverty the same amount (1.3 percentage points) via higher wages of the employed poor would require a 20 percent increase in their wages.

Measures for the Unemployed

The unemployed poor are 21 percent of the unemployed in Jordan—the other 79 percent of the unemployed are not poor. Though there are no unemployment benefits, we estimated the effect on poverty if such benefits existed. To eliminate poverty among households with unemployed workers, the unemployed would need, on average, an additional JD 302/year (JD 25/month).

Assume that unemployment benefits were introduced at rates of JD 25, JD 35, and JD 45 per month and for up to six months.[7] Under these three alternative payments, the percentage of poor would be reduced only marginally, by 1.4, 1.8, and 2.4 percentage points, respectively. The explanation for this low figure is that the relevant group in this case, poor persons living with unemployed or with unemployed and employed household members, constitutes only 5.2 percent of the population.

The cost of lifting one person out of poverty using this measure would vary from JD 76 to JD 83 per annum. The public cost of providing unemployment benefits to all unemployed below the poverty line would be, respectively, JD 4.5 million, JD 6.3 million, and JD 8.0 million per year. Further, unless benefits were targeted to the poor, there would be much larger transfers to the 79 percent of the unemployed who are not poor: JD 16.9 million, JD 23.7 million, and JD 30.0 million, respectively, if benefits were paid to all unemployed persons.

Contributory Pensions

Recall that 17.2 percent of the population are poor and 2.4 percent could not be reached through payments to employed or unemployed workers. In the case of making contributory pensions as the policy instrument, the poor who cannot be reached rise to 15 percent (that is, only 2.2 percent of the poor are pensioners or live with a pensioner). Poor pensioners account for 21.8 percent of all pensioners in Jordan. Pensions for those in poverty in our sample are on average about JD 74/month. (Compare this to earnings for employed workers among the poor who earn on average JD 42 per month.) The average household size of poor pensioners is 10.8.

To eliminate poverty among households with an older person who is in receipt of a pension, pensioners, should be given on average an additional JD 366/year (JD 30/month). This amounts to an increase in their current pensions by 40 percent. Again, we ask what would happen to pensioners in poverty if we gave them an additional JD 10 per month. In this case 0.4 percent of the population would move out of poverty (that is, the percentage of the population in poverty is reduced only to 16.8 percent). The cost of lifting one person out of poverty using the JD 10 pension-top-up is JD 65/annum. The public cost of this payment to poor pensioners would be JD 2.9 m/year. To get the same reduction in poverty using a proportional increase in the pensions of all pensioners living in poverty, a 10 percent increase in pensions would be required.

Noncontributory Pensions

Another way to alleviate poverty is lump sums to poor households with persons above the age of 65 who are not in receipt of a pension. These households have on average one older man (accounting for 1.7 percent of the population) and one older woman (accounting for 1.4 percent of the population). The per capita income in these households is on average JD 94 in the case of older men and JD 99 in the case of older women. The household size is 8.1 for older men and 8.4 for older women.

To eliminate poverty among households with an older person who does not receive a pension, old persons in these households should be given on average JD 349/year (if the older person is a man) or JD 316/year (if the older person is a woman). If all such households were given JD 40/month, poverty among these households would be reduced by 72.5 percent, if this money were targeted to older men, and 75.0 percent, if it were targeted to older women. But the poor would still be 16 percent of the population, if such pensions were given to older men, and 16.2 percent, if they were given to older women. At a pension level of JD 50, the percentage of those below the poverty line would be reduced only marginally to 15.8 percent and 16.1 percent, respectively, of the total population.

The cost of lifting one person out of poverty using a noncontributory old-age pension of JD 40/month is about JD 80/annum per person. If the pension were set at JD 50/month, the cost rises to about JD 90/annum (these figures apply equally to pensions given to older men and older women).

The results of the previous simulations suggest that poverty cannot be reduced to any significant extent through income support policies or wage interventions. Lump sum payments to poor workers, wage increases, increases in existing pensions, or the introduction of noncontributory old-age pensions can have only a marginal effect and at great budgetary costs. These conclusions hold even in the absence of secondary effects that would arise from the distortions introduced by these policies.

CAN INEQUALITY IN LABOR EARNINGS BE DECREASED?

The previous analysis examined the effects of various labor market policies on poverty assuming that the distribution of earnings remained constant. It would, however, be instructive to identify the underlying factors that contribute to earnings inequality and see whether policies can affect the distribution of individual earnings rather than to attempt to increase directly the level of household incomes. To do this, the effects of various factors that determine individual labor earnings, such as education, age (a proxy for experience), rural/urban residence, public/private sector of employment, and sex of the worker, are estimated using conventional earnings functions. There was no information in EURPS about incomes from employment on an individual basis; that is, labor income was reported as total labor income in the household. Therefore, we now use the data from the Household Income and Expenditure Survey 1992 (HIES), which contains information on 7,600 households and 52,000 individuals.[8]

As a measure of the distribution of labor earnings we use the variance of the logarithm of individual earnings, the latter being the conventional dependent variable in earnings functions (Mincer 1974; Dougherty and Jimenez 1991). Statistically, the variance of the logarithm of earnings can be exactly decomposed using regression analysis. In a conventional earnings function, with the logarithm of wages (w) on the left-hand side and education (E, measured as schooling in years), age (A), age-squared (ASQ), and other variables on the right-hand side

$$ln\,(w) = a + bE + cA + dASQ + \ldots + e$$

the log variance of wages is exactly equal to the sum of the absolute contributions to inequality of the explanatory variables.[9] Each explanatory factor's percentage contribution to inequality thus measured can be expressed in terms of the regression coefficient of the variable in question, its standard deviation, its correlation with the dependent variable, and the standard deviation of the dependent variable. For example, the percentage contribution(s) of education to inequality is equal to

$$s = b^* \, SD_E^* \, CORR_{E,ln(w)}/SD_{ln(w)}$$

which shows that the effect of education on earnings inequality will be greater the higher is the regression coefficient, the standard deviation of education, and the correlation between education and log wages.

By using this method, we can examine each explanatory variable's contribution to inequality. Table 9.1 presents the results in two ways: first, as a percentage of total variance (column 1) and, second, as a percentage of the explained variance by the regression (that is, the coefficient of determination, R^2).

The results suggest that the single most important factor in earnings inequality is age. Age alone explains almost one-fifth of the total variance of earnings or two-thirds of the explained variance. Education differences are

Table 9.2
Explained Variance of Log Earnings by Selected Variables in Jordan, Indonesia,
and Thailand

	Jordan	Indonesia	Thailand
Sex	2.2	5.9	1.7
Age	17.9	7.7	10.4
Schooling	6.2	20.8	35.9
Public Sector	2.7	6.3	4.2
Urban	-0.1	9.8	-0.2
Total explained(R-sq)	28.8	50.5	52.0
Explained by other variables	Na	6.5	9.7
Unexplained	71.2	43.0	38.3
Total	100.0	100.0	100.0

second in importance, and this effect comes predominantly from postsecondary education. Sex and public/private wage differentials (urban/rural) are a distant third and account for less than 10 percent of the explained variance of earnings. Urban/rural differentials contribute insignificantly to inequality, as was expected for a small country like Jordan.

The nature of the results indicates that there is little that redistributional policies in the labor market can change with the possible exception of education. A caveat applies to the extent that age reflects a seniority-based system of wage determination that is affected by spillover effects of public sector pay schemes that are not adequately captured by the additional public sector variable in the regression. Though we cannot examine this issue further here, we attempt to put these results in context by presenting additional information for two fast-growing East Asian economies, namely Indonesia and Thailand. Table 9.2 provides suitably summarized results of regression analysis for the three countries. In particular, Table 9.2 presents more or less the complete results for the three countries based on the total variance of earnings. However, given the substantial difference between the coefficients of determination (R^2) in Jordan and the other two countries, Table 9.3 attempts some "standardization" by expressing each variable's contribution to inequality in terms of the explained part of the variance in earnings.

The difference in the specification and the explanatory power of the regressions in Jordan and the other two countries restricts the validity of the comparison. However, the results indicate that in Indonesia and Thailand difference in schooling is the prime determinant of earnings inequality. In other words, an egalitarian education policy in Indonesia and Thailand is bound to have greater impact upon the distribution of earnings than in Jordan. This is, in effect, an acknowledgment of Jordan's significant education record—with universal enrollment in education and practically no gender differences in the education attainment of younger cohorts.

Table 9.3
Contribution of Selected Variables to Log Earnings Inequality in Jordan,
Indonesia, and Thailand as Percentage of Explained Variance Only

	Jordan	Indonesia	Thailand
Sex	7.8	11.7	3.3
Age	62.0	15.2	20.0
Schooling	21.4	41.2	69.0
Public sector	9.2	12.5	8.1
Urban	-0.3	19.4	-0.4
As % of explained variance	100.0	100.0	100.0

Source: Jordan: see source for Table 9.1. For Indonesia the results are based on the Labor
Force Survey (SAKERNAS 1992) and for Thailand on Round 1 of the Labor Force Survey
1992. The complete results are reported in Tzannatos (1996) and Tzannatos and Dar
(1996).

CONCLUSION

The results in the previous two sections suggest that poverty cannot be
reduced to any significant extent through direct or indirect income support
interventions via the labor market or some obvious redistributive policy.
Lump sum payments to poor workers, wage increases, unemployment benefits, increases in existing pensions, or the introduction of noncontributory
old-age pensions can have only a marginal effect at great budgetary costs
and distortions in the economy at large.

In the case of payments to the employed poor or the introduction of
unemployment benefit, poverty would be reduced by only 1 to 2 percentage
points (from 17 percent). If existing pensions are increased by the amounts
mentioned here, poverty will be reduced by less than half of 1 percentage
point. If noncontributory pensions are introduced for those over 65 who
are not in receipt of another pension, poverty will be reduced by only 1
percentage point. At the same time, the results show that increases in wages
are less effective than lump sum payments in reducing poverty, and economic analysis suggests fixing wages has a distortionary effect on the economy. Also, increasing existing pensions, even in the form of lump sum
payments, is not as effective as means-tested transfers to older persons.

These results call for a more sophisticated study that can incorporate
administrative costs of alternative instruments and will take into account
second-round effects of policies (such as effects on labor supply and unemployment). For current purposes, it suffices to say that poverty in Jordan
has been associated with economic contraction and continuing high population growth (3.7 percent per annum in the 1980s). In this respect, appropriate policies are programs based on trade and financial reforms,
deregulation, and rationalization of the government's role in the economy

and its employment size. In addition, a reduction of the high fertility rates could be desirable. However, it is beyond the scope of this chapter to expand on these general macro and population policies.

In terms of more direct labor market policies, it should be first recognized that the education system in Jordan is relatively equitable, and education policies have effectively reached the poor. The poor have good access to primary and secondary education even though the relatively few dropouts are mostly among the poor. Public spending on education has generally grown markedly or has been well protected during periods of recession. This explains in part the fact that education does not have the high inequalizing effect upon earnings as, say, Indonesia, where university education is pursued almost exclusively by students from the top two deciles (Tzannatos and Sayed, 1995). Also, Thailand is a statistical outlier with respect to educational attainment for a middle-income country (Tan, 1991). However, the significant contribution of graduate earnings to inequality in Jordan, the strong association between poverty and education, and the high unemployment rates of university graduates justify prima facie the gradual increase in cost-recovery in higher education while allocating the increased revenue to support needy students (World Bank 1996, p. iii).

With respect to gender differences in the labor market, only a part of the wage gap can be attributed to the (small) differences in the educational attainment between women and men. However, differences in the labor force participation rate between women and men are significant—in effect, most women withdraw from the labor market upon marriage. Part of the gender differences in participation and the subsequent gender pay gap are due to social security regulations, maternity provisions, and income taxation of the family (World Bank 1995). Women's lower attachment to the labor force, for family reasons or because of discrimination, reduces their experience and earnings ability while it discourages employers from offering them training and seniority. Giving equal opportunities for women and men in all aspects of the labor market will not only increase efficiency and reduce poverty through growth but will also reduce inequality.

Finally, the role of government as an employer deserves separate attention. Most of the employees are in the government sector. Though our analysis suggests that public/private wage differences account for 10 percent of the explained variance of earnings, this may be an underestimate, if the public sector is acting as a de facto "leader" for wage setting in the rest of the economy. Also, this estimate ignores significant parts of civil service remuneration in the form of noncash benefits such as various allowances, subsidized pensions and health insurance, benefits in kind, housing loans, bonuses, education grants, preferential tax treatment, and provident funds. To some extent the large government sector in Jordan is the result of high priority given to social services. Given the sizable presence of the government in education, health, housing, and other social services (including social safety nets programs), the efficient provision and/or finance of such services seems to be more promising in the creation of a growth-oriented environment and the battle against poverty than the labor market policies examined here. Still, more research will be required to confirm the validity of this proposition for Jordan and examine its applicability to other countries.

NOTES

This is a revised version of a paper presented at the Conference on Earnings Inequality, Unemployment, and Poverty in the Middle East and North Africa at the School of Business, Lebanese American University, Byblos, Lebanon, November 5–7, 1998.

The findings, interpretations, and conclusions expressed in this chapter are entirely those of the author and should not be attributed in any manner to the World Bank, to its affiliated organizations, or to the members of its Board of Executive directors or the countries they represent.

1. The paper uses survey information on Jordan from the 1991 Employment, Unemployment, Returnees, and Poverty Survey (48,000 households) and the 1992 Household Income and Expenditure Survey (7,600 households).

2. Additional estimates for the severe poverty line are available from the author. However, the results for the poverty line of JD 103 differ only in magnitude compared to the reported ones for the poverty line at JD 137 and this does not affect the main conclusion; that is, poverty cannot be reduced to any great extent via labor market policies. For example, the wage increase required to eliminate poverty in households with employed poor would be 47 percent and 50 percent, respectively, under the JD 103 and JD 137 poverty lines. Both increases are unrealistically high.

3. This analysis is based on per capita incomes (instead of expenditure) because the relevant variable in labor market analysis is "income from employment" (wages). The percentage of the population below the poverty line (JD 137) is practically the same on both the income and expenditure criteria, that is, approximately 17 percent. There may, however, be some distributional effects, if the propensity to consume differs according to income sources of the household.

4. For simplicity "living" from now means "living with or being" a labor force participant.

5. This low monthly wage may reflect reduced work effort as well as bad data.

6. This estimate is low as it assumes perfect targeting, zero administrative costs, and no fraud or abuse. Also, it is assumed that this pure income transfer would not result in any changes in the behavior of beneficiary households. These assumptions apply to other estimates in the current section.

7. Most unemployment insurance schemes pay about 40 to 60 percent of pre-unemployment labor earnings and end within a few months; the average income from employment per employed worker living in poor households is about JD 42/month.

8. For a description of these data see World Bank (1995).

9. Fields and Yoo (1995) show that this decomposition holds not only for the

log variance but for any inequality index that is continuous and symmetric, including the Gini coefficient, the Atkinson index, and the generalized entropy family.

REFERENCES

Al-Saquor, M. (1990). "The Poverty Line in Jordan," in K. A. Jaber, M. Buhbe, and M. Smadi, eds. *Income Distribution in Jordan*. Boulder, CO: Westview Press.

Dougherty, Christopher R. S. and Emmanuel Jimenez (1991). "The Specification of Earnings Functions: Tests and Implications," *Economics of Education Review* 10 (2): 85–98.

Fields, Gary S. and Gyeongjoon Yoo(1995). "Analyzing the Sources of Korea's Falling Labor Income Inequality." Initial results prepared for the Northeast Universities Development Conference, Harvard University, November.

Mincer, Jacob (1974). *Schooling, Experience and Earnings*. National Bureau of Economic Research. New York: Columbia University Press.

Ravallion, Martin, D. Gurav, D. van de Walle, and E. Chen (1991). "Quantifying the Magnitude and Severity of Absolute Poverty in Developing Countries in the Mid-1980s." Background paper for the 1990 *World Development Report*. Washington, DC: World Bank.

Tan, Jee-Peng (1991). "Thailand's Education Sector at a Crossroads," in *Decision and Change in Thailand—Three Studies in Support of the Seventh Plan*. Washington, DC: World Bank.

Tzannatos, Zafiris (1996). *Labor Earnings Inequality in Indonesia 1976–1992: Evidence from SAKERNAS*. World Bank Poverty and Social Policy Department. Washington, DC: World Bank.

Tzannatos, Zafiris and Amit Dar (1996). *How Do Workers' Earnings Change under Fast Growth? Eight Questions and One Answer for Thailand in the Last Decade*. World Bank Poverty and Social Policy Department. Washington, DC: World Bank.

Tzannatos, Zafiris and Haneen Ismail Sayed (1995). "Training and the labor market in Indonesia: Policies for productivity growth and employment gains. Report No. 14413-IND. Washington, DC: World Bank.

World Bank (1990). *Poverty—World Development Report*. Washington, DC: World Bank.

——— (1994). *Hashemite Kingdom of Jordan: Poverty Assessment* (in two volumes: Volume 1 *Main Report*; Volume 2 *Labor Market*). Report No. 12675-JO. Washington, DC: World Bank.

——— (1995). *Hashemite Kingdom of Jordan: Women and the Labor Force*. Report No. 14592-JO. Washington, DC: World Bank.

——— (1996). *Jordan Higher Education Development Study*. Report No. 15105-JO. Washington, DC: World Bank.

10

Unemployment, Low Wages, and Income Inequality: The Triangle of Poverty in the Middle East and North Africa

Berch Berberoglu

INTRODUCTION

This chapter examines the relationship between unemployment, low wages, income inequality, and poverty in selected Middle Eastern and North African (MENA) countries. Providing an analysis that places the study of socioeconomic phenomena in the MENA region in comparative-historical perspective, I argue that rapid urbanization accompanied by economic stagnation and a decline in the standard of living has led to an enormous increase in poverty among a significant segment of the local population living in and around major cities throughout the region.

Examining aggregate data on the sectoral distribution of the labor force, wage levels, unemployment, income inequality, and various quality-of-life indicators in a number of Middle Eastern and North African countries— including Egypt, Syria, Iraq, Jordan, Lebanon, Algeria, Tunisia, Morocco, and Libya—this chapter provides an analysis of the major sources of poverty that have contributed to a significant decline in living standards for a substantial segment of the urban population.

Examining data obtained from the United Nations Economic and Social Commission for Western Asia, the World Bank, and other sources, the chapter attempts to explain the depth and extent of poverty in the Middle East and North African region through an analysis of relevant social and economic indicators that contribute to an understanding of this pervasive problem that affects the fabric of social life in this important region of the world.

THEORETICAL AND SUBSTANTIVE ISSUES

In a market-oriented capitalist economy, the accumulation of capital, and wealth in general, is a product of the exploitation of labor for private profit. Since ownership of private capital gives control over the production process to those who directly benefit from private accumulation—by controlling the labor force and the employment structure, by determining wage levels and overall earnings, and by setting the parameters of consumption levels (all of which affect the standard of living of the working population)—poverty and wealth are the outcome of social relations that are unequal and contradictory. The contradictions embedded in such relationships lead to the polarization of society along economic, social, and political lines such that the nature and outcome of these unequal socioeconomic relations become reflected in (political) relations of domination.[1]

At the heart of this process that leads to growing wealth or impoverishment of opposing segments of the population lies the nature and source of income that determines the social position of various classes in society. Thus, at one end of the poll we find the owners of capital accumulating wealth through the exploitation of labor, while at the other end we find workers and the laboring population subjected to the dictates of the owning class, which determines the latter's socioeconomic position and, in effect, the position of the great majority of the population.[2]

The class relations engendered by this process are affected by certain macroeconomic factors that are the product of the existing socioeconomic system. These include the structure of employment, wage levels, and the nature of income inequality. Together, these factors determine the standard of living of the broader population and the nature and extent of poverty among various segments of contemporary society.

In this context, I would argue that unemployment, low wages, and heightened income inequality serve as three decisive pillars of poverty affecting the social condition of the laboring population. High rates of unemployment, declining wages in the formal sector, and bare survival with below-subsistence-level earnings in the informal sector are the determinants of the high incidence of poverty exacerbated by rapid urbanization and marginalization of a large segment of the population that suffers from a variety of ill effects that this process generates and reproduces. These conditions are the outcome of property-based class relations that continue to polarize society into opposing social classes. Such class opposition, which emanates from disparities in income and wealth in capitalist society are as developed in the Middle East and North Africa as they are in the advanced capitalist countries. In fact, given the severity of the economic downturn that has led to declining wages and shrinking incomes for the majority of the population in the MENA region, the situation in most Middle Eastern and North African countries has reached crisis proportions.[3]

THE REALITIES OF LIFE IN THE MIDDLE EAST AND NORTH AFRICA IN THE 1980s AND 1990s

"The economies of most Arab countries have gone from boom . . . to bust," states a widely circulated World Bank report published in 1995:

Public sectors have stopped hiring. Labor opportunities in the oil-rich economies are stagnant. And growth in the modern private sector has remained marginal in most countries. The region seems stuck in a low-productivity trap. Workers have paid dearly in falling real wages, soaring unemployment, and shattered expectations.[4]

Such a prognosis by a leading conservative global organization that advocates the interests of international business raises some important questions regarding the nature, extent, and depth of unemployment, income inequality, and poverty in the Middle East and North African region in recent decades.

This section provides data on a variety of economic and social indicators for countries of the MENA region, including GNP per capita, the structure of production, sectoral distribution of the labor force and employment structure, urbanization and growth of the urban population, unemployment, inflation, wages, poverty line, income distribution, and various health-related quality-of-life statistics.

Data on these and other similar socioeconomic indicators provided in this chapter illustrate the gravity of the situation in the Middle East and North African region.

Level of Economic Development

An important, though not sufficient, indicator of living standards for broad segments of the population is the level of development of the productive forces, which, in a significant way, determines the overall level of economic development. However, the unequal distribution of the productive forces, hence the unequal distribution of wealth, leads to increased income inequality and, depending on the severity of the case, this leads to heightened levels of poverty.

One dimension of the seriousness of this problem is revealed by the performance of the national economy as reflected in the gross national product per capita, as shown in Table 10.1. Data on GNP per capita for Egypt, Syria, Jordan, Lebanon, Algeria, Tunisia, and Morocco show a gap of some 10 to 20 times between non-oil-producing MENA countries and the advanced capitalist countries, with the extreme poles of $1,080 for Egypt at the one end and $40,940 for Japan at the other end.[5] The recalculation of these figures on a GNP PPP per capita basis (that is, using purchasing power

Table 10.1
Gross National Product Per Capita in Selected Middle Eastern and North African
Countries, 1996

Country	GNP per capita Average annual Dollars (1996)	Growth (%) (1995-96)	GNP PPP Per capita $ (1996)
Egypt	1,080	3.5	2,860
Syria	1,160	0.6	3,020
Iraq	n.a.	n.a.	n.a.
Jordan	1,650	2.8	3,570
Lebanon	2,970	0.6	6,060
Algeria	1,520	1.8	4,620
Tunisia	1,930	0.4	4,550
Morocco	1,290	10.4	3,320
Libya	n.a.	n.a.	n.a.

Note: GNP PPP is gross national product converted to international dollars using purchasing
   power parity rates. An international dollar has the same purchasing power over GNP as
   the U.S. dollar in the United States.

Source: The World Bank, World Development Indicators, 1998 (Washington, DC: The World
   Bank, 1998), pp. 12–14.

parity rates) does improve the situation somewhat, but the levels still remain low.

Another indicator of the general level of economic development is the
sectoral distribution of the gross domestic product. Data on the share of
various sectors of the economy as a percentage of the GDP of MENA
countries are provided in Table 10.2, which shows the relative distribution
of national income in agriculture, industry, and services.

The data show that while industry accounts for less than one-third of
the GDP in most of the MENA countries (except for Libya and Algeria,
where oil and natural gas, respectively, account for the bulk of industrial
activity), the services sector accounts for more than half (and in some cases,
such as Jordan and Lebanon, nearly two-thirds) of the GDP of most MENA
countries.

The continuing prevalence of the agricultural sector in national income,

Table 10.2
Structure of Output: Gross Domestic Product by Sector in Selected Middle Eastern and North African Countries, 1980 and 1996

Country	GDP ($ millions) 1980	GDP ($ millions) 1996	Agriculture(%) 1980	Agriculture(%) 1996	Industry(%) 1980	Industry(%) 1996	Services(%) 1980	Services(%) 1996	Manufacture(%) 1980	Manufacture(%) 1996
Egypt	22,913	67,691	18	17	37	32	45	51	12	24
Syria	13,062	17,587	20	n.a.	23	n.a.	56	n.a.	n.a.	n.a.
Iraq	47,562	n.a.	n.a.	n.a.	n.a.	n.a.	n.a.	n.a.	n.a.	n.a.
Jordan	3,962	7,343	8	5	28	30	64	64	13	16
Lebanon	n.a.	12,997	n.a.	12	n.a.	27	n.a.	61	n.a.	17
Algeria	42,345	45,699	10	13	54	48	36	38	9	8
Tunisia	8,742	19,516	14	14	31	28	55	58	12	18
Morocco	18,821	36,820	18	20	31	31	51	49	17	17
Libya	35,545	n.a.	2	n.a.	76	n.a.	22	n.a.	2	n.a.

Source: The World Bank, *World Development Indicators, 1998*, pp. 180–82; The World Bank, *World Development Report, 1997*, pp. 236–37.

the low level of industrialization, and the rapid expansion of the services sector have led to major distortions in the domestic economy that are a product of the manner in which the MENA countries have become incorporated into the global economy dominated by the advanced capitalist countries. The nature of this incorporation and the direction of development that has been pursued have, as a consequence, impacted the growth and expansion of the domestic labor force in different sectors of the national economies in the MENA region in a way that has made the situation worse when considering the effect of these developments on poverty and living conditions in many of these countries—an outcome that is closely related to the nature of employment and the labor force structure.

The Structure of the Labor Force and Employment

An aspect of the low level of industrialization in the MENA countries, relative to the advanced capitalist countries, is the prevalence of agriculture, which continues to be an important part of the national economies in the MENA region. Another aspect of this is the enormous growth of the service sector, where wages remain the lowest. Table 10.3 provides data on the sectoral distribution of the labor force for the MENA countries for the years 1980 and 1990.

As the data show, there has been a substantial growth in the labor force in six of the nine MENA countries. Moreover, while a substantial shift has occurred out of agriculture, the flow has been mostly into the services sector, with minimal expansion (and in some cases a drop) in the industrial sector.[6]

Given that the rural-to-urban shift has meant a swelling of the ranks of workers in the services sector, where wages are substantially lower than they are in industry, the rise in urban poverty in most of these countries during this period has been a product of this shift from the agricultural to the services sector.[7]

Table 10.4 provides a breakdown of the economically active population by gender and economic activity for the years 1980 and 1994. It shows that in most cases women are primarily concentrated in agriculture and services, while men continue to be concentrated in the industrial sector. While there are some notable exceptions, such as Tunisia and Lebanon, where women constitute an important segment of the industrial work force, women in the service sector constitute more than two-thirds of the economically active female population in Lebanon and Libya, and more than half that in Jordan and Iraq. Still, the great percentage of women in the labor force in Syria, Morocco, and Algeria, followed by Egypt, Tunisia, Jordan, and Iraq, continue to labor in the agricultural sector (see Table 10.4).

The strong presence of women in the agricultural and service sectors of

Table 10.3
Sectoral Distribution of the Labor Force in Selected Middle Eastern and North African Countries, 1980, 1990, and 1996

Country	Total (millions) (1980)	Total (millions) (1996)	Agriculture(%) (1980)	Agriculture(%) (1990)	Industry(%) (1980)	Industry(%) (1990)	Services (%) (1980)	Services (%) (1990)
Egypt	14	22	61	43	17	23	22	34
Syria	2	4	39	34	28	24	33	42
Iraq	4	6	n.a.	30	n.a.	22	n.a.	48
Jordan	1	1	24	21	32	32	44	47
Lebanon	1	1	13	5	26	22	61	73
Algeria	5	9	36	26	27	31	37	43
Tunisia	2	3	39	28	30	32	31	40
Morocco	7	11	56	45	20	25	24	30
Libya	1	1	n.a.	18	n.a.	31	n.a.	51

Note: Data on the labor force in the services sector calculated on the basis of World Bank data on the labor force in agriculture and industry.

Source: World Bank, *World Development Report, 1997* (New York: Oxford University Press, 1997), pp. 220–221; World Bank, *World Development Indicators, 1998* (Washington, DC: World Bank, 1998), pp. 50–52.

Table 10.4
The Structure of Employment in Selected Middle Eastern and North African Countries, by Gender and Economic Activity, 1980 and 1994

Country	Adult (15+) economic activity rate, 1994		Agriculture				Industry				Services			
	Male	Female	% of economically active male population (1980)	(1994)	% of economically active female population (1980)	(1994)	% of economically active male population (1980)	(1994)	% of economically active female population (1980)	(1994)	% of economically active male population (1980)	(1994)	% of economically active female population (1980)	(1994)
Egypt	71	22	43	32	8	43	20	23	10	9	32	38	56	31
Syria	77	16	27	22	78	69	35	30	7	6	39	49	15	25
Iraq	77	23	21	12	62	39	24	19	11	9	55	69	27	52
Jordan	78	10	11	10	58	41	27	28	3	4	62	63	39	55
Lebanon	74	25	13	6	20	10	29	34	21	22	58	59	59	68
Algeria	75	8	27	18	69	57	33	38	6	7	40	44	25	36
Tunisia	79	26	33	22	53	42	30	33	32	32	37	44	16	26
Morocco	81	21	48	35	72	63	23	28	14	19	29	37	14	18
Libya	77	9	16	7	63	28	29	27	3	5	55	66	34	68

Source: United Nations, Economic and Social Commission for Western Asia, *Survey of Economic and Social Developments in the ESCWA Region, 1996–1997* (New York: United Nations, 1997), p. 140; World Bank, *World Development Indicators, 1998* (Washington, DC: World Bank, 1998), pp. 58–60.

most MENA countries indicates the lopsided nature of employment and explains the prevalence of high levels of poverty, especially among women, as wage levels in these sectors are much lower than in industry.[8]

The increasing level of women's participation in paid employment in the MENA region, and in the Third World in general, indicates the growing feminization of the labor force and the changing role of women in the international division of labor—a development that has immense implications on the employment structure, gender roles, and the nature and extent of poverty.[9]

To place these data in proper perspective, we next turn to an analysis of population growth and urbanization in the MENA countries.

Population Growth and Urbanization

There has been a tremendous growth of population in most countries of the Middle East and North African region, with average annual growth rates ranging from 1.9 to 4.3 percent, and a cumulative total of 50 percent or more for most of the MENA countries for the 16-year period from 1980 to 1996 (see Table 10.5).

Consequently, this has meant a swelling of the ranks of the urban population, which has grown at a much higher rate, due in large part to the added impact of the rural-to-urban migration, which has continued at an alarming pace during the decade of the 1980s and in the early 1990s. Added to this is the high growth rate of the working-age population during the 1970s to the 1990s, such that the Middle East and North Africa region has become the region with the fastest-growing working-age population in the world.[10]

Table 10.5 provides data on the urban population over the period 1980 to 1996. In most cases, we find a doubling of the urban population during this 16-year period, such that by 1996 three-quarters or more of the total population of Lebanon, Libya, and Iraq and more than half the population of Jordan, Tunisia, Algeria, Morocco, and Syria lived in urban areas—a situation similar to that of the advanced capitalist countries, but without the necessary economic infrastructure to support this rate of growth and expansion.

The urban population explosion has further contributed to the rise in unemployment, decline in wages, and increase in income inequality and poverty affecting millions of people in cities throughout the Middle East and North African region. Data on these and other related aspects of life in the MENA countries are presented and discussed in the next section.

Unemployment, Low Wages, and Income Inequality

In looking at the unemployment situation, we find that the MENA region has the highest rate of unemployment in the world, averaging 15 percent of the labor force in 1993.

Table 10.5
Urbanization in Selected Middle Eastern and North African Countries, 1980 and 1996

Country	Total Population Average annual			Urban Population Average				
	Millions		growth rate (%)	Millions		As % of total Population		Annual growth rate
	(1980)	(1996)	(1980-96)	(1980)	(1996)	(1980)	(1996)	(1980-95)
Egypt	41	59	2.3	17.9	26.6	44	45	2.5
Syria	9	15	3.2	4.1	7.6	47	53	4.1
Iraq	13	21	3.1	8.5	16.0	66	75	n.a.
Jordan	2	4	4.3	1.3	3.1	60	72	5.8
Lebanon	3	4	1.9	2.2	3.6	73	88	3.7
Algeria	19	29	2.7	8.1	16.2	43	56	4.5
Tunisia	6	9	2.2	3.3	5.7	51	63	3.0
Morocco	19	27	2.1	8.0	14.2	41	53	3.3
Libya	3	5	3.3	2.1	4.4	69	86	n.a.

Source: World Bank, *World Development Report, 1997* (New York: Oxford University Press, 1997), pp. 230–231; World Bank, *World Development Indicators, 1998* (Washington, DC: World Bank, 1998), pp. 42–44, 154–156.

Table 10.6
Unemployment Rate in Selected Middle Eastern and North African Countries, 1990 and 1996

Country	Total Unemployment (percent of total labor force)	
	(1990)	(1996)
Egypt	8.6	9.4
Syria	6.8[a]	12.0[b]
Iraq	n.a.	n.a.
Jordan	16.8	13.0
Lebanon	n.a.	20.0
Algeria	19.7	27.9
Tunisia	15.0[a]	16.2[c]
Morocco	15.4	16.0
Libya	n.a.	n.a.

Note: (a) 1991; (b) 1997; (c) 1993.

Source: World Bank, *World Development Indicators, 1998* (Washington, DC: World Bank, 1998); U.S. Congress, Senate, Committee on Foreign Relations, *Country Reports on Economic Policy and Trade Practices* (Washington, DC: U.S. Government Printing Office, 1998), pp. 329, 338, 351, 362, 377; U.S. Department of Commerce, STAT-USA, Country Commercial Guides, Lebanon: Domestic Economy.

Focusing on various countries in the region, we find that nearly all MENA countries had high double-digit unemployment rates throughout the 1990s, ranging from 12 to 28 percent of the labor force in 1996—the latest year for which we have data (see Table 10.6).

The rate of inflation has been another concern as a factor contributing to the rise of poverty in the MENA region. During the period 1990 to 1996, most countries in our sample registered double-digit average annual inflation rates, ranging from 11 percent to 37 percent. Only Jordan, Tunisia, and Morocco registered rates below 6 percent (see Table 10.7).

Table 10.8 provides data on trends in real manufacturing wages in most MENA countries for the period 1970 to the early 1990s. As the data show, except for the period 1975–80, real manufacturing wages have been declining across the region during much of the 1980s, such that by 1990–92 they had further dropped to the 1970 levels.

Table 10.7
Inflation Rate in Selected Middle Eastern and North African Countries, 1990–1996

Country	Consumer Price Index (average annual % growth) (1990-96)	Food Price Index (average annual % growth) (1990-96)
Egypt	12.4	9.5
Syria	11.3	8.9
Iraq	n.a.	n.a.
Jordan	4.2	4.1
Lebanon	36.8	n.a.
Algeria	27.0	28.6
Tunisia	5.3	5.0
Morocco	5.5	8.4
Libya	25.0[a]	n.a.

Note: [a] 1993.

Source: World Bank, World Development Indicators, 1998 (Washington, DC: World Bank, 1998), pp. 230–232.

An inevitable consequence of high unemployment and declining real wages within a high-inflationary environment has been the maldistribution of income, which has contributed to increased polarization and a rise in the poverty population. As Table 10.9 shows, during the early 1990s, the top 10 percent of income earners in Egypt, Jordan, Algeria, Tunisia, and Morocco (countries for which we have data) accounted for 27 to 35 percent of total income, and the top 20 percent of income earners accounted for 41 to 50 percent of all income. The distribution at the lower end of the income spectrum is similarly skewed in the opposite direction, such that the bottom 10 percent of income earners accounted for between 2.3 and 3.9 percent of all income and the bottom 20 percent accounted for between 5.9 and 8.7 percent of all income (see Table 10.9).

These figures approximate the pattern of income distribution in the advanced capitalist countries, except that at the higher levels of income (in the top 10 to 20 percent range) the distribution is more skewed in favor of the wealthy in the MENA region. In both instances, however, it is clear that a small segment of high income earners account for a disproportionately larger share of total income than those in the lower end of society.[11]

Table 10.8
Index of Real Manufacturing Wages in Selected Middle Eastern and North African Countries, 1970–1992
(1970 = 100)

Country	1970	1975	1980	1985	1990	1991	1992
Egypt	100	116	155	181	127	124	114
Syria	100	78	136	123	95	92	n.a.
Iraq	n.a.	n.a.	n.a.	n.a.	n.a.	n.a.	n.a.
Jordan	100	96	157	157	125	115	111
Lebanon	n.a.	n.a.	n.a.	n.a.	n.a.	n.a.	n.a.
Algeria	100	87	89	80	76	n.a.	n.a.
Tunisia	n.a.	n.a.	n.a.	100	91	94	100
Morocco	100	n.a.	113	93	86	88	90
Libya	n.a.	n.a.	n.a.	n.a.	n.a.	n.a.	n.a.

Source: World Bank 1995.

Table 10.9
Distribution of Income or Consumption in Selected Middle Eastern and North African Countries,
Various Survey Years, 1986–1995

| Country | Survey year | Percentage share of income or consumption | | | | | | | |
		Lowest 10%	Lowest 20%	Second quintile	Third quintile	Fourth quintile	Highest 20%	Highest 10%
Egypt	1991	3.9	8.7	12.5	16.3	21.4	41.1	26.7
Syria	n.a.	n.a.	n.a.	n.a.	n.a.	n.a.	n.a.	n.a.
Iraq	n.a.	n.a.	n.a.	n.a.	n.a.	n.a.	n.a.	n.a.
Jordan	1991	2.4	5.9	9.8	13.9	20.3	50.1	34.7
Lebanon	n.a.	n.a.	n.a.	n.a.	n.a.	n.a.	n.a.	n.a.
Algeria	1995	2.8	7.0	11.6	16.1	22.7	42.6	26.8
Tunisia	1990	2.3	5.9	10.4	15.3	22.1	46.3	30.7
Morocco	1990	2.8	6.6	10.5	15.0	21.7	46.3	30.5
Libya	n.a.	n.a.	n.a.	n.a.	n.a.	n.a.	n.a.	n.a.

Source: World Bank, *World Development Report, 1997* (New York: Oxford University Press, 1997), pp. 222–223; World Bank, *World Development Indicators, 1998* (Washington, DC: World Bank, 1998), pp. 68–70.

This raises some serious questions regarding the living standards of low-income groups, for it has a direct impact on the nature and extent of poverty in the Middle East and North African region. In the next section of the chapter I address these questions and draw some conclusions on the nature, extent, and causes of poverty in the MENA region.

The Nature and Extent of Poverty

Poverty in the Middle East and North Africa, and in the Third World in general, has reached crisis proportions. Structural adjustment policies imposed by international lending agencies, intended to promote a favorable economic environment for global business interests, have further exacerbated the precarious position of marginal populations and led to greater poverty throughout the region.[12]

Table 10.10 provides data that shed light on the situation regarding the level of poverty in the MENA region to a considerable extent. As the data show, in the early 1990s the percentage of people living below the poverty line, as calculated by national governments, ranged from 12 to 14 percent in the North African countries, 19 to 23 percent in Lebanon, Egypt, Syria, and Jordan, and 45 percent in Iraq (see Table 10.10).

In looking at data on the percentage of people living on less than $2 a day at 1985 international prices, adjusted for purchasing power parity, the figures become more alarming. In Egypt, for example, 52 percent of the population was living on less than $2 a day in the early 1990s. In Jordan and Tunisia nearly one-quarter of the total population lived below the poverty line during this period. The figures for Morocco and Algeria are not much better at around 20 and 18 percent, respectively. If the national poverty data are any indication, a commensurate average percentage increase would put well over half of Iraq's total population below the poverty line (a situation due in large part to the devastation inflicted on Iraq by the Gulf War of 1991).

The crippling effects of poverty on broad segments of the population can be delineated by data on health-related indicators, such as life expectancy, malnutrition, infant mortality, and other related dimensions of health, which are given in Table 10.11.

In looking at 1996 life expectancy data for men and women for countries in the MENA region, we find that except for Iraq (which was greatly affected by the Gulf War), the average age for men is 67 years and for women 70 years—levels that are much lower than those in the advanced capitalist countries. Moreover, since these figures are for the population as a whole, and are not broken down by income and wealth, the longevity figures are bound to be even worse for the poverty population (as compared with well-off segments of society). Longevity data based on income would provide a

Table 10.10
Poverty Levels in Selected Middle Eastern and North African Countries, 1990–1991

Country	Poverty Line National [a] (1990-91)	Poverty Line International [b] (1990-91)
Egypt	22.0	51.9
Syria	22.0	n.a.
Iraq	45.0	n.a.
Jordan	23.0	23.5[c]
Lebanon	19.0	n.a.
Algeria	12.2[d]	17.6
Tunisia	14.1	22.7
Morocco	13.1	19.6
Libya	n.a.	n.a.

Note: Data for the national poverty line in Egypt, Syria, Iraq, Jordan, and Lebanon are for 1992.
   [a] Percentage of the population living below poverty line deemed appropriate for the country by its authorities;
   [b] Percentage of the population living on less than $2 a day at 1985 international prices, adjusted for purchasing power parity; (c) 1992; (d) 1988.

Source: World Bank, World Development Indicators, 1998 (Washington, DC: World Bank, 1998), pp. 64–66. United Nations, Economic and Social Commission for Western Asia, Survey of Economic and Social Development in the ESCWA Region, 1995 (New York: United Nations, 1996), p. 149.

better assessment of life expectancy for different segments of the population, but such data are not readily available.

The prevalence of child malnutrition, however, gives a good measure of the general health level of the broader population, which would more closely correspond to the position of those in poverty. According to available data for the period 1990 to 1996, 9 to 10 percent of children under five were malnourished in most countries of the MENA region. These data can be supplemented by infant mortality rates and under-five mortality rates to obtain a clearer picture of life affecting the poverty population.

As can be seen in Table 10.11, infant mortality rates for MENA countries range between 25 and 53 per thousand live births—except for Iraq, where the rate is 101 per thousand (due primarily to the effects of the UN sanc-

Table 10.11
Health Indicators for Selected Middle Eastern and North African Countries, 1990–1996

Country	Life expectancy at birth (years) (1996) (Male)	(Female)	Prevalence of child malnutrition (% of children under 5) (1990-96)	Infant mortality rate (per 1000 live births) (1996)	Under-5 mortality rate (per 1000)(1996)
Egypt	64	67	9	53	66
Syria	66	71	n.a.	31	36
Iraq	60	63	12	101	136
Jordan	69	72	10	30	35
Lebanon	68	71	9	31	36
Algeria	68	72	10	32	39
Tunisia	69	71	9	30	35
Morocco	64	68	10	53	67
Libya	66	70	5	25	30

Source: World Bank, *World Development Indicators, 1998* (Washington, DC: World Bank, 1998), pp. 16–18, 20–22, 64–66, 100–102.

tions, which have caused shortages of medical supplies). For most countries, however, infant mortality rates fall between 30 and 32 per thousand live births. Even if we were to take this last set of data as our base, the rates for the MENA countries still remain five or six times that of advanced capitalist countries.[13]

The under-five mortality rate in the MENA region is even worse, ranging between 30 and 39 per thousand in 1996, with Egypt and Morocco showing the highest rates at 66 and 67 per thousand, respectively, and Iraq at an alarming 136 per thousand—again, due in large part to the effects of the Gulf War. These figures are substantially above the rates in the advanced capitalist countries where they range between 6 and 8 per thousand, with most registering a 6 per thousand rate—a difference of 5 to 11 times![14]

These health-related data, together with data on the labor force structure, unemployment, wages, income distribution, and poverty, give a good indication of the position of the great majority of the working population, which suffer from poverty and destitution in countries that are, paradoxically, endowed with resources that place them among the richest countries in the world—a situation that can only be explained in terms of the system of production and distribution of wealth and income in these countries. It is the maldistribution of national wealth and income that, in the end, explains the material disparity among people, which, as has been the case in the MENA region, leads to further social and economic polarization.[15]

CONCLUSION: THE ROOTS OF POVERTY

To conclude, I have argued here that poverty is the outcome of unequal socioeconomic relations of production and distribution, and that the accumulation of wealth at one poll has meant the accumulation of misery and impoverishment at the other poll. The great wealth of the dominant classes today has come about through the intensified exploitation of wage labor. And this is true for countries of the MENA region. Under a market-oriented capitalist economy, unemployment and low wages are characteristic features of contemporary capitalist society that are systemic and cannot be changed in any fundamental way short of a major social transformation.

Poverty today cannot be readily eradicated as long as a disproportionate segment of the wealth created by the working class ends up in the hands of the owners of capital, with only a fraction of that wealth returned to the workers in the form of wages—and that wage is only slightly above the minimum subsistence required for the reproduction of labor—while the rest ends up in the pockets of the capitalists in the form of profits.

We have seen that the condition of the laboring population in the Middle East and North African region has significantly deteriorated in recent decades, and that such deterioration is manifested in high rates of unemployment, declining real wages, and a general drop in the standard of living of the great majority of the population.

What the future holds for working people in the Middle East and North Africa will be an outcome of what they decide to do—to endure the difficult conditions that chain them to perpetual poverty and destitution, or to organize and express their will through increased political activity aimed at improving their immediate condition, while at the same time charting a course that advances their long-term class-based interests in effecting social change and social transformation across the Middle East and North African region.

NOTES

This is a revised version of a paper presented at the Conference on Earnings Inequality, Unemployment, and Poverty in the Middle East and North Africa at the School of Business, Lebanese American University, Byblos, Lebanon, November 5–7, 1998.

1. See Berberoglu (1994) for an analysis of the origins and development of social classes and class conflict as an outcome of unequal socioeconomic and political relations.

2. A theoretical discussion on income and wealth inequality as the basis of class inequality is provided in Szymanski (1983).

3. For an analysis of the nature and contradictions of development in Middle Eastern and North African countries, see Richards and Waterbury.

4. World Bank 1995, p. 1.

5. See World Bank, *World Development Indicators* (1998, pp. 12–14).

6. The drop in industrial production in Lebanon and Syria between 1980 and 1990 can be attributed to the civil war in Lebanon and Syria's role in it during this period, which was exacerbated by Israel's invasion and occupation of Lebanon in 1982 and in the subsequent period, when much of industrial activity had come to a virtual halt for a number of years.

7. The problem is compounded by the fact that much of the activity within the service sector is directly linked to the growth and expansion of the informal sector, where a precarious hand-to-mouth existence at below-subsistence levels is the order of the day.

8. This is similar to the situation in the advanced capitalist countries, where wages of farm workers and service workers are much lower than that in industry, due in large part to the lack of unionization and the effects of deindustrialization stemming from a drop in the wages of previously unionized high-wage industrial workers who are now employed in nonunion, low-wage, service-oriented occupations. While the logic of the shift toward the service sector is different in the two cases, the low wages prevalent in the service sector of both Third World and advanced capitalist countries yield the same result in increased levels of poverty and destitution.

9. See Moghadam (1998); Cagatay and Ozler (1995); Stichter and Papart (1990).

10. World Bank (1995, p. 8).

11. See Tabatabai (1996). For data on income distribution in the advanced capitalist countries, in particular the United States, see Jerry Kloby (1993, pp. 27–42).

12. See Van Eeghan (1998); Vander Hoeven (1995).

13. See World Bank, *World Development Indicators* (1998).

14. Ibid.

15. For an analysis of the political implications of socioeconomic polarization in countries of the Middle East and North African region, see Berberoglu (1999).

REFERENCES

Berberoglu, Berch (1989). *Power and Stability in the Middle-East*. London: Zed Books.

———(1994). *Class Structure and Social Transformation*. New York: Praeger Publishers.

———(1999). *Political Turmoil in the Middle-East*. New York: State University of New York Press.

Cagaty, Nilufer, and Sule Ozler (1995). "Feminization of the Labor Force: The Effects of Long-Term Development and Structural Adjustment," *World Development* 23 (11): 1883–1894.

Kloby, Jerry (1993). "Increasing Class Polarization in the United States: The Growth of Wealth and Income Inequality," in Berch Berberoglu, ed. *Critical Perspectives in Sociology*, 2nd edition. Dubuque, IA: Kendal-Hunt Publishing Company.

Moghadam, Valentine (1998). *Women, Work and Economic Reform in the Middle-East and North Africa*. Boulder, CO: Lynne Rienner Publishers.

Richards, Allen and John Waterbury (1996). *A Political Economy of the Middle-East*. Boulder, CO: Westview Press.

Stichter, Sharon and Jane Papart, eds. (1990). *Women, Unemployment and the Family in the International Division of Labor*. Philadelphia: Temple University Press.

Szymanski, Albert (1983). *Class Structure: A Critical Perspective*. New York: Praeger Publishers.

Tabatabai, Hamid (1996). *Statistics on Poverty and Income Distribution: An ILO Compendium of Data*. Geneva: International Labor Office.

Vander Hoeven, Rolph (1995). "Structural Adjustment, Poverty and Macroeconomic Policy," in Gerry Rogers and Rolph Vander Hoeven, eds. *New Approaches to Poverty Analysis and Policy* III. Geneva: International Labor Office.

Van Eeghan, Willem (1998). "Poverty in the Middle-East and North Africa," in Nemat Shafik, ed. *Prospects for Middle-Eastern and North African Economies*. New York: St. Martin's Press.

World Bank (1995). "Will Arab Workers Prosper or Be Left Out in the Twenty-First Century?" *Regional Perspectives on World Development Report*. Washington, DC: World Bank.

———(1998). *World Development Indicators*. Washington, DC: World Bank.

11

Ideology, Economic Restructuring, and Women's Work in Iran (1976–1996)

Fatemeh E. Moghadem

INTRODUCTION

This chapter examines women's labor market participation in Iran during the last three decades, with a focus on the postrevolutionary (1980–1996) period. The period under the study will be divided into three subperiods, each corresponding to a distinct economic growth/structural change and gender policy approach by the state. During the 1970s, oil revenues were rising, the Iranian economy was rapidly growing, and the public sector was expanding. The explicit policy of the state was the utilization of female labor referred to in official government documents as an "untapped supply of labor" for economic growth. This period was followed by the Islamic Revolution (1978–1979) and the subsequent rise of the Islamic government.

The revolution created changes in property relations, and the state undertook confiscation and control of many large industrial and agricultural operations. The state also assumed an active role in rationing and subsidizing food and other necessities. Thus there was an increase in the scope of state intervention in the economy. The period of the 1980s was also accompanied by a substantial decline in Iran's oil revenues. Thus a combination of factors—falling oil revenues, insecurity and uncertainty in property relations, and its impact on investment, as well as a general state of inefficiency in the management of state and para-state (foundations) operations in Iran—generated a deep recession. This period is also marked by a strong attempt by the government to Islamize the society. Thus female employment policy was designed in this context, and constituted a reversal of what was perceived to be the "immoral and Westernized" policies of the Shah. In this context, women's primary occupation was perceived to be wifehood and motherhood, and in the labor market in female occupations such as teaching and health-related services.

In general, Iran has pursued a policy of normalization and reconstruction of the economy since the death of Ayatollah Khomeini in 1989. This policy includes a liberalization and privatization component: returning or selling state and para-state firms to the private sector, reduction in subsidies, encouragement of foreign investment, and a failed attempt to float the exchange rate system. While the explicit ideology of the state continues to be that of Islamization of the society, there is an ongoing process of debate, reinterpretation, and adjustment of religious texts to what is perceived to be the requirements of a modern society. Thus the proper role and rights of women in an Islamic society have become subject to controversy and change. In comparison to the earlier years, the ideology and policy approach is more open and flexible in relation to women and their role in society and in the labor market.

This chapter argues that the structural changes in the economy resulting from growth, migration, urbanization, and education have impacted women's participation. Furthermore, state policy and ideology have had a significant impact on labor force participation and occupational segregation. I will, however, argue that the limited scope of the structural adjustment policies, together with the specific institutional, demographic, and ideological characteristics of the Iranian economy in the 1990s, have not allowed for a significant impact stemming from privatization and liberalization policies.

FRAMEWORK

In this study, I will focus on a number of demographic, economic, and structural variables that according to other global studies have impacts on female labor. I will then identify variables that were subject to explicit gender-biased ideological changes, and will separate them from those that changed primarily through economic and structural factors. Within the latter category, I will aim at identifying impacts that could stem from privatization and liberalization policies. In doing so, I am aware of the data limitations and the difficulties in separating ideological from structural, economic, and liberalization factors. Admittedly, the approach adopted in this chapter is exploratory.

Global studies on female labor have found significant relationships with the following variables: education, fertility, age of marriage, growth and structural changes in the economy—urbanization growth of service and industrial sectors, and changes in the agricultural sector.[1] The following factors have positive impacts: increase in the level of educational attainments of women, decline in fertility, and increase in the age of marriage for women.[2] In the case of developing countries, however, increase in the years of schooling may initially cause a decrease in the labor participation, as a larger percentage of young women will go to school instead of participating in family or low-wage labor. The impact of growth on participation is less clear, is not always positive, and there is no consensus on trends associated with development on women's labor force participation.[3] While there are indications that sluggish growth may contribute to a decrease in the relative share of female employment, empirical findings are not conclusive.[4] Liberalization and privatization policies may positively affect participation as foreign investment and growth of export sector may employ women. The negative impact stems from the downsizing of the state enterprises and in cutting education, health, and other social services that employ women.

Women participating in the labor force are clustered around certain jobs and their entry in other types is usually slow. In general two factors are considered as major contributors to occupational segregation: human capital—education and skills—and discrimination. Based on social and cultural perceptions concerning the appropriate role of women in society and the job market, women may be discriminated against.[5]

In this chapter, I will examine labor participation in the context of the following factors: changes in the level and structure of the Iranian economy, education, fertility, age of marriage, cultural and legal factors, and government ideology and policy, including privatization and liberalization. I will demonstrate that the postrevolutionary changes in fertility, age of marriage, legal status of women, access to higher education, and emphasis on traditional cultural values are part and parcel of a broad gender ideology. As the ideological factor was more pronounced during the earlier stages of the revolution, the impact was stronger at that period. Over time, however, the ideological factor has become modified, and the impact is less pronounced.

The empirical evidence presented here is based primarily on five available cross-section population surveys for 1956, 1966, 1976, 1986, and 1996. I have also used the results of a sample survey for 1991. It is worth noting that in all surveys, the data underestimate female labor participation and the design of the questions leads to an underestimation of unpaid labor in agriculture.[6] However, since the same approach is used for all surveys, the cross-section data are comparable. Also note that the inadequacy of the data does not allow for statistical tests of significance to be carried out. Thus the study is descriptive and exploratory.

Unless otherwise stated, I have used the same definitions and categories of labor force as those provided by the *ILO Yearbook of Labour Statistics*.

OVERVIEW

Iran experienced rapid growth during the oil boom of the 1960s and 1970s. Since the revolution, however, performance of the economy has been generally poor, with modest improvements since 1989. A somewhat similar pattern is observed in female employment. The total number of active women in the population of 10 years and older was about 1.45 million in 1976. It fell to 1.31 million in 1986, rose to 1.63 million in 1991, and to 2.0 in 1996. The percentage shares of active women in total female population of 10 years and older were 12.9, 8.2, 8.7, and 9.1 for 1976, 1986, 1991, and 1996, respectively. These numbers give the impression that economic factors had an impact on participation. For the period 1976–1986, in which the largest decline is observed, however, male employment grew by an average annual rate of nearly 4 percent (Table 11.1).[7] Thus female labor as a percentage of total active labor declined from 20 in 1976 to 10 in 1986, as the share of male labor increased (Table 11.2). The decline is clearly gender biased, and cannot be explained solely by economic stagnation. We need to explore the changes beyond economic growth.

LEGAL AND IDEOLOGICAL ASPECTS OF FEMALE EMPLOYMENT

Female labor laws did not change significantly during the postrevolutionary period. Comparisons of the pre- and postrevolutionary labor laws pertaining to work at night, maternity leave, breast feeding rights, day-care facilities, and the like indicate marginal changes in positive as well as negative directions, and the laws are generally protective.[8] Taken at its face value, the Constitution of the Islamic Republic does not appear gender biased. It states that no one can be forced into a specific type of occupation, and no one is allowed to exploit others in the job market. Irrespective of race, language, and sex people are entitled to equal access to voluntary employment, provided such access is not contrary to Islamic principles, public welfare, and the rights of others.[9] However, the reference to Islamic principles can be gender biased. Islamic ideology emphasizes the complementary aspects of the biological differences between men and women, and considers family—not individual—as the basic social unit. It is argued that the objective of an Islamic state is to bring about maximum social harmony.[10] In spite of an appearance of gender equality in the choice of occupation, the qualification concerning adherence to Islamic principles can be used as an obstacle for equal access. It can be argued that the proper place for women is at home, men as heads of households should be given priority to women in employment, and women are biologically unfit for certain occupations. Indeed a large segment of the conservative tradition-

Table 11.1
Employment and Education of Population of 10 Years and Older

	1956	1966	1976	1986	1991	1996
Total Population (1000 persons)	12785	17000	23002	32874	38655	45401
Male	6542	8794	11796	16841	19997	23022
Female	6242	8206	11206	16033	18658	22379
% in Total Male						
Active	83.9	77.4	70.8	68.3	65.5	60.8
Employed	81.5	70.2	64.3	59.5	59.3	55.6
Student	7.6	15.1	23.5	23.0	26.9	29.0
% in Total Female						
Active	9.2	12.6	12.9	8.2	8.7	9.1
Employed	9.2	11.5	10.8	6.1	6.6	8.7
Home-Maker*	79.5	73.3	68.8	68.7	63.7	58.4
Student	3.0	7.4	14.8	16.6	22.0	26.6
% in Total Urban Male						
Active	78.5	69.2	63.9	66.8	64.5	58.5
Employed	74.6	65.1	60.7	57.7	58.6	53.6
Student	16.1	23.7	29.6	24.5	27.3	30.9
% in Total Urban Female						
Active	9.3	9.9	9.0	8.3	8.9	8.1
Employed	9.2	9.6	8.5	5.1	6.9	7.1
Home-Maker	77.0	68.1	64.2	66.5	61.5	56.3
Student	8.4	16.4	23.7	20.5	25.2	30.9
% in Rural Male						
Active	86.6	82.9	77.9	70.3	66.9	64.5
Employed	85.0	73.6	68.1	61.8	60.1	58.9
Student	3.4	9.4	17.2	21.2	26.6	25.9
% in Total Rural Female						
Active	9.2	14.3	16.6	7.9	8.6	10.7
Employed	9.1	12.7	13.0	6.3	6.1	9.6
Home-Maker	80.8	76.7	73.0	71.8	66.6	61.9
Student	0.4	1.7	6.5	11.8	17.6	19.7

Note: *This category is not exclusive to housewives and includes family members whose primary occupation is homemaking.

Source: Markaz-e Amar-e Iran, *Salnameh Amarye Keshvar*: 1369 (1990), Markaze Iran Preliminary results of 1991 population Survey. Markaz-e Amar-e Iran, *Sarshomary-e Omoomy-e Nofus of Maskan 1375: Natiyeg-e Tafssili.*

alists has persistently argued that women's labor should be spent exclusively in the family.

At the outset, one of the main ideological objectives of the revolution was to end what was perceived by the clergy as un-Islamic and "morally decadent" public appearance and position of women under the Pahlavi regime, and a desire to return to "true Islamic values" that would "elevate" the social and moral position of women. Thus the Islamic regime intro-

Table 11.2
Active Population

	1956	1966	1976	1986	1996
Males	90	87	80	90	87
Females	10	13	20	10	13
Total	100	100	100	100	100

Source: ILO Yearbook of Labor Statistics; Markaz-e Amar-e Iran, Sarshomary-e Omoomy-e Nofus of Maskan 1375; Natiyeg-e Tafssili.

duced forced veiling and segregation in public places. This change was accompanied by considerable rhetoric and revolutionary fervor. During the 1980s, many women working under the Pahlavi regime were viewed as morally decadent. The government undertook a campaign to expel them from work, and to purify (paksazy) the government offices and factories. The government also used early retirement incentives to persuade women to leave the job market. A law passed in 1979 allowed workers to ask for early retirement after 15—instead of 25—years of service. Although the law included male as well as female workers, it persuaded a larger number of women than men to retire.[11] Data concerning the impact of these policies are not available, but the anecdotal evidence suggests a significant impact.

In recent years, however, the work environment has become more friendly to women.[12] In contrast to the earlier period when day-care facilities in some government institutions were closed down,[13] many workplaces have now set up day-care systems for their employees. A law passed in 1990 allows women to retire after 20, instead of a minimum of 25, years in government service. While this law shows a pattern similar to the earlier policies of keeping women at home, it was a response to the demands of women workers in the public sector, and was a recognition of the double burden of women. Furthermore, the law explicitly states that no woman should be coerced to retirement, and that the law is applicable only if a woman voluntarily asks for early retirement.[14] From the discussions advanced by working women in Zan-e Rooz, it is evident that women fought to have this law passed by the majles.[15] This law also indicates that in spite of modifications in ideology and in treatment of working women, the system continues to consider household labor the primary occupation of a Muslim woman.

Ideology, Age of Marriage, and Fertility

After the Islamic revolution, there were important changes in the family law. Under the previous regime, the legal age for girls to become eligible for marriage was initially 16, and was raised to 18—although 16-year-old women could marry provided a special permit was obtained. Following the early Islamic practices, the present regime reduced the legal age to 9 years,

Table 11.3

Female Population by Age Categories and by Marital Status

Age	1976*		1986		1991		1996	
	Total 1000 Persons	Married at Least Once** %	Total 1000 Persons	Married at Least Once %	Total 1000 Persons	Married at Least Once %	Total 1000 Persons	Married at Least Once %
10-14	3034	0.00	2704	2.43	3619	2.21	1739	2.19
15-19	1782	34.25	2456	34.29	2831	25.46	1401	20.00
20-24	1451	79.31	2056	74.50	2414	68.37	1044	59.61

Note: *Includes married, widowed, and divorced.

　　**There is a total recorded number of 112, or 0.00369 percent, of the total in the age category.

Source: Markaz-e Amar-e Iran, *Sarshomary-e Omoomy-e Nofus va Maskan*, Kolle Keshvar, Sale 1355; Markaz-e Amar-e Iran, *Sarshomary-e Omoomy-e Nofus va Maskan*, Kolle Keshvar Sale 1365: Natayege Tafssili; Markaz-e Amar-e Iran, Iran; Statistical Yearbook, 1370; Markaz-e Amar-e Iran, *Sarshomary-e Omoomy-e Nofus va Maskan*, Kolle Kesh var Sale 1375: Natayeg-e Tafssili.

provided the girl had reached puberty and a special court and the girl's guardian approved the marriage. These courts, however, are lenient in approving such permits.[16]

As indicated in Table 11.3, in 1976, the total recorded number of married girls in the age category of 10 to 14 was 112, which as a percentage share of all girls in that age category is negligible. However, this share was about 2.4, 2.2, and 2.2 percent for 1986, 1991, and 1996 respectively. If we compare the age category of 15 to 19 years, the percentage shares are almost identical for 1976 and 1986; however, the shares are declining for 1991 and 1996. Furthermore, the data suggest a declining trend in the percentage share of married women in the age category of 20 to 24. Thus the numbers indicate a sharp decrease in the age of first marriage for 1986, a factor that contributed to a decline in female labor participation. Although the practice of child marriage is still significant, the data show a general tendency toward an increase in the age of first marriage for 1991 and 1996.[17] Fertility is another factor affecting female employment. Population growth figures are about 2.7 percent annual average for 1966–1976.[18] For 1976–1986, the average annual growth was estimated to be 3.9 percent.[19] This rate declined to less than 2 percent for 1986–1996 (a lower 1.5 percent for 1991–1996).[20] Some scholars have challenged the accuracy of the 1976–1986 population growth, and have estimated it to range between 3.3 and 3.6 percent.[21] Nevertheless, there is consensus that Iran experienced an explosive population growth during the initial years of the establishment of the Islamic Republic.

These changes reflect a change in government policy. After the revolution, abortion became illegal and other measures of population control were considered immoral, against the principles of an Islamic society, and an attempt by the Western countries to reduce the number of Muslims in the world.[22] The revolution vowed to protect the oppressed (*mostazafeer*), promises of free urban housing for the *mostazaf*s were made, and it was declared that families with a larger number of children would have precedent. In mosques and through media, the clergy urged people to get married and to have children.

An explosive population growth, however, alarmed the ruling clergy. In 1989, just before his death, Ayatollah Khomeini made a religious declaration (*fatwa*) that considered use of contraceptives and sterilization of men and women acceptable. Since then the government has pursued an aggressive policy of population planning, accompanied with free distribution of contraceptives in health clinics, as well as active use of mosques, the media, educational institutions, and other sources to persuade people to have fewer children.

Officially, abortion remains illegal. In practice, however, legal loopholes and clerical interpretations have made abortion highly accessible, and available free of charge in government hospitals and clinics. According to the law, abortion can be performed if pregnancy is harmful to a woman's health. Furthermore, according to clerical interpretation, if an abortion takes place during the first 120 days, before the "ensoulment" of the fetus, it is not a crime. If challenged, the person who performed abortion has to pay a penalty (*dieh*) to the fetus's lawful heirs: the parents. After that period, however, it is a crime, and a higher blood money should be paid to the fetus's heirs. This interpretation is a guarantee for physicians that the potential penalty does not involve imprisonment. According to attestation of doctors and nurses, however, abortion is frequent, and no one had heard of a single case of a doctor being reprimanded.[23]

Government policy concerning subsidies has also undergone change. Only the first three children in each family are eligible for food and other subsidies.[24] Furthermore, the entire policy of food and other subsidies is being reexamined with the tilt toward privatization.

From the above, it can be hypothesized that government ideology and policy that led to the decline in the age of first marriage and the explosive rise in fertility are likely to have had a negative impact on women's participation during the 1980s. Furthermore, the modification in ideology and the sharp change in policy concerning fertility have positively contributed to participation. The census data support this hypothesis (Tables 11.1 and 11.2). However, the data are not sufficiently specific to allow for a separate measurement of these effects.

EDUCATION

The Islamic government has pursued a policy of expanding the provision of basic education. There is a general increase in the percentage of female students in the population 10 years and older, from 14.8 percent in 1976 to 16.6, 22.0, and 26.6 percent for 1986, 1991, and 1996, respectively.

This increase in part explains the decline in women's labor participation, especially that of teenage girls. The increase in the number of female students is more pronounced in the rural areas: 6.5, 11.8, 17.6, and 19.7 percent for 1976, 1986, 1991, and 1996, respectively. However, the combined total percentage shares of female students and active female labor for 1976—27.8—is larger than that of 1986—24.7—indicating that factors other than the increased share of women students account for the decline in female labor participation. However, this share is 30.7 and 35.7 for 1991 and 1996, respectively, indicating an increase over the 1976 share (Table 11.1).

During the first decade after the revolution, higher education was characterized by a gender-based discriminatory policy that aimed at segregating men and women, and reflected an ideological perception of the proper occupations for women. In general women were considered suitable for the profession of teaching and for health-related services; female students should be taught by women, and female patients should be cared for by other women. Furthermore, such fields as engineering were considered to be against the nature of women. In spite of a significant growth of secondary education from 1976 to 1986, the level of tertiary female education remained constant. Because of the ideology of segregation, coeducational technical schools were closed. Thus women could no longer have access to technical education. Although special female technical schools have been established, they were limited to the fields of hygiene, first aid, sewing, cooking, and knitting. For 1984–1985, 91 fields of study (54 percent out of the 169 areas offered by some 120 institutions of higher education were not available to women, mostly in the technical and scientific fields. In other areas maximum quotas ranging from 20 to 50 percent were applied to women students. Marginal modifications were introduced in 1989, increasing the areas open to women by about 10 percent.[25] Further changes in 1994 allowed women to participate in all fields of higher education.

Women are also discriminated against for graduate studies abroad. According to a law passed by the Iranian parliament in April 1985, a woman holding a bachelor's degree from one of the Iranian universities has to be married in order to qualify to go abroad for graduate studies.

FEMALE EMPLOYMENT: A SECTORAL AND OCCUPATIONAL EXAMINATION

As indicated in Table 11.4, women's economic activities are heavily concentrated in agriculture, manufacturing, and public and private services for both pre- and postrevolutionary periods. The combined share of all other economic sectors is 4.8, 9.4, and 4.4 for 1976, 1986, and 1996, respectively. Furthermore, female labor participation in economic sectors such as construction, mining, wholesale, and transport is primarily in the area of

Table 11.4
Distribution of Employed Women by Economic Sectors (10 years and older, 1,000 persons)

	1976		1986			1996
	Total	%	Total	%	Total	%
Total	1212	100.0	975.3	100.0	1765.4	100.0
Agriculture	227.9	18.8	259.0	26.6	294.2	16.7
Industry	639.1	52.7	210.8	21.6	583.2	33.0
Public, Social & Private Services	286.6	23.6	414.2	42.5	809.7	45.9
All other categories *	58.4	4.8	91.3	9.4	78.4	4.4

Note: *In each of the economic sectors included in this category women's participation is less than 2% of the total. However, the category "activity not classified" accounts for 4.6 percent and 2.9 percent of the total for 1986 and 1996, respectively.

Source: Baqerian, M. and Markaz-e Amar-e Iran, Sarshomary-e Omoomy-e Nofus of Maskan 1375: Natiyeg-e Tafssili.

clerical and office work. Therefore, this study will focus on agriculture, manufacturing, and public, social, and private services. I will also examine female employment in terms of occupational categories that will be inclusive of all active female labor.

Agriculture

An examination of female active labor in agriculture for the period 1956–1996, shows a peak for 1976; the absolute number of active women for 1976 is about four times that of 1966, and more than three times that of 1986. For all other years the data indicate a continuously rising trend in the absolute number of active women (Table 11.5).[26] Thus female labor as a percentage of total active labor in agriculture is 4.3, 6.4, 22.8, 8.2, and 8.9 for 1956, 1966, 1976, 1986, and 1996, respectively (Table 11.6). The 1976 peak can be explained in terms of the oil boom. The number of active male laborers in agriculture declined for 1976 and then rose in 1986 (Table 11.5). The booming construction and industrial activities provided jobs for rural male workers that paid higher wages than agriculture. Thus women filled the jobs abandoned by men.

Another difference between the pre- and postrevolutionary period is the role of large-scale farms. In 1976, about 13 percent of the cultivated area was farmed by production units that relied on wage labor for at least 50 percent of their labor force.[27] After the revolution, the legal status of many large farms became ambiguous and subject to dispute, and they became nonoperative.[28] Thus demand for wage labor in agriculture declined, a factor that is reflected in the decline in the share of female wage labor from 2.1 in 1976 to 0.9 in 1986.[29] This share, however, rose modestly in 1996, 1.3 percent (Table 11.6). Although the increase is small, and perhaps in-

Table 11.5
Active Population in Agriculture, Hunting, Fishing, and Forestry

1000 Persons						
		1956	1966	1976	1986	1996
All Categories	Total	3325.7	3168.5	3615.3	3208.6	3318.5
	Males	3182.5	2965.3	2791.0	2945.8	3024.4
	Females	143.2	203.2	824.3	262.8	294.1

Source: ILYO, *Yearbook of Labor Statistics*; Markaz-e Amar-e Iran, *Sarshomary-e Omoomy-e Nofus of Maskan 1375: Natiyeg-e Tafssili.*

significant, a possible explanation is privatization, return, or sale of large farms to the private sector. Thus many of the large farms became operational and employed workers. This argument can be further supported by the changing shares of male wage labor: 16.2, 9.4, and 12.8 percent of the total for 1976, 1986, and 1996, respectively (Table 11.6). Thus privatization may have had a marginally positive impact on female employment in agriculture.

It is worth noting that rural women were not an ideological target of the Islamic regime, and there is no indication of a direct ideological impact on participation in agriculture.

Manufacturing

As indicated by Table 11.7, in 1976, the absolute number of active women in manufacturing was about three times that of 1986. In comparison to 1986, there is a sharp increase for 1996; nevertheless participation is lower than that of 1976. This occurred while the absolute number of active men showed an increasing trend; the number for 1996 is nearly twice that of 1976. Thus female labor as a percentage of total in manufacturing accounted for 38.4, 14.8, and 22.9 for 1976, 1986, and 1996, respectively. The largest decline occurred in unpaid family labor. In 1976, the absolute number of unpaid female workers was more than six times that of 1986, and nearly twice the figures for 1996. The share of these workers in total manufacturing was 21.3, 3.7, and 7.9 percent for 1976, 1986, and 1996, respectively. Note that a similar trend can be observed for unpaid male labor. These changes can be explained by economic recession and recovery, rural-urban migration, education, and other structural changes in the economy that have generally reduced the share of unpaid family workers.

The sharpest decline in participation is observed during 1976–1986. Traditionally textiles have been the largest employer of women in manufacturing. In comparison to 1976, the number of women employed in this industry declined by 419,000 in 1986, which accounts for 97.4 percent of the total decline in manufacturing. For the same period, however, male employment in this industry declined by only 16,000.[30] Exclusive estimates

Table 11.6
Active Population in Agriculture, Hunting, Fishing, and Forestry

		% in Total				
		1956	1966	1976	1986	1996
All Categories	Total	100.0	100.0	100.0	100.0	100.0
	Males	95.7	93.6	77.2	91.8	91.1
	Females	4.3	6.4	22.8	8.2	8.9
Employers & Own Account Workers	Total	54.9	58.1	48.2	75.6	68.7
	Males	54.1	56.8	47.6	73.3	66.1
	Females	0.8	1.3	0.5	2.3	2.6
Employees	Total	28.7	25.2	18.3	1.0	14.1
	Males	27.7	23.1	16.2	9.4	12.8
	Females	1.0	2.1	2.1	0.9	1.3
Unpaid Family Workers	Total	16.1	16.3	16.2	12.2	14.6
	Males	13.6	13.4	12.5	7.3	9.9
	Females	2.5	3.0	3.7	4.8	4.7
Not Classified By Status	Total	0.3	0.3	17.3	1.9	2.6
	Males	0.3	0.2	0.8	1.8	2.4
	Females	0.0	0.0	16.5	0.1	0.2

Source: ILO, Yearbook of Labor Statistics; Markaz-e Amar-e Iran, Sarshomary-e Omoomy-e Nofus of Maskan 1375: Na-tiyeg-e Tafssili.

Table 11.7
Economically Active Population in Manufacturing

		1976 (1000)	%	1986 (1000)	%	1996 (1000)	%
All Categories	Total	1682.2	100.0	1460.1	100.0	2552	100.0
	Males	1035.8	61.6	1243.8	85.2	1968.8	77.1
	Females	646.4	38.4	216.3	14.8	583.2	22.9
Employers & Own Account Workers	Total	357.6	21.3	505.4	34.6	767.7	30.1
	Males	255.3	15.2	414.6	28.4	558.8	21.9
	Females	102.3	6.1	90.8	6.2	208.9	8.2
Employees	Total	900.9	53.5	818.1	56.0	1457.7	57.1
	Males	724.5	43.1	761.7	52.2	1305.7	51.1
	Females	176.3	10.5	56.4	3.9	152.0	6.0
Unpaid Family Workers	Total	411.2	24.4	73.7	5.0	242.0	9.5
	Males	52.2	3.1	18.4	1.3	42.3	1.6
	Females	359.1	21.3	55.2	3.8	199.7	7.9
Not Classified by Status	Total	12.5	0.7	63.0	4.3	84.5	3.3
	Males	3.7	0.2	49.1	3.4	62.0	2.4
	Females	8.7	0.5	13.8	0.9	22.5	0.9

Source: ILO, Yearbook of Labor Statistics; Markaz-e Amar-e Iran, Sarshomary-e Omoomy-e Nofus of Maskan 1375: Nattyeg-e Tafssili.

of the total job loss for women in small textile family workshops are not available. As indicated by Table 11.7, however, there was a decline of about 300,000 in total active female labor in the category of unpaid family workers, most of which probably occurred in the textile industry. Also note that the total decline in active male labor in the category of unpaid family workers accounted for nearly 34,000. As many of these job losses are likely to have resulted from the closing of small carpet workshops, the net job loss of 16,000 for men in the textile industry may be entirely or largely in this category rather than in wage labor. As shown in Table 11.7, female wage labor in manufacturing declined to one-third of the 1976 level, and its share in total dropped from 10.5 to 3.9 percent. For the same period, however, male wage labor rose and its share in total increased from 43 to 52.2 percent. As mentioned earlier, textiles are the largest employers of female wage labor, and the total decline of 120,000 in female wage labor is largely due to this sector.

During 1976–1986, no significant changes in technology and use of machinery were introduced in the textile industry.[31] Therefore, the decline in women's participation cannot be attributed to job obsolescence resulting from technological change. It seems that the government, through a combination of institutional reorganization, harassment of women workers, as well as early retirement and other monetary incentives, contributed to the decline. In textile and apparel industries, the number of cooperatives in which men could join as own-account workers rose significantly; thus the reorganization of factories resulted in job loss for women. During the early postrevolutionary period, many large textile factories came under public control. In addition to the early retirement incentives, according to another law passed during the early postrevolutionary years, the husbands of women who resigned from their jobs became eligible to a lifetime salary increase of Rls. 10,000, roughly $100 at the time of the passage of the law. This law persuaded many poor working women to resign from their factory jobs.[32] Thus government ideology and policy was an important contributor to the decline of female wage labor in the textile industry.

In contrast to 1986, the share of female wage labor rose to 6.0 percent of the total in 1996. Its absolute number as well as its share in total manufacturing, however, remained below the 1976 figure of 10.5 percent. The relative increase, in comparison to 1986, can be explained in terms of economic recovery and modification of the ideological factors that contributed to the earlier decline in participation. It is worth noting that there is an increase in both absolute and relative share in total of the category employer and own-account worker for 1996: 8.2 percent of the total in contrast to 6.1 and 6.2 for 1976, and 1986, respectively. This rise can also be explained by modifications in ideology as about 90 percent of these workers are independent workers in the textile and apparel industry, indicating that the earlier attempts to discriminate against women in cooperatives have been modified.

The 1996 evidence, however, does not suggest a significant negative impact from privatization on participation. Manufacturing operations that came under state control and were privatized in the 1990s were large enterprises. The only operation in which women had a significant share was the large textile factories. Since women became subject to ideological discrimination and many were forced out during the 1980s, it is unlikely that privatization and downsizing may have had a further negative impact. It is also worth noting that exchange control continues to persist in Iran. Export promotion policies have not brought significant changes. With the exception of the oil sector, which is not a significant employer of women, the government has not succeeded in attracting foreign investment. Thus there are no indications that privatization policies may have had a positive impact on female employment.

Services

In contrast to manufacturing, the absolute number of women active in community, social, and personal services has shown a consistent increase for 1986 and 1996, in comparison to 1976. The absolute number of women employed in this category in 1996 is about three times that of 1976 (Table 11.4). This is largely due to increased female employment by the public sector. The share employed by the public sector in total female employment accounted for 30, 42, and 39 percent for 1976, 1986, and 1996, respectively.[33] The increase in employment of women by the public sector is largely due to employment of women teachers, and to a lesser extent, women health service providers. In 1986, about 83 percent of the women employed by the public sector were listed under the category of education, and 9 percent were involved in the health-related services.[34] For 1996, however, the respective shares are 60 and 13 percent[35] indicating a relative availability of other employment opportunities in the public sector. The following factors contributed to an increased demand for women teachers: the ideology of segregation, the young composition of the population and thus the need for teachers, and the state's commitment to expand elementary and secondary education. During the 1990s, the state has continued its commitment to education and health. Thus privatization policies have not had a negative impact on employment of women by the public sector.

Occupational Categories

As indicated in Table 11.8, the absolute number of women employed in the category of professional and technical shows a continually rising trend

Table 11.8
Active Female Labor by Occupation Categories

	1976	1986	1996	1976	1986	1996
	1000 Persons			%		
All Categories	1985.7	1319.7	1765.4	100.00	100.00	100.00
Professional, Technical	188.2	343.3	566.5	9.48	26.01	32.3
Administrative	1.3	1.5	41.4	0.06	0.11	2.4
Executive, Manager, Clerical	63.5	46.8	104.1	3.20	3.55	6.0
Sales Work	8.4	11.3	77.7	0.42	0.86	4.5
Skilled Farmers	822.8	263.2	254.9	41.44	19.94	14.6
All Other Categories	901.5	653.5	720.8	41.95	47.09	40.2

Source: ILO, Yearbook of Labor Statistics; Markaz-e Amar-e Iran, Sarshomary-e Omoomy-e Nofus of Maskan, Kolle Keshvar Sale 1375: Natiyeg-e Tafssili.

and its share in all occupational categories rises from 9.5 to 26.0 and 32.3 for 1976, 1986, and 1996, respectively. The largest share in this category, just under 90 percent, however, is in the combined education and health-related professions. As mentioned earlier, increased demands for female teachers and health care professionals are important contributors. In comparison to 1976, there is also a slight increase in the total number of women in the category of administrator, manager, and executive for 1986, from 1356 to 1534. For 1986, nearly all women in this category are school principals,[36] and the number of women in any other managerial sector is near zero. For 1996, however, education-related managerial positions accounted for about 76 percent of the total, indicating that the system has been comparatively more open to women.

During the 1980s, a female occupation that became subject to ideological scrutiny was the secretarial position. The presence of well-dressed secretaries in the offices was regarded as "prostitutionization" of women. This ideological position is reflected in a 37 percent decline in the absolute number of women employed in the clerical position for 1986 in comparison to 1976 (Table 11.8). Again the data for 1996 indicate an increase in employment in this occupation.

CONCLUSIONS

In this chapter I have explored the possible impacts of a combination of economic, structural, and ideological factors on female labor participation in Iran. The findings of the chapter suggest that a host of economic and ideological factors have impacted female employment in Iran. As economic stagnation and ideological fervor were stronger during the 1980s, the data suggest a general decline in female employment in this period. The decade of the 1990s, however, is a period of relative recovery, normalization, and modification of the state's ideology. Thus, labor force participation indicates a generally positive trend. The data, however, do not show a significant impact stemming from privatization and liberalization policies of the 1990s.

NOTES

1. Among other sources see: Stichter and Papart (1990, pp. 1–9); World Bank (1993, pp. xi–xxiii, 10).

2. The latter two variables reduce women's domestic responsibilities and increase in education improves possibilities for employment and earning power of women outside the home.

3. Some writers have argued that during the earlier years of industrialization and growth female employment declines, and begins to rise at later stages. Thus they argue that female employment over time is U-shaped (Cagatay and Ozler

1995). Iran appears to be an exception to this pattern. During the earlier decades of 1950s, 1960s, and 1970s the participation rate rose and then started falling. In the case of Iran, it is worth noting that the survey methods have consistently underestimated women's work in agriculture. Thus the extent of decline in agricultural labor is also underestimated. Furthermore, the rapid growth and policies of the 1960s and 1970s, as well as the ideological changes of the 1980s, appear to have overshadowed other factors.

4. Schultz (Working paper 1989); Boserup (1970, p. 53); Becker (1991, p. 55).

5. *The New Palgrave; A Dictionary of Economics* (1987, pp. 492–498).

6. On each survey, the respondents are asked if they worked on a farm during the last 10 days, and only one annual visit is undertaken by the survey team. If, for seasonal reasons, women did not perform agricultural tasks, their overall participation is not reported. By contrast, in Turkey, for each survey more than one visit during different seasons is carried out. Thus the latter may reflect a more accurate picture of labor participation.

7. Estimates by Baqerian (1990, p. 10) are about 3.2 percent annual average.

8. Kar (1992).

9. The Constitution of Islamic Republic of Iran, amendment number 4, principal number 43, amendment number 2, and principal numbers 19, 20, and 21, cited in Kar (1992).

10. Nasr (1987, pp. 47–53).

11. Baqerian (1990, pp. 75–76).

12. Personal observations and comparisons between my visits to Iran in 1989, 1992, and 1994.

13. For example, the Agricultural Development Bank had an excellent day-care system, and right after the revolution the day-care facility was closed.

14. *Zan-e Rooz*, Esfand 1369 (1990, no. 1304, pp. 6–10).

15. *Zan-e Rooz*, Mehr 1369, no. 1286.

16. *Zan-e Rooz*, number 1235, Sept. 29, 1989, and number 1236, Oct. 6, pp. 14–15, 54–55.

17. This information can also be detected from various articles in the daily newspaper *Ettella't*, as well as, *Zan-e Rooz*, in which young people and their parents complain about problems of housing, inflation, and heavy initial costs of weddings as obstacles to marriage.

18. Markaz-e Amar-e Iran, *Iran dar Ayineye Amar*, Tehran (1989, p. 11).

19. Markaz-e Amar-e Iran, *Salnameh Amary-e Sal-e 1370* (Annual Statistics of Iran: 1991), Tehran (1991, p. 34).

20. Markaz-e Amar-e Iran, *Gozydeh-e Mataleb-e Amary*, Tehran (1992, p. 4).

21. Hakimian (1998).

22. Hoodfar (1994).

23. Ibid., p. 13.

24. *Iran Times*, no. 1027, July 19, 1991.

25. Shahidian (1991, pp. 6–38, 12–14, 17–20).

26. The continually increasing trend in women's participation rate in agriculture appears contrary to the experience of other developing countries, which is usually decreasing. This is particularly striking when we consider the rising number of female students in rural areas: from 3.4 percent of the female population of 10 years and older in 1956 to 25.9 in 1996 (Table 11.2). As mentioned earlier, how-

ever, survey methods grossly underestimate the participation rates, usually in single digits. Thus the omission may include teenage girls who are seasonally and marginally active, who drop out as a result of education. Rural women were not an ideological target of the Islamic regime. The data does not lend itself to a conclusion that ideological factors had a significant impact on the decline of female labor in rural areas.

27. Moghadam (1985, pp. 755–776).

28. Bakhash (1989, pp. 186–201).

29. It should be noted that the large number of active female labor in the category "not classified by status"—16.5 percent of total active labor in agriculture for 1976—is probably due to the fact that women in this group performed both unpaid family and wage labor. Thus the actual decline in female wage labor is probably much sharper than is suggested by the category "employee" that shows a decline from 2 to 0.95 percent of total active labor in agriculture (Table 11.5).

30. Baqerian (1990, pp. 74–76).

31. Ibid., pp. 74–76.

32. Ibid., pp. 21, 34, and 37.

33. Ibid.; and Markaz-e Amar-e Iran, *Sarshomary-e Omoomy-e Nofus va Maskan 1375: Nataiyeg-e Tafssil.* (Population Census, 1996: Detailed Results), Tehran (1997, p. 196).

34. Ibid.

35. Markaz-e Amar-e Iran, *Sarshomary-e Omoomy-e Nofus va Maskan 1375: Nataiyeg-e Tafssili.* (Population Census, 1996: Detailed Results), Tehran (1997, p. 198).

36. Baqerian (1990).

REFERENCES

Bakhash, S. (1989). "The Politics of Land, Law, and Social Justice in Iran," *Middle East Journal*, (Spring): 186–201.

Baqerian, Mitra (1990). "Bar-ressye Vigegyhaye Eshteqali Zanan dar Iran" (1355–65). Tehran: Plan and Budget Organization, unpublished.

Becker, Gary (1991). *A Treatise on the Family*. Cambridge: Harvard University Press.

Boserup, E. (1970). *Women's Role in Economic Development*. London: George Allen & Unwin.

Cagatay, Nilufer and Sule Ozler (1995). "Feminization of the Labor Force: The Effects of Long-Term Development and Structural Adjustment," *World Development* 23 (11): 1883–1884.

Hakimian, Hassan (1998). "Population Dynamic, in Post-Revolutionary Iran: A Re-examination of Evidence." Working paper.

Hoodfar, Homa (1994). "Devices and Desires: Population Policy and Gender Roles in the Islamic Republic," *MERIP* (no.190): pp. 11–17.

Iran Times. Various issues.

Kar Mehrangiz (1992). "Yek Gozaresh Darbareh Hoquqi Kari Zanan," unpublished.

Markaz-e Amar-e Iran (1997). *Sarshomary-e Omoomy-e Nofus Va Maskan 1375*, Tehran.

————(1992). *Gozydeh-e Mataleb-e Amary*, Tehran.

————(1991). *Salnameh Amary-e Sal-e* 1370, Tehran.

————(1989). *Iran dar Ayineye Amar*, Tehran.

Moghadam, Fatemeh (1985). "An Evaluation of the Productive Performance of Agribusinesses: An Iranian Case Study," *Economic Development and Cultural Change* (July): 755–776.

Nasr, Sayyed Hossein (1987). *Traditional Islam in the Modern World*. London: Routledge.

The New Palgrave: A Dictionary of Economics. Vol. 2. 1987.

Schultz, Paul (1989). "Women's Changing Participation in the Labor Force: A World Perspective," World Bank, Working paper, December.

Shahidian, H. (1991). "The Education of Women in the Islamic Republic of Iran," *Journal of Women's History* (Winter): 6–38.

Stichter, Sharon and Jane Papart (1990). *Women, Employment and the Family in the International Division of Labor*. Philadelphia: Temple University Press.

World Bank (1993). *Turkey: Women in Development*. Washington DC: World Bank.

Zan-e Rooz. Various issues.

Index

About the Editors and Contributors

DR. BERCH BERBEROGLU is Professor and Chairman of the Department of Sociology and Director of the Institute for International Studies at the University of Nevada, Reno. He has published 16 books and many articles on international political economy, development, and problems of Third World societies, including several books on the Middle East—*Turkey in Crisis; Power and Stability in the Middle East*; and *Turmoil in the Middle East: Imperialism, War, and Political Instability.*

DR. SALIM CHISHTI is Research Scientist at Kuwait Institute for Scientific Research. He has published many articles on education, labor, energy, and macroeconomics in international journals.

DR. E. MINE CINAR is a Professor of Economics at Loyola University of Chicago. Her research interests and numerous publications are in the areas of economic development, financial markets, and gender. Dr. Cinar is a member of several professional associations and is widely known for her work in the Middle East Economic Association. She is the editor of the electronic MEEA proceedings journal *Topics in Middle-East and North African Economies* and is currently working on the fourth research volume of MEEA, *Women and Work in the Middle-East and Africa.*

DR. GHASSAN DIBEH is the chairman of the department of economics and management at the Lebanese American University in Byblos, Lebanon. His research interests include business cycles, political economy, and economic and financial crises in capitalist economies. He has published articles on business cycle theory and mathematical methods in economics.

DR. MUHAMMAD Q. ISLAM is Associate Professor of Economics at Saint Louis University. His research interests include the incidence and welfare cost of taxation, causes and consequences of public expenditure growth, and the impact of public expenditures and taxes on economic growth. His work has appeared in international refereed journals such as *Southern Economic Journal, International Tax and Public Finance, Public Finance Review*, and *Economics Letters*.

MR. AYMAN KANDEEL is a Ph.D. student in Economics at the University of Southern California. His B.A. and M.A. degrees are from Cairo University and American University in Cairo, respectively. Much of his work is at the intersection of two subject areas, income distribution and financial markets.

MS. BADRIA KHALAF is an Assistant Research Scientist at Kuwait Institute for Scientific Research. Her main areas of interest are labor economics and project appraisal.

DR. HANS LOFGREN is a Research Fellow in the Trade and Macroeconomics Division of the International Food Policy Research Institute (IFPRI), Washington, DC. Before joining IFPRI in 1995, he taught economics at the American University in Cairo. His research is focused on the application of general equilibrium modeling to the analysis of agricultural and trade policy in developing countries, with particular emphasis on the Arab World.

DR. FATEMEH E. MOGHADEM is Professor of Economics and Department Chairperson at Hofstra University and President of Middle East Economic Association 1996–present. Her publications include a book entitled *From Land Reform to Revolution: The Political Economy of Agricultural Development in Iran 1962–1979* and several articles in journals such as *Economic Development and Cultural Change, Cambridge Journal of Economics*, and *Oxford Bulletin of Economics and Statistics*.

DR. JEFFREY B. NUGENT is Professor of Economics at the University of Southern California. He has worked extensively on a variety of issues in the economics of development in several Middle Eastern and North African countries. He is coauthor of a recent book on institutions and development, the subject of much of his recent research.

DR. KAREN PFEIFER is Professor of Economics at Smith College, in Northampton, Massachusetts, and an editor of Middle East Report. She served as series editor of the annual volume *Research in Middle East Economics*, 1995–1999. With support from the Fulbright Middle East Program, the Social Science Research Council, and Smith College, her research has focused on socioeconomic transformation in the Middle East, including the evolution of the state-capitalist economies in Turkey, Egypt, and Algeria, the behavior and performance of Islamic versus non-Islamic business firms, and the impact of economic liberalization on private investment in Egypt.

DR. WASSIM SHAHIN is Dean of the School of Business at the Lebanese American University in Byblos, Lebanon. He is the author of *Money Supply and Deficit Financing in Economic Development* (Quorum Books, 1992). Dr. Shahin's articles and reviews have been published in scholarly journals such as the *Journal of Banking and Finance, Southern Economic Journal, Journal of Money Credit and Banking, Quarterly Review of Economics,* and *Finance and World Development.*

DR. ELIAS H. TUMA is Professor of Economics, Emeritus, at the University of California, Davis. He has published several articles and many books including *The Persistence of Economic Discrimination, European Economic History,* and *Economic and Political Change in the Middle-East.*

DR. ZAFIRIS TZANNATOS works for the World Bank where he is the Manager for Social Protection in the Middle East and North Africa region and the leader of the Bank's Program on Child Labor. He published/co-published more than 50 articles and seven books including *Women and Equal Pay* (Cambridge University Press, 1985), *Socialism in Greece* (Gower, 1986) *Current Issues in Labour Economics* (Macmillan, 1990), *Women's Employment and Pay in Latin America* (World Bank, 1992), *Case Studies on Women's Employment and Pay in LAC* (World Bank, 1992), *The Economics of the Labour Market* (Macmillan, 1993), *Out of the Margin: Feminist Perspectives on Economics* (Routledge, 1995).

DR. SOURUSHE ZANDVAKILI is Professor of Economics at the University of Cincinnati. He is also a Fellow at the Institute for Data Analysis and a Faculty Consultant at the Center for Social Policy and Evaluation Research. His research in labor and public economics, welfare and poverty, human resources management, research methodology, and applied econometrics has been published in journals such as *Journal of Econometrics, Economica, Journal of Applied Econometrics, Economics Letters, Applied Economics, Empirical Economics, Journal of Income Distribution, Journal of Socio-Economics,* and *Research on Economic Inequality.*

ISBN 0-313-30977-9

EAN

9 780313 309779

90000>

HARDCOVER BAR CODE

DATE DUE

~~APR 2004~~		
~~JAN 2004~~		
~~FEB 20 2004~~		
		Printed in USA

HIGHSMITH #45230